From Dawn
to Dusk

Other books by Judith Hubback

Islands and People
Wives Who Went to College
People Who Do Things to Each Other: Essays in Analytical
   Psychology
The Sea Has Many Voices

From Dawn to Dusk

Autobiography of Judith Hubback

Chiron Publications • Wilmette, Illinois

Library of Congress Catalog Card Number: 2003012118

Printed in the United States of America.
Project management by Linda Conheady.
Book design by Ellen Scanlon.
Cover design by D. J. Hyde.

Library of Congress Cataloging-in-Publication Data:

Hubback, Judith.
    From dawn to dusk : autobiography of Judith Hubback.
        p. cm.
    Includes bibliographical references and index.
    ISBN 1-888602-25-2 (pbk.)
    1. Hubback, Judith. 2. Jungian psychology—England.
3. Psychoanalysts—England—Biography. I. Title.

BF109.H77A3 2003
150.19′54′092--dc21

2003012118

Contents

Acknowledgments

The following publishers and individuals have generously given permission to use quotations from their copyrighted works. From a letter from Jenifer Williams, Oxford, in *Time and Tide*, summer 1935. From 'Do Not Go Gentle Into That Good Night', by Dylan Thomas, from *The Poems of Dylan Thomas*, copyright © 1952 by Dylan Thomas. Reprinted by permission of New Directions Publishing Corp. Extract from *The Times Second Leader*, London, on 5 April 1954, "Political and Economic Planning broadsheet". ©NISyndication Limited, London (1954). From *The Economist Newspaper Limited*, London (17 April 1954). From a letter to *The Manchester Guardian* on *Graduate Wives* by Judith Hubback (1954). © Guardian. From articles on education in Modern Schools in England by Judith Hubback which first appeared in the *New Statesman*, London, in the mid-1950s. From T. S. Eliot's *Four Quartets, Burnt Norton*, Faber & Faber. Excerpt from "Burnt Norton" in *Four Quartets* by T. S. Eliot, copyright 1936 by Harcourt, Inc. and renewed 1964 by T. S. Eliot, reprinted by permission of the publisher. Excerpts from "East Coker" in *Four Quartets*, copyright 1940 by T. S. Eliot and renewed 1968 by Esme Valerie Eliot, reprinted by permission of Harcourt, Inc. 'To My Unwritten Poems', published in the *San Francisco Jung Institute Library Journal*, Vol. 8, no. 1, p. 65, 1988. From 'The Dynamic Self' by Judith Hubback, first published in the *Journal of Analytical Psychology* in April 1998 (Vol. 43, 2:277–285).

The cover design was inspired by a Navaho weaving hanging in Judith Hubback's consulting room. The two colours suggest dawn at the top and dusk below.

One

Family Background: Roots and Origins

Autobiography is bound to be self-centred: it is about me. And that has been difficult all my life, since when I was a child my parents often stressed that it was wrong to be self-centred or selfish. They rubbed it in more than was necessary, perhaps not realising that unselfishness has to be developed gradually. So in this story the me-person is me in relation to many other people, what they and I were, are, and have done. My ideas have developed in connection with my activities, so I am writing about how life and I have got on together.

As well as what I as an individual have been fortunate enough to inherit materially, and some of the collective events of the twentieth century and beyond—wars, dictatorships, the women's movement, social changes, technology and so on—what I have done and what I have felt and thought all go together. Since I became a psychologist in mid-life, my story has to begin with my origins and childhood.

Circumstances have been like composted garden soil, in which my views and ideas have grown. Sometimes the gardeners have been other people: sometimes I have learned from them, imitated them or even resisted them. When I have been anxious and depressed, I have needed friends as flexible stakes, and appreciated their support. To continue the garden imagery, the modern view on staking trees and shrubs is to tie them low down: they will make stronger and deeper roots than if the ties are attached higher. I think that in my youngest years I found life more difficult than the grown-ups realised: so, metaphorically, it is I who have had to pay attention to getting better grounded. In writing this I am selecting some of the events, people, thoughts, emotions and atmospheres which have influenced me and contributed to how my life developed. I describe how one thing led to another, and how I became the person I am now.

My mother, Marjorie Murray, and father, John Fischer Williams, were both very scrupulous people, and conveyed that honesty was the virtue almost higher than any other. The subtleties of that emerged later, when some white lies turned out to be acceptable: they might be kinder than the truth. Those were some of my early impressions of morality. Each of my sisters may have had a different view, and certainly their life experiences have been different from mine. There were five of us: Barbara, my half-sister, born in 1902, during my father's first marriage; Prudence (Prue), born in 1912, when he had remarried; Jenifer, in 1914; myself, early in 1917; and Mariella, at the end of 1920.

Unselfishness and honesty: fine of course. And since there was always enough money, the realm of those virtues was personal relationships. Within the family there were sins, we could be naughty, but never criminal. What happened was that, of the various ways of relating to the world, thinking was the most highly valued. My father was a great thinker, essentially intellectual, scholarly, a barrister and an international lawyer. I admired him greatly and was considered to be like him—as was Jenifer. She and I later differed in several ways, since she became a Civil Servant and then a successful Oxford history tutor. But during childhood we had a lot in common, more than the obvious fact of both being red-headed. My mother once told me I was Father's favourite. It was an odd thing for her to say, since both our parents made great play of treating all their children equally; I think it was wrong of her, and remember feeling embarrassed rather than flattered or impressed. I felt that he understood me well, and I was not sure whether she did, especially when I was young.

From early childhood I observed people closely; a drawing I did when I was just over three is entitled "Happy and cross people" (see illustration, p. 3). Of course I knew both emotions. Interestingly, it is not very easy to tell which person is which; also there is a figure with no eyes, to the left of the two main ones, and it looks distinctly phallic. As the child I was then cannot

Happy and cross people

now be questioned, or encouraged to speak freely about it, the third "person" remains rather enigmatic. Consciously, I knew nothing about male bodies, let alone symbolic phallic objects. I had no brothers and we never saw my father nude. Several years later, in the gallery of the Louvre, in Paris, I was hurried quickly past a statue of a hermaphrodite with breasts and a penis. My questions about it were not answered. My mother kept the drawing, so it still features in my large book of family photographs and other items such as letters and school reports. She did one such collection for each of her four daughters. Observing people's expressions was useful in my first profession, teaching, and also from mid-life onwards, when I had become an analytical psychologist.

Mother enjoyed the way Father adored her, but I never saw any displays of physical affection. He wrote to her daily when

3

they were apart, and composed a poem every year for her birthday and another on the anniversary of their marriage. She also wrote to him every day, with detailed and enthusiastic descriptions of what was going on. She was his second wife, and had helped him very much in his unhappiness after he divorced Barbara's mother, who had left him. A divorce was unusual early in the twentieth century, as well as being only for those who could afford it.

Some time during my childhood I came to know that my father's mother had died shortly after he was born, in 1870. His only sister was ten years older, and took little interest in him. His widowed father was probably a rather distant figure. My father was sent to an all-boys boarding school, the traditional and conventional Prep School at Elstree, at about the age of seven, then to Harrow, which was also of course an all-boys school. He got into New College at Oxford young, did very well academically and in sports, also in University politics, where he became a Liberal and made many long-lasting friends.

I do not remember him bemoaning the lack of female or feminine influences in his upbringing, but I think it must have contributed significantly to his marrying an attractive young woman after they had known each other for only a few weeks. It is easy to assume that what turned out to be a major mistake was partly due to his having so little family experience of girls or women. The impulsiveness also conveys that he had had very little opportunity to become aware of the minor unconscious feminine factor within his largely masculine personality. The breakdown of his first marriage contributed significantly to him and my mother getting extremely anxious when each of their daughters was growing up and finding boyfriends, but they were so paralysed with fear that they could only hint at the reason. There is an amusing footnote to that: Mother told me, many years later, that she and her four sisters, all good-looking and lively girls, had between them had thirty-five *lovers*, her way of referring to men who were significantly attracted to them. There was indeed a complete prevalence of girls for two generations.

My father's father had been a successful business man, who had made quite a lot of money from the China tea trade, in the firm of Jardine Matheson. Before him, my father's grandfather had been the captain of a topsail schooner, Cutty Sark vintage, trading with the Far East. My romantic picture of that mariner was of him as captain on the bridge of a large sailing ship, in a gale. The firm quite likely dealt in opium as well. That was never mentioned in the family. Perhaps it was not really known, until recent research threw light on the matter. My son Christopher was gleeful and sarcastic when he discovered that was one of the origins of the family's comfortable bank balance.

When my father inherited his share of the fortune, he explored the coast of Cornwall, on a bicycle, and bought a farm, its many acres and a rocky point going round to the then small village of Gorran Haven. The impressive and dramatic stone house that he built a short way above the cliff was the first commission for a young architect, called Coleridge. When I was a teenager I thought that was a suitable name for him, since the house he designed has to stand up to all the winds like the ship of the *Ancient Mariner*, but the poet Coleridge's addiction to opium is an irrelevant coincidence. Planning permission for the house would not be granted now. In our childhood we often saw beautiful ships sailing across the wide bay, and learned the names of all the rigs. There were also majestic transatlantic liners, smoky freighters and local fishing boats. There was no shortage of fish, crabs and lobsters. We easily caught a great many prawns. There were no utilitarian rectangular container-boats.

My mother's character and personality were very different from my father's. Theirs was a marriage of opposites: they were complementary to each other. She most likely inherited her varied artistic gifts from her Victorian mother, of whose work I think all that remains is a framed piece of embroidery, and two gentle sketches of Perugia and Florence, which I now have. Mother herself painted wild flowers and ones from the garden, places she had visited, landscapes, workshops, churches, cathedrals and castles. They were meticulously drawn, well composed and sensitive. She produced a Christmas card every winter, with inscriptions chosen by my father. Her woodcuts and especially her etchings are outstanding examples of the work she did over many years. It was always individual in its creativeness. She had more than amateur talent, and had been much encouraged by high praise in the studio where she studied in Paris in the months before getting married, which was in 1911. Marriage and children hardly deterred her at all, since my father could always afford ample domestic help for her. She painted a frieze to go round the nursery walls, slightly naïve versions of animals, each in its appropriate setting. Father composed a rhyme for the last panel, which was framed to go with it:

> Child, before you go to bed
> Look and count from *A* to *Z*,
> All the beasts and birds that you
> See on Sunday at the Zoo.
> Most are wild, a few are tame,
> All have French and English name.
> But not one of all the lot
> Has half such a Mummy as you have got.

I see myself as having been a rather nasty, unappreciative child, since I did not like her having painted the last two complimentary lines about herself. But my children, grandchildren and now a great grandson, in whose rooms the frieze has been at various times, appreciate it greatly. An example of my criticising my mother for not imagining a likely reaction (but not daring to voice my disappointment) was when she made me a linocut bookplate as a birthday present, with these words on it: 'Black is the raven, black is the rook, but blacker the child who steals this book'. Yet it left its imprint: I have to confess that I am still annoyed when friends forget to return books they have borrowed from me.

Mother also did a few portraits, which have a period value. Later in life she took to embroidery, most successfully. She did her own designs, painstakingly adapting for her needs something from some other art form, such as a Persian tile drawn in a museum, or flowers, birds, and animals from French medieval tapestries. She was a traditionalist, but an enterprising one. Though denigratory opinion might see her art as ladylike, that would be wrong. It was much better than that sounds. Her hands were square, the hands of someone who understood pencils and all tools, unlike my father's: he had elegant long fingers and I cannot remember seeing him use any garden or household tool, hammer, gimlet or whatever. Mother once told me she did not like van Gogh at all: he could not draw, she said. That was serious criticism from her. Naturally, in contrast, she admired Dürer.

As my mother was modest about her work, she did not publicise it much. And, most of all, higher status was always given to what my father did. It is sad that we children, except perhaps the youngest, Mariella, who was the one of us most emotionally attached to her, followed unthinkingly. My view is now that in almost everything there was an implicit value judgement, an unacknowledged competitiveness. Yet the world is like that. In our childhood language, Father was brainy and we thought Mother was not. Brainy was what we tried to be. As I write that, I hesitate a little: was it what I made of the atmosphere of family life, of the unspoken messages and not what my sisters felt or our parents meant to convey? At the time it was certainly regrettable, it made me impatient of stupidity, an attitude which has lasted all too long. But it had a valuable outcome because more or less unconsciously I reacted against it: it played an important part in my becoming a feminist when I grew up and it imbues much of what I have written. Gradually I came to see that Father and Mother were different, complementary, not the one better than the other. I was not fond of my mother in childhood, or later. Love from me to her did not develop. A friend once said I had "lost" her when I was very young, and had held it against her, unconsciously, for ever.

If much of that sounds sad, well, so it was. But not always: I can remember many cheerful games. There was one incident, when Mariella and I played what seemed to us a clever April Fool's Day trick on our father. We sent him a letter purporting to come from a neighbour, according to which two children had trespassed in his garden and damaged something or other—I forget just what. We were not often "naughty", but I expect we longed to be. The neighbour was demanding an apology. Father started writing a suitable letter, having already told us off severely. He did laugh, when we confessed, and there was no question of a reprimand. April Fool tricks were within the limits of the permissible, within the established order of things. Old photographs all show him looking severe. But behind the severity he was very kindly, and we knew he was affectionate.

Father was anyway more serious than our mother, who did convey, just occasionally, that she found the atmosphere rather heavy. Somewhere inside her was the original child she had been, lively, energetic, enthusiastic. She told us about her childhood, at first in London, then in a small Surrey village, with four sisters younger than herself, where they were very happy in a carefree way. She always enjoyed the country deeply and knew a lot about flowers and birds; indeed, she collected birds' eggs, an occupation not in the slightest disapproved of then. One of her uncles helped her. The surroundings were beautiful, which certainly influenced her. She and her sisters were brought up unconventionally and sensibly, given that they were children in the 1880s and 90s. At one stage, their hair was cropped short, easy to look after, almost as boys' might have been. I got the impression that she did not love her mother as much as her father: she conveyed that her mother was certainly beautiful but somehow not as warm as her spontaneous father. The truth may have been that her mother had to manage a large household without much money to spare, on the standards of the country class to which they belonged. I should call it county, really, with so much of the character that that word now trails behind it.

My mother's family lived in what had once been a family farmhouse, with a good-sized flower and vegetable garden, which I think was designed by the well-known woman gardener of the time, Gertrude Jekyll. They had chickens, ducks, cats, dogs, three horses and a donkey. There were of course trains for long distances, but mostly they walked, rode or drove in the pony trap. The girls looked after the horses and came to know much of the surrounding country very well. My mother and her sisters were not coddled, but encouraged to be outgoing. One summer, in the early 1890s, when my mother was ten and the next girl, Muriel, was nine, they travelled alone to stay with cousins who lived on an island off the coast of Norway, coping effectively with trains, boats and a hotel on the way.

My mother went to school only for about a year and then was educated at home, by a strict governess. The next two sisters after her may have gone to a small boarding school for a while.

It is remarkable how widely she educated herself. She also drew wherever she went and taught herself lettering. As I remember her, she had a deep enjoyment of poetry and literature in general, for example, classical nineteenth-century novelists such as Thackeray and Meredith, but she also kept up with at least some contemporary writers, especially serious ones rather than lighter or excessively romantic ones. Her reading did not include what she considered dangerous or disreputable books, overtly sexy, such as those of D. H. Lawrence or James Joyce. But I can remember her reading, much later of course, Virginia Woolf's *To The Lighthouse* when we were in Cornwall and identifying closely with the matriarchal but anxious Mrs. Ramsey, whose husband was always deep in philosophical thought. She much enjoyed both well-known English poetry and ancient Greek plays in Gilbert Murray's lyrical translations. That aspect of her may have been inborn, but I expect it was fostered by either or both her parents, as well as many years of close friendship with the rector's daughter, since it was more pronounced than would perhaps have been usual in a county family at that time. She had an energetic mind which would have benefited from what would now be called a good education. I cannot find a better word to describe what seems to have been her family atmosphere than to say it was cultured.

One benefit to me of her enjoyment of poetry was that, at just the right time, she introduced me to Robert Louis Stevenson's *A Child's Garden of Verses*, and I still remember several of them. I especially enjoyed the image of the stars reflected in the bucket of water, in *Escape at Bedtime*, since sometimes I wished that I dared do just that.

> The lights from the parlour and kitchen shone out
> Through the blinds and the windows and bars;
> And high overhead and all moving about,
> There were thousands and millions of stars.
>
> There ne'er were such thousands of leaves on a tree,
> Nor of people in church or the Park,
> As the crowds of the stars that looked down upon me,
> And that glittered and winked in the dark.

The Dog, and the Plough, and the Hunter, and all,
And the star of the Sailor, and Mars,
These shone in the sky, and the pail by the wall,
Would be half full of water and stars.

They saw me at last, and they chased me with cries,
And they soon had me packed into bed,
But the glory kept shining and bright in my eyes,
And the stars going round in my head.

My love of poetry flourished, and from my teens onwards I have often written poems. Some of them have been good enough to be published, in a small way.

My mother's father came from the minor, or perhaps I should say not so minor, aristocracy: he was one of the many descendants of the early eighteenth-century Scottish third Duke of Atholl. Being a member of the Murray clan through her father enabled my mother to revere its tartan, but I thought its colours were gloomy, and I cannot remember ever being moved by that sort of thing. I may be reading my views backwards when I see myself already as a child indefinably refusing to be impressed by rank or its trappings. I suppose it was part of trying to be different from my sisters, who enjoyed wearing tartan kilts. Also the culture of work had already become part of my personality: what had been inherited was somehow less to be admired than what had been achieved through effort.

A detail comes to mind, which illustrates another factor that there always was in the background: My aunt Rhona, my grandparents' third daughter, had what I thought was a bad squint, which I noticed when she came to visit my own family on some occasion. I was told, it seemed to me belatedly, since my mother had often talked about her childhood, that Muriel, the second girl, had pushed Rhona off a wall they had climbed onto. She had fallen onto a holly hedge, and lost the sight of her eye. This story illustrates how a tragic event, resulting from fairly ordinary childhood aggression between sisters, had had to be concealed.

The same thing operated in a big way over my father's first marriage, during which he had had a son who was either still-born or who lived only a few days. All through my childhood there was a sepia photograph of a baby, lying in what looked like a christening robe. It hung above the washbowl in the dressing room where my father shaved. I felt it conveyed unspeakable sadness. I could sense but not understand his daughter Barbara's unhappiness until many years later. Her mother had left her when she was only about four years old, and when Barbara asked her nanny where Mummy was, she was told "You cannot see your mother, she is a bad woman".

All in all it was easy for me to believe that girls were failed boys, disadvantaged from the beginning. I was told openly that I as well as Jenifer had been "meant to be" boys.

As well as those selected illustrations of some of the atmosphere in my family, which I feel conditioned me and contributed to my becoming an analyst, the other important thing was that our parents had spent all their formative years before the First World War. Our father was born in 1870, and our mother in 1880. Like many of his Liberal contemporaries, he had found the Boer War of 1899–1902 very disturbing. He was a deeply reflective man, with a wide circle of friends and colleagues in pre-war London, mainly Liberals, who were well informed about public affairs and politics in general. Being forced by that World War to give up his belief in progress and reason was a great blow to him. He hated the War, but supported it as inevitable and even necessary. There was something important to me about the way in which the phrase "before the War" occurred very often. It was not, I think, simple nostalgia. It felt as though it was something to do with an irreversible loss of standards in all areas of life. His education in the ancient classics steeped him in the history of the Greek city-states, their wars and the defeat of the civilised Athenians by the cruder Spartans, so that those events were always in the back of his mind.

Part of the "before the War" theme was the disappearance of the guinea, the golden coin, which both parents lamented. But I have the impression that that was actually less important than the lower morality in collective life, politics and so on, which seemed to be what they were referring to. Atmospheres as well as facts were inevitably comparative. Things had moved from having in general been better, to what had become worse. Of course, when I started noticing such matters in the Nineteen Twenties, the war being over was wholly good. But my parents criticised the vulgar "newly rich" profiteers, who had made money from armaments, and silly, girl 'flappers'. Father minded that Barbara had not completed her degree at Oxford, and that she appeared to lead a rather "fast" life. She loved the brash New York of the Twenties. She went on the stage, which worried him, and when that was not successful enough she became a beautician for a while. Her childhood had been traumatic: she was a difficult step-daughter with an unwelcoming step-mother who had hated her being around so much early in her marriage. Growing up in a way to please Father was far from easy for her. Much later she enjoyed being a journalist in the U.S.A., became happier, joined the staff of the United Nations and wrote knowledgeably about opera.

Where my father's views on public affairs were concerned, I soon picked up that the Treaty of Versailles was full of major shortcomings. He worked throughout the Nineteen Twenties as one of the legal advisors on the international Reparations Commission, which was based in Paris, so we all lived there, apart from Barbara. In his opinion, the Germans could not possibly pay what the victorious Allies demanded. Knowing something of his work and his views on the dangers of nationalism is the basis of my life-long interest in international matters. Nationalism sounded like blown-up parochialism, but among the *isms* patriotism was probably an acceptable emotion to him.

I have selected facts and anecdotes about my parents to convey some of what got built in to my original personality and led to the various things I have done. Much of how I was influenced by them of course also contributed to the lives of my sisters, but from what I know of them we were each of us affected differently and are all individuals, even at times aggressively so. Outsiders saw us collectively as 'the Fischer Williams girls'. Our father's Christian name was John and he used his middle name, Fischer (his mother's maiden name), along with his basic surname, Williams, but from our teens onward Jenifer and I did not use Fischer. We had not been given that name at baptism. Being accurate but also rather puritanical, we explained that anyway the names were not hyphenated. I considered hyphens were snobbish, and I did not want that label, especially as I was developing strongly left-wing sympathies.

My elder sister Prue once complained to Mother that Williams was a "common" name, which shocked that very loyal wife. Irrespective of the undistinguished name, she considered we were "top drawer" people. That is, of course, now a dated term, and already at the time she used it I found it uncomfortable. Jenifer, even more fiercely than I, did her best to dissociate herself from such views, trying to wipe out the stain of class superiority. Both blatant and subtle social classes certainly do exist, and are much written about, though they are less differentiated now than they were when we were young. But we had chosen neither our parents nor our genes. The currently fashionable term *elitism* has taken the place of my mother's "top drawer" attitude. I now see that where the "top drawer" theme is concerned she was openly stating her inherited views, and had the right to. She expected Jenifer and me to agree with her, which we did not. She would have liked us to be grateful, but we were not.

Having described the family background, I will move on to my personal childhood in the next chapter.

Two

The Nineteen Twenties: Mostly Paris

I was born in London in the winter of one of the most stressful of the First World War years, 1917, my mother's third child. My father wrote a poem for each of the babies when they were born, usually containing elaborate references to learned and classical matters. The one for me includes his hope that I would pay attention to history, and would combine the symbolic olive branch with 'Wisdom's sword'. It is worth reproducing the poem, cryptic and dated though it may seem to modern people, since it is typical of my father's learnedness.

To Elais Judith   born 23rd February 1917

The Persian burnt the citadel
Shrine of the wise, the shielded, Maid,
Naught would he have of power to tell
The grace that freemen's hands had made;

But when by pious feet again
In joy the Virgin's shrine was trod,
An olive sprouted, token plain
Freedom was not forgot of God.

So, little olive-plant, you came
To this most vexed of all the stars
To witness with your double name
Things that abide beyond our wars.

Olive and corn shall flourish free
If, taught by history's sternest word
You and tomorrow's race decree
War's head must fall to Wisdom's sword.

Incidentally, wisdom is still hidden in the future.

The name Judith comes from a character in the Old Testament, the patriotic murderess of Holofernes, who was the Saddam Hussein of her time. The other name, Elais, was derived from the ancient name of Greece, Hellas, which also meant olive branch: and the intellectual virgin goddess Athene gave her name to Athens. According to the myth of Noah's Ark, the dove found the branch, which showed God was going to get the Flood to recede and stop punishing sinful humans. A little of my father's scholastic ways of thought rubbed off on me, which I sometimes find inconvenient, and I try to conceal them.

Many years later I wondered, but not superstitiously, whether the poem might have been a kind of cryptic forecast of my interest in inner conflicts, the concerns of psychology, as well as the history of wars and revolutions. I saw the poem as an aspect of my secret ambitions, though I suspected correctly that they would never be achieved in actuality. In my teens I discovered that Shelley put it well when he wrote:

> The desire of the moth for the star,
> Of the night for the morrow,
> The devotion to something afar
> From the sphere of our sorrow.

My father did not approve of Shelley, nor of the company he kept, such as Byron, whose biography I was forbidden to read in my teens.

It is possible, though not certain, that on present-day standards my mother's diet during pregnancy was far from good, though she was in Cornwall with the benefit of garden-fresh vegetables. My father was working in London, where there were many air raids, which made her anxious for his safety. Perhaps I was extra vulnerable, since I was the only one of the children to have mild rickets leading to knock-knees. I can remember hearing someone using the word *rickety*, which sounded unpleasant, and I sensed that they were talking about me. I somehow managed to catch ringworm, it was on my head, so all my hair had to be shaved off, which further offended my incipient girl's vanity.

By the time I was three, there had been five successive nannies to look after us children. The next one was taken on when the youngest child was on the way, and would come to Paris with us. She stayed for ten years: she had recently worked in an aristocratic Belgian family so she could already speak French and was very competent. But I hated her. It was unfortunate for me that the baby was very charming and became so to speak "hers". In the early days there was also a nursery-maid. I sided staunchly, to no avail, with one of them, Thérèse, when she was sacked for stealing. For there to be nursery quarters, and an attendant nanny living in, was usual in families of our kind, early in the last century. I think it would be an anachronism to condemn my mother automatically for not looking after us herself, even if that social system is widely criticised now, especially by women who give up some of their years in professional work for the sake of their young children. I myself stopped regular work outside home when my children were young. I had a certain amount of domestic help in various minimally equipped houses which by modern standards would be considered very un-labour-saving, and some of what follows later in this memoir illustrates the whole theme. The problems have not melted away.

Having had so many changes of nannies made me deeply insecure. I developed a tendency to suspect the grown-ups of making life difficult. I remember lots of fusses and eating troubles, and I discovered too early that I could hate people. It seems to me that I was really rather a nasty little girl, bad-tempered, biting my nails, grinding my teeth and that sort of thing. "They" tried to stop me with punishments: though they were not seriously unkind, they were unimaginative. It is obvious now that I was trying to demonstrate that I would have liked to bite them and not my nails. I could not obey the apparently simple request to stop those annoying practices.

There was an unbridged gap between my mother and me, I never thought I could turn to her when I was in trouble or that she had the slightest idea of what it was to be me. There were no cuddles. In all the time between my fourth and fourteenth years, I can only remember one occasion when she had tea in the nursery with us children.

Nanny never came to a meal in the dining room with our parents. They had one or two of us, in turn, to lunch with them. Nanny had alternate Sunday mornings and afternoons off duty and Thursday afternoons. On Sunday morning the three older children read parts of the Bible (one chapter from the Old Testament, another from the Psalms, and one from the New Testament) in the drawing room with our parents. On Christmas Day we went to the English establishment church, St. George's, near the British Embassy, but Nanny sat separately from us. Just possibly she preferred it that way, but it felt invidious. She did not come with us on weekend expeditions, so the class system was intrinsic to the way of life. She made no secret of not getting on well with Mother, "She has thin lips, she is ungenerous, your father is a nice man", she said. She belonged to the generation of post-war women who found no man to marry. She told us that her only much loved brother had tragically been lost, missing, never found, on the Western Front. That was very affecting: I sensed or perhaps simply observed her sadness, but there was no one to tell about these frightening and unhappy things. I got into the habit of hiding them inside myself, where they festered. I also never mentioned that I sided with the cook and the parlour maid when there was friction between the kitchen and the dining room.

Since the family lived in Paris all through the Nineteen Twenties, when I was aged between three-and-a-half and thirteen, there was plenty of opportunity to get to know the differences and the similarities between English and French people. Home was basically English in way of life and language, between us sisters, with Nanny and with our parents, who never got rid of their English accents. All the maids were French and I learned to speak French from them. It was because I could already speak French, but tried to conceal the fact, that I was sent to the kindergarten of the large Lycée where my older sisters already were. I think it was run on kindly Montessori lines, and retrospectively I cannot help feeling ashamed of how scornful I was of the manual tasks we were set to do, which I considered I could easily manage. In the next class up I was among 53 pupils. We sat in tiers, as in a university lecture hall. There was a great shortage of teachers, but I can remember clearly that it was satisfying to be incorporated with children of my own age, whose mannerisms I easily adopted, and somehow or other I learned to read in French. I had learned to read English at home.

After perhaps two more years my parents began to criticise the rigid methods of teaching and what even they considered was too much homework, and we were sent to a private school, the Cours Fénelon. I imbibed a lot of information of a factual kind; everything had to be done very accurately and marks were handed out continually for work done correctly. Grammar of course was central, and as I am obsessional I enjoyed it, and it has often been useful. Arithmetic was also a matter of accuracy, and geography was mostly learning just where every French town was, large and small, and drawing maps was fun. The whole world came in then, coastlines, rivers and mountain ranges. Essays had to be done to a formula. There was a lot of learning by heart, and skill acquired in doing that compulsorily acted as a basis for voluntarily enjoying poetry in my teens.

Each week marks were totted up, and small medals were earned, which we pinned onto our coats. The superior ones had blue enamel insets, and the best were white in a gilded setting. The system was intensely competitive, the medals advertised our academic prowess as we walked down the street, and there were prizes at the end of the school year. Our basic pocket money at home was augmented by good school marks, yet the family ethic was clearly that "showing off" was wrong.

It now seems odd that I did not find such contrasted atmospheres and experiences confusing. Probably I absorbed them both and accepted them as equally valid aspects of daily life. I was not so to speak hybridised, I simply felt both English and French. I would certainly have liked to look like a neat little French girl, to fit in completely with my contemporaries. I thought pullovers knitted by Nanny were not at all fashionable, and our party clothes were never trimmed with frills or lace. Such fripperies therefore became enviable. But living a double life must have felt to some extent normal, more than the usual school–home contrast. Children of the kind I met all seemed to be obedient conformists on the surface, although on another level they were totally French in the way they shrugged their shoulders at rules and conventions. I hope they were among those who were brave enough to become Resistance fighters when most of France was occupied by the Nazis.

As well as school in French, I had Latin lessons at home, from about the age of ten, alone with a tutor, the idea being that I should learn how it would be pronounced in what would be my next, English, school, and also learn some elementary maths. He had an interesting mind, full of miscellaneous information which I found more stimulating than what he was meant to be teaching. He gave me the impression that, mysteriously, Latin was not only dry but worthwhile, so knowing the origins of words has been useful ever since. Also in addition to school I had to go for hour-long walks, speaking German all the time, with a woman who had come from somewhere in South Russia after the 1917 Revolution. She seemed very depressed and I took neither to her nor to her Russian-accent German. It must have been an implicit introduction to the complications of European history. In 1926, I saw the headline for an article about education in my parents' copy of the daily paper, *Le Figaro*. It read: *Il faut abolir L'Esclavage des Enfants* ("the slavery of children should be abolished"). No wonder I cut it out, and my mother preserved it, among the photographs of that year! In contrast to all the intellectual education, the activity I really enjoyed was painting and varnishing small whitewood objects with intricate ancient Celtic patterns which I found in my mother's embroidery design books. I now see that those interweaving patterns demonstrated both dynamism and containment, most of them had a focal centre and they held psychological meanings which I only perceived many years later, when I had become a psychologist.

I think the valuable aspect of living in Paris for ten certainly formative years was that I did not so much compare the two main kinds of people in my life at that time and find the one or the other more admirable as I noticed, imbibed and learned to observe. It was not difficult to gather that my father was very critical of the French politicians connected with trying to enforce the harsh terms of the Treaty of Versailles; he disliked their excessive anti-German views. That was complicated for me, since the prizes for good work at school often took the form of luridly illustrated books detailing the cruel misdeeds of '*les Boches*', the

Germans, in the parts of France they had invaded in the recent war, and the provinces of Alsace and Lorraine annexed after the Franco-German war of 1870–71 and re-incorporated into France in 1919. The teacher of German had come from there. There were also frightening posters displayed on many streets, picturing terribly damaged faces (*les gueules cassées*), appealing for donations to funds for helping disabled old soldiers. It was not that I was subjected to conflicting kinds of emotion—I *thought* my parents were right in their opinions, but I *felt* deeply affected by the French point of view. The contrast just had to be accepted. It became an ingredient of the life-long struggle, and contrast, between thought and emotion, and that has coloured much of what I have done and written.

As it can be for many children, I benefited from going to a school where there were girls who I found were of a different religion from what I had at home. Most were Roman Catholics, who went to confession every week (they used to joke about simply working down a list they had been given of possible peccadilloes) and enjoyed being dressed up as little brides on the day of their First Communion. I knew a few of the girls were Jewish, but at that time I had not come across any anti-Semitism, nor even heard of the "Jewish question". Later I often wondered anxiously what happened to them during the Nazi occupation of France. A few, very few, were Protestant. That led to an interest, during history lessons, in learning about how their Huguenot ancestors had had to flee from France under Louis XIV, in the seventeenth century, benefiting the countries which would accept them: an introduction to the poignant subject of refugees.

My parents knew several Russian aristocrats who had managed to escape during the Communist Revolution. The men had become taxi drivers and the women dressmakers, and there was a girl who I remember at school, called Olga, who regaled and horrified me with stories of living in a cellar with only rats to eat. I felt uncomfortable when I met anyone with that name for many years, a misapplied kind of guilt at not having had to go through such experiences.

Besides miscellaneous pieces of knowledge acquired that way and in school books, I knew that my mother and several of her friends in London had, early in the then-recent war, worked in an organisation set up for Belgian refugees driven from their homes by the German invaders. Another intriguing aspect of history was that the patriotic school text books described the wickedness of the fifteenth-century English, who were so cruel to Joan of Arc (the idea and the imagined sensation of being burned at the stake were acutely terrifying), but my father told me she had done England a great service by helping to turn us out of a country where we did not belong. Learning about the two different interpretations of historical events has been important, ever since.

In terms of quality of life, Paris meant being cooped up in a flat, though we walked to and from school, about twenty minutes each way, and Nanny took the two younger ones for walks after morning school, to the Bois de Boulogne, the Paris version of Hampstead Heath. Mariella was the youngest, I was almost four years older. My intolerance of boring stupidity was painfully reinforced by those walks. The route taken was almost always the same. I can see now that there was probably not much choice, but I used to display my imagined superiority to the two of them by walking a little ahead, with slightly rounded shoulders. That was of course an unavailing way to demonstrate in action something that could not be spoken. Nothing would change, power lay somewhere else, and sulking had its own stupefying effect: no one tried to find out the cause of the sulks, which anyway I could probably not have explained convincingly. I was sent, the only child there, to what were called Swedish gym classes (why Swedish?) to make me hold myself better. They were unsuccessful. There were magazines on the table in the waiting room which hinted at mysterious and unmentionable dangers. I guessed later that they must have been venereal diseases. It felt like a guilty and puzzling secret, so I did not dare ask the teacher, a man, for enlightenment, nor anyone at home.

One important mitigating factor emerged from the walks during the second half of the Twenties: a smooth-haired terrier picked us up and followed us home from the Bois, in defiance of Nanny's efforts to shoo him away. He had an oil stain on his back, so he had presumably been hit by a car. After pleading desperately with my parents not to insist that he should be taken to the police, who I was sure would be heartless and have him put down, I succeeded in being allowed to keep him. He became mine, on condition that I exercised him twice a day, bathed him regularly and accepted to be generally responsible for him. I called him Peter, and he turned out to be an incurable fighter, so at first I had to extricate him from other dogs, and after that I had to make sure he always wore his muzzle. I had a link with him through discovering empathy with how he seemed to be trying to express anger openly, so he became my close companion, a wordless confidant. My sulks decreased.

When we were living in Paris, there was at least one winter when it was much colder than usual. The Grand Canal in the grounds of the magnificent palace at Versailles froze hard enough and long enough for us to be able to skate there, and on many memorable days. To my child's eyes it looked as though it stretched for miles and miles. Looking back now, it stands out in my mind as almost a dramatic experience of living in history. I knew that every winter the canals froze in Holland and other European countries, without realising that it was at that time also frequent to be able to skate long distances in the Fens. Ice skating was not only for Christmas card reproductions of Dutch paintings.

Another memory of childhood days in Paris was the man who came from somewhere in the outskirts with his herd of goats. He used to attract people out of their flats, piping old country tunes, and sell milk and cheese. My mother had several ocarinas, terracotta wind instruments on which she also played folk tunes, and she much enjoyed the times he came along the streets, and always went out to talk to him.

The windows of the nursery part of the flat looked out onto a courtyard, a stale smell often rose from it, especially on warm days. It was impossible to see the sky without leaning right out, over the edge of the balcony, which of course we were not meant to do. I do not think the sun ever came into our rooms and I considered my parents' sunnier ones, looking out over the street, were superior. Another version of the class system! The maids had bleak bedrooms at the top of all the flats, which I felt was shocking, but I knew my parents did too, and that was a comfort.

The lack of sky in the nine Paris months was splendidly compensated by my intense pleasure in the wide views of sea and sky in Cornwall during the three summer ones. The garden was large enough for good and inventive games; the fields were freedom, providing cow-pats were avoided; the farm horses became friends, though the geese on the pond were alarming enemies to be braved, on the way to collecting fish from the village or milk and freshly clotted cream from the farm. The milk was in an aluminium can, it had been more or less cooled, and the rich clotted cream was always in its traditional, open, glass bowl. Once I had got over my earliest fears of the crash of waves on the steep beach at high tide (which Jenifer says led to screams at the noise of bath water), the daily swim, whatever the weather and however rough the sea, laid the basis for life-long physical and aesthetic satisfaction.

Many of the fields were still cultivated then, and the corn was stacked to dry in little pyramids, the stooks, before being carted ("carried") to the farmyard and threshed by a noisy, dust-producing but exciting machine. Chickens pecked about in the yard, there were ducks as well as geese, and elms half-overhanging the pond. At that time, too, the hedges and zigzagged stone walls were rich with all sorts of flowers and butterflies, most of which have since disappeared. In the sky the endless gyrations of wind-loving gulls were deeply woven into all my other pleasures, the cliff jackdaws, rock pigeons, sparrow hawks, kestrels, buzzards; the oyster catchers, wagtails and little shore birds, each with their ways of communicating, warning or aggressively fighting off rivals. Before returning to the narrowness of life in the Paris flat, we usually saw brilliant white gannets, flying westward, high and far out at sea, then diving to the delight of watchers (we did not side with the fish!).

All those aesthetic pleasures provided a perfect contrast to what felt to be the banalities of nursery life. I know I am nostalgically idealising how it was for me, and I realise I knew only a little of how life was in the farmworkers' and fishermen's cottages, or how hard their lives were in the winter. When I went down to the village, I often met Tommy, the unfortunate old-seeming man, with his shambling gait, his loose and slobbering mouth and his talk which was difficult to understand. I was helped not to be frightened of him, and most likely he was happier living in the village with tolerant people around than if he had been sent off to the large asylum up at Bodmin, many miles away. Another member of his family, called Dorothy but known as Dotty, used to bring a hot-water-bottle down to the beach, to pour into the sea just where she was going to bathe. I thought it was a plausible idea.

Back in Paris, during the Easter break from school, Mariella was usually left with Nanny, and for the three older ones there were marvellous holidays with lots of mountain walks. Twice we went to the Pyrenees. It rained most of the time, but on one memorable day we walked through high bleak country over the frontier between France and Spain, with the help of a pony and a mule. We talked about the epic medieval *Chanson de Roland*, with the great friendship between those unavailingly chivalrous knights, Roland and Oliver, killed at the pass of Roncevaux fighting against the Saracens, the feared Moslems of the Middle Ages. What we did not know, of course, was that many years later, during the Spanish civil war in the Thirties, hundreds of Basque children would cross those mountains, fleeing from the armies of General Franco. Another year we stayed on the edge of the Italian lake of Orta, where we learned to row small boats. Father wrote lectures on many mornings, and told us about Mussolini's Fascism by drawing our attention to the malevolent-looking policemen, with their black patent leather headgear. Mother sketched and I think we found ample ways of enjoying ourselves. We played various games which even included such apparently over-serious or highbrow pastimes as practising irregular Latin verbs, daring each other to get them right. As there was of course no radio or TV, we did not feel the lack of them and probably benefited from devising our own quizzes. We were largely ignorant of popular culture, and did not know we were.

My father's eldest daughter, Barbara, did not feature much for me, as she was so many years older, except that when she visited Paris she and Nanny used to talk about how they both disliked my mother, her step-mother. I do not remember feeling uncomfortably disloyal, I suppose I learned to hear and indeed to listen but not to comment, which sounds cold-hearted now, though sensible. It was just how things were. In any case I knew

I was emotionally ambivalent towards Mother. Barbara conveyed the existence of men friends, but I took no notice.

My two elder sisters, Prue and Jenifer, went to the Berkshire country boarding school, Downe House, in 1927, and I remained in Paris with the rest of the family until 1930. So I had more years of French education than those elder sisters, both born before the First World War, and than Mariella, born after it. There were only eighteen months between Prue and Jenifer and it was convenient for the grown-ups to consider them a pair. They had shared a bedroom, while I slept with Nanny and Mariella for many years. My memory of them before they left was of frequent bitter rivalries, quarrels and fights (there were often scratched faces at breakfast, which was rather exciting), since their characters were very different and they found each other deeply uncongenial.

I had minded a lot that I was not allowed to form a trio with them but had been paired with Mariella, who was nearly four years younger. She was always very kind to me, for example, when she sensed, correctly, that there had been some sort of unfairness, but that did not feel to be enough help. For children, a few years seem far more significant than they become later: we indulged in rigid beliefs of superior/inferior according to age. Moreover, I imagined, after reaching Downe House, that escape from the family would grant me a safe kind of anonymity. Within a week or so I overheard another girl criticizing, all too perceptively, something about my character, so the fantasy had to be given up that only at home did everybody know everything there was to be known about me. The lack of emotional privacy there had been combined with painful inner loneliness. Sensing that particular kind of loneliness in others, and being concerned for them, was important much later, during the years when I practised as a psychologist. Of course it is essential not to misuse such subjective knowledge, and to "see" it where it is not. But it does mean that empathising with fundamentally lonely people is part of relating to them. They may be different from me in all sorts of other ways, but if they want to conceal their loneliness and at the same time try to give the impression of being generally all right, I know personally and privately what they mean.

When my sisters left the Paris flat, at least in term-time, I achieved a bedroom of my own, which became a kind of study. It was a respite from being the in-between one, and some years later I discovered that during most of the time through childhood and the teens I had thought that I was, in a mysterious way, not a real separate person at all, but a tenuous and cloudy mixture of somebody called Prue-and-Jen. As they had quarrelled and fought, so the struggle between what I felt were two aspects and versions of me went on inside. The long journey towards becoming a full individual, with ideas of what I wanted to do in life, perhaps quite different things from anyone else in the family, was of course completely unknown, not contemplated. It was not even 'a wild surmise', to use Keats' words about Cortez's sailors when they first glimpsed the Pacific. That journey, that struggle, are the warp and weft of this book. Much later I came across two remarkable books by women, each a genius in her own way, Virginia Woolf's *A Room of One's Own*, and Marion Milner's *A Life of One's Own*, and admired them profoundly for breaking new ground when they were struggling with the problem of who they were.

Three

The Nineteen Thirties

The international Reparations Commission was wound up in 1930 without having dealt satisfactorily with the after-effects of the defeat of Germany. I was old enough to understand my father's disappointment that it had not been as successful as he and others had hoped. His time as a Civil Servant came to an end. He was sixty by then. Ten years earlier he had left the Aliens Department of the Home Office, where he had worked in the First World War, trying hard but not very successfully to liberalise policy there. He had also left his London practice as a Chancery barrister. The work in Paris had in effect made him into an international lawyer. Behind the scenes his opinion was valued in Liberal circles in London, and his views were used anonymously, in leading articles in the then *Manchester Guardian.*

On his return to England, however, he had no practice or academic post or work in any legal institution. The world economic system began to go downhill: in America there was the stock market crash of 1929, and trouble spread to Europe. First it was called the Slump, then it became the Depression of the Thirties. Unemployment was increasingly serious, with its dreadful effects on so many millions of people. The rise of the Nazis was inexorable. There was war in the Far East, the Japanese invasion of Manchuria. For my father, gloom set in and he felt under-employed, although at different times he was on various committees: he was Chairman of the Royal Commission on Tithe, lectured at The Hague on international law, ran several interesting arbitration cases and became well known as an authority in those fields. I do not remember him being really happy, except in relation to my mother and his high expectations for his daughters, for the rest of his life.

For my mother, I think the move to a house they built outside Oxford, with a good view of its famous university buildings (but no intrusion from the manufacturing ugliness of the Cowley motor-works), gave her leisure to continue her etching, her wood engraving, her embroidery, some gardening and singing in the local Bach Choir. She had a few like-minded friends. I am sure she sympathised with my father's disappointment at not getting in to much of the Oxford academic life, but they were both able to spend more time in Cornwall than before. They bought a radio (a "wireless") and a car. Mother became a better driver than Father. His activities in international affairs fuelled my hopes for myself. I was already aware of my unspoken ambition of becoming something much more than what would have been merely a background wife and mother, a helpmeet for an impressive man. I did not know the word *feminist*, but it would have been useful for describing what I imagined for my future. I wanted to get away from the depressing atmosphere at home, where I was still mostly in the nursery.

Almost at once my wishes were granted: Nanny left. I felt I could step forth into freedom, away from her after ten long years and away from the claustrophobic flat. Coming back to England involved a sad parting from the terrier, Peter, but it led to my going to Downe House, in the country.

Downe House was an excellent school for me, for many reasons. Its first home, when founded with only a few girls in 1907 by the outstanding Miss Olive Willis, was in what had been Charles Darwin's house in Kent. Although it had moved to Berkshire, the indirect connection with him gave me a sense of learning the subjects which rapidly became important to me in an establishment where, earlier, a significant piece of history had been made. I cannot remember any member of staff suggesting I should read either *On the Origin of Species* or *The Descent of Man*, and I wish someone had, since they would have been history and literature for me as well as science. The sciences were not given much real attention when I was there, the labs were not up-to-date and the science staff were not of as good quality as were those on the Arts side.

One of Miss Willis' aims was that Downe should be more appropriate for twentieth-century girls than were other schools, which aped boys' public schools slavishly. She wanted to allow room for attention to be given to emotions as well as to the intellect. Downe had many points in common with the very progressive co-educational Bedales, and since I came from an all-girls family, I might have benefited from that. But I think that I was not ready for what would have been too much strain. It was more restful in my teens not to be interacting or competing with boys when I had so many other developmental things to cope with. Near to us in Cornwall there was a family of three very congenial boys, with whom I spent a lot of my time in joint activities in the Easter and summer holidays.

The atmosphere at Downe was fully liberal and democratic: we met and talked with the staff at meals and in free time. Hierarchy was at a minimum since the prefects, who were at that time staff-chosen in most other schools, were elected by all the girls. There were very few rules, only minimal punishments, no internal exams, no prizes or 'houses' which might have engendered competitiveness, unlike the often-bitter sisterly rivalries at home.

In the summer term we wore tunics of any colour we wanted, which looked good at collective events such as the annual "massed gym", which was a little like what was fashionable in Czechoslovakia at that time. We also had picturesque country dancing displays in the big cloister square: the whole place had earlier housed an eccentric religious Order. The tunics were helpful for the development of individuality, allowing us to choose colours which suited each of us. Most of us appreciated the slightly cranky winter uniform, which was kind to girls whose figures were elemental rather than elegant. Jenifer has reminded me that the unflattering school colours of moss-green and heather-purple, chosen by Olive Willis when she founded Downe, were the same as those of the Suffragettes who ran the Women's Social and Political Union. Miss Willis was herself more a scholar than a militant feminist. Women had only been fully enfranchised as recently as 1928, achieving the vote at the age of twenty-one, like men, and I think we took that victory for granted. I cannot claim that the Downe school colours were my introduction to feminism. We changed into our own clothes after the daily games. I took to lacrosse avidly, especially as it was played in a large field, the boundaries were the natural hedges and it involved running very fast. The other winter game, netball, was too constricted to my liking. The company of those who also enjoyed games was a good contrast for me to that of my closer friends, who were most of them as academically inclined as I was. One who I knew well hated daily lacrosse so much that she played as badly as she could, but did not achieve dispensation.

Downe is in a beautiful hilly and wooded part of the country, and there were wide views in most directions. Provided there were three of us, we walked and biked as far as we could in the safety which was taken for granted then. Many of us slept out on camp beds in the summer with the intense pleasure of watching the planets and stars. The French phrase, à *la belle étoile*, conveys the beauty of sleeping out better than does the simpler *under the stars*.

As the number of girls increased, various buildings were added higgledy-piggledy onto what they had originally been. As well as the cloister, with its simple arches, there was also an outdoor theatre, with sloping stone seats as in an ancient Greek one, so that unconventionality was expressed in material ways as well as in the general atmosphere. Plays were produced every summer. The building works were done under the direction of Miss Nikel, an eccentric woman refugee from Poland, whose variegated earlier life had included, she told me, historical research work in the Vatican Library.

Being at Downe was a marvellous contrast to the restrictions of the flat in Paris and to the attendant conventions of town life there. Being liberated from the narrow daily company of Nanny (which had admittedly been mitigated at week-ends by my parents' civilising influence) was very stimulating to my budding interests, especially English and History, which were very well taught. I learned much too little "hard" science. As my present interest is less in material facts (of which anyway there are now too many to cope with) than in the psychological interaction between the scientific method and the ways of thinking of arts people, I am belatedly trying to catch up. Since we did not have to spend any time going to and from home, as my daughters did in their time at their London day school, there were clubs and societies in the early evenings. Discovering that I could take part in them and write papers to be discussed in the group was one of the first excitements.

I can remember the subjects of two of the papers I wrote, which are relevant here since each of them was a precursor of my later studies and interests. One, presented to the History Society, was on the life, beliefs and influence of the sixteenth-century Ignatius Loyola. He had gone through a deep psychological crisis after nearly dying from war-wounds, later founded the high-powered if narrow-minded Jesuit order and wrote for its members a book of strict instructions on how to meditate. The probably over-ambitious philosophical paper was on symbolism, extracted and eagerly developed from a learned book about the architectural symbols of Chartres cathedral. There was also a debate about capitalism and socialism in which my left-wing efforts to introduce a lot of information about international politics and economics had little effect on the listeners. It was certainly useful to have been taught to plan my writing, and at the same time to be encouraged to develop spontaneity. I look back now with mild affection on those early efforts, including poetry in the school magazine, composed in a free manner so different from the kind of formulaic compositions required in Paris. I can recapture some of the excitement and anxiety felt then, which still, so many years later, came with presenting professional work to colleagues, or even when simply proposing a friend's health. I usually make some kind of slip, and can privately trace its significance, which is not necessarily "Freudian" or sexual.

For the first two years at Downe I was adapting to how congenial life had become, in the main. One adolescent feature, though, on the shadowy side, was characteristic of that time of life for many young people and by then I knew its name: depression. I used to get apparently causeless but low and bad phases, which usually lasted several weeks. I did not know there were angry emotions locked up in them. Then, without having been able either to meditate on them (as perhaps Loyola might have) or examine them in an analytical way, I did nothing but live through them. They were not connected with periods, which my mother had unfortunately introduced me to some years earlier with the gloomy name of "the Curse", and instructed me not to swim at that time or take other strenuous exercise. I felt that as a girl all I could do was to tolerate such major deprivations. I realise she held the then-fashionable view about menstruation, and at Downe it was called "being off games", so I was resentful if I missed playing in a match.

When the depression had mysteriously gone, I would wake up without it: it felt as though it had burnt itself out and energy had returned. Presumably there was now enough good stuff in life to counteract the bad. Some kind of healing trust had been engendered, or a lower level reached, where there were reserves of vitality. It was as though I was a field which had lain fallow for a while. I could not have known that the recurrence of such difficult experiences was what took me into analysis later, and led to what became my major career.

In November 1933, under the aegis of our excellent history specialist, Jean Rowntree, a group of us started producing a newspaper for circulation in the school. It was called *The Times Explained* (we liked the pun) and ran until I left Downe a year later. She had it typed and duplicated to be sold in the school. She taught us Current Events as well as history, and told me recently, in very old age, that she still has all her notes for those lessons. And she remembers all about the newspaper. We wrote articles on a wide variety of public affairs, and I find that in the copies I kept many world events were covered as well as some of what was happening in the British Isles. There were pieces on Parliament, agricultural subsidies, naval negotiations, the Welsh coal dispute, the Austrian problem, the rise of the Nazi movement (including reference to concentration camps), Spain's latest crisis, Church conflict in Germany, war between Bolivia and Paraguay, the murder in Marseille of King Alexander of Yugoslavia, conflicts between Serbs, Bosnians and Macedonians; and so on. Reading those articles now puts me in touch with the Thirties background of many tragic contemporary events. I and another girl were the Editors and we enlisted about nine other writers. There were at least ten issues, of which I can now find only six.

The year-long effort was well worthwhile, even if it may now sound oppressively serious as a spare-time occupation for school-girls. It has to be remembered that we were living in deep country with no radio, TV or access to movies, let alone pop music. For me personally it is interesting to look back on that time, since it contains and illustrates several of my later pursuits: world affairs, writing, editing the *Journal of Analytical Psychology* from 1977 to 1986, and generally co-operating with contemporaries. It combined information, ideas and practical work. It must have helped us towards emerging from narrower school affairs. And it was fun doing it.

Another member of staff also enabled my generation to do something rather adventurous, she was the French mistress, Mlle Agobert. Nobody dared tell her that she did not wash often enough, and smelled disgustingly of stale sweat. She was no model for French couture, wearing the same black dress all the year round, with three different detachable collars, but she was brilliant in her own way. She was a slave-driver, producing acts from several plays by Molière, Corneille and Racine. She ran them in as close a way as possible to productions of classical plays in Paris and made us perform as though we were budding French actresses. I was usually given male parts, but did not mind too much when that included strutting about as the emperor Nero in a purple toga, wearing a bay-leaf wreath. The plays were boldly taken to three northern French towns, acted to audiences in the *Lycées* and reported with approval and amusement in the local press. At the time it was an extraordinary enterprise, which conveyed to us indirectly that out-of-the-ordinary things could be attempted.

A very important aspect of life at Downe was morning and evening prayers in the austere concrete chapel. At the Sunday morning service the girls from the top form, known as Seniors rather than prefects, took turns to read the passages selected from the Old Testament. As I was already aware, at least in theory, of how poor millions of people were, in England as well as further afield, I was very pleased that the first piece I was given was from Isaiah, chapter 55:

> Ho, every one that thirsteth, come ye to the waters, and he that
> hath no money; come ye, buy and eat; yea, come, buy wine and
> milk without money and without price.

The sense of power in declaiming those words still comes to
mind, and I felt Isaiah was my friend. Not long after, I began to
have serious misgivings about being a Christian, and confused
that with any and all kinds of religion. Since going to church
regularly both at Downe and in the holidays was compulsory, I
needed to revolt. Hypocrisy and living a lie had to be challenged. As it has been for countless people, Pilate's reported
question, "What is truth?", obviously appealed to me, and I
could not answer it. When I went to admit my loss of faith to
Miss Willis, she simply asked me to tell her more, in a very tolerant way, and never held it against me. She did not add that
perhaps one day I would come to see it all differently, which is
characteristic of how she treated her pupils as equals, and did
not talk to them from on high.

In my family it was an assumption that we would all go to
University. We would then be well-educated women. I cannot
remember any discussion of what would happen after that,
which, in the event, was sensible.

My sisters and I were lucky that at that stage our mother
wisely made no rueful complaints about not having gone to
school and a lack of formal education, as compared with all the
opportunities we had. In fact, she had learned how to work
hard from lessons with very few other girls, including what now
seem monstrously unimportant parts of the Old Testament, but
she had taught herself a great deal of literature and the history
of art. My parents did not appear to know there were any other
possible places for us than Oxford or, at a pinch, Cambridge. Father had been happy at New College as well as successful, and
they had chosen to live near Oxford after the Paris work finished. Barbara had not fitted in well with academic life, and
Prue had married during her second year at Somerville College.
Where I was concerned, those factors combined to turn my attention keenly towards Cambridge. I felt strongly that I had had
enough of fitting in with what was expected of me.

But the major factor was that Jenifer was well on the way to achieving a First Class degree in what was also my chosen sub-ject, history. I thought I would be tagging along behind her if I aimed at Oxford, since the implicit competitive atmosphere which seemed to envelop everything in our family dictated that I would continue to be the less successful younger sister.

At that time we only used the telephone in major crises, and most exceptionally I was allowed to ring up my parents from the school office as the deadline approached for filling in an appli-cation form. I wanted to insist that I was going to disobey them by applying only to Newnham, and not to Girton also (the only other women's college), since Girton was two miles out from the main part of the University, and sounded more 'schooly'. I felt it was a dramatic and major defiance, over and above the revolu-tionary rejection of Oxford. Fortunately Newnham offered me an exhibition, a kind of grant I had never heard of, so my defiance was vindicated.

At the end of the autumn term, 1934, school was over. Having read Milton's *Paradise Lost* not long before, I knew my personal version of two of its nearly last lines,

> The World was all before them, where to choose
> Thir place of rest, and Providence thir guide. [*sic*]

In spite of the rapidly worsening state of the world and doubts about Providence, I felt personal optimism. Downe had given me confidence, not indeed to rest, but to go forward.

The months between leaving school—where I had enjoyed stimulating company, safely separate from family life—and the years at Cambridge were spent at first with my parents in what I felt was a dull house in the uninspiring suburbia of Headington Hill just outside Oxford. I believed the desirable intellectual peo-ple lived on Boar's Hill, on the other side of that damp town. Mariella, who was much friendlier to Mother than I was, and who appreciated the romantic view of Oxford spires and towers in the valley below, was by then at Downe.

There were many dim misty days, very little company of my own age and my father's increasing depression about the state of the world seemed to colour everything grey. If I had been more alert to what was actually available, I would perhaps have

explored the riches of the Ashmoleum Museum. I did go to see
what had been Shelley's room in University College and bought
a pocket copy of his atheistic prose works. I got to know the
second-hand book-shops well, looking for such bargains. But
the pattern developed of not being good at finding out what I
could do alone, apart from reading.

The convention was very strong that in the evening we all sat
reading in front of the economically small coal fire while Father
also read and Mother silently persevered with her embroidery. I
thought her stitching was obsessional, like the ticking of the
grandfather clock, and somehow a reproach to me. Perhaps I
had forgotten that for many years I had enterprisingly designed
and knitted various garments, scorning the patterns I could have
bought in shops. I did not buy women's magazines which I considered represented the wrong kind of femaleness. Without realising it, I wanted the real thing, with men of my age.

I turned up my nose at the idea of being interested in anything Mother did, and was full of nasty distaste and scorn to-
ward her, with whom I seemed to have nothing in common. I
could sense she longed for intimacy, but I could not give it. I
dropped into bored unenterprising moods, not realising that
what was lacking was any opportunity of getting to know young
men. There was no contact with undergraduates, who were of
course all occupied to the full with their own work, sports and
love affairs with women students. I cannot remember any conscious awareness of sexual longings.

As my parents' house was outside Oxford, and they were not
interested in the cinema, it was difficult to get to see films,
though going by bike would have been possible: but again, who
with? In those days before any, let alone several, TV sets in
every house, films might have shown me what was missing.

On Sundays there was usually a solemn expedition to what
was then called Morning Service in St. Mary's, the University
church. The resident vicar, Canon Cockin, gave intellectual sermons, which could be worked in somehow with my atheism.
And though I rejected the doctrine, I enjoyed the poetical words
of the sixteenth-century prayer book. But in the evening we
went to the service in New College chapel, grudgingly on my
part and telling my parents they were hypocritical. I switched

into my scorning mood, maintaining that going there had nothing to do with real religion, that they only went because it was Father's old college and Mother wanted to hear the organ and the singing, which was indeed exquisite. Since she was a keen member of the Oxford Bach choir, and organised some good-quality out-of-the-ordinary carols every Christmas, that was typical of how I viewed her. I was not, as Jenifer had been at that stage of her life, three years earlier, openly rude or insulting, but coldly unloving, ungiving, unappreciative.

At some stage in the winter, I had told Ka Arnold-Forster, a family friend in Cornwall, of whom I was very fond, that I would like to try rock climbing. She told me about a party of climbers and walkers who had been going to North Wales at Easter for many years, staying at a famous old inn, Pen-Y-Pass. The path to Snowdon starts from there, and there are countless climbs on all the mountains round about. She was sure that I could simply write to Geoffrey Winthrop-Young or his wife, to ask if I could join them.

They were mostly Cambridge people, who had started climbing before the war. The leading spirit was Geoffrey, who had lost a leg below the knee while driving ambulances in the North Italian campaign during that war, but had climbed the Matterhorn in the Twenties, with a guide he knew well. He had a nailed leather piece fitted to his wooden leg, and he was almost dauntless. He was a poet, and had collected round him several well-known climbers, (including, earlier, George Mallory, who had been killed on Mount Everest). Jack Longland, who was very warm-hearted, had also climbed on Everest, was there too. He was camping with his young wife: that was considered exceptional behaviour, in those now far-off days.

Mallory's brilliant daughters were at the Easter party: Clare, already reading history at Girton College, who sometimes took risks, and Berridge, who was going to be a doctor and who was the more careful of the two. Their mother hovered anxiously in the background. I made friends with them at once and found to my great joy that the whole party included me easily, though I was a raw and absolute beginner. I had acquired some nailed climbing boots (no-one wore rubber-soled ones then: they thought they would slip on the wet Welsh cliffs, though Jack

Longland broke old conventions, scaling up exposed rock slabs like a monkey, in gym shoes). I had never owned what was then called a wind-jacket: as soon as I arrived I saw that everybody else was properly equipped, so, using my nail-scissors, I cut my raincoat short with no fears of my mother's disapproval.

It rained most of the time, and in spite of the water, which of course ran up my sleeves as I reached hopefully skywards, trying to find the next almost nonexistent crack, I was exhilarated by it all. The atmosphere of the group of mainly very experienced climbers was totally receptive to such a young beginner as I was. They were prepared to help, instruct and encourage in a way that amazed me. It was a kind of brotherhood. At that stage in the history of rock climbing, I think more or less everybody was Oxbridge, or similar in background. The war opened up the mountains to anybody prepared to enjoy them, so that now the old snobbishness has disappeared.

In the evenings, after a surprisingly conventional dinner with much talk, not only about mountains, everybody sat round the fire singing sentimental songs, many of them being poems of Geoffrey's set to music. I got to know one or two University lecturers, young dons who drew me into their circle at Cambridge when I got there the following autumn. My friendship with Clare Mallory flourished, and has lasted all the rest of our lives. The war got in the way of my continuing to climb, but Clare and Berridge both moved to America, went on climbing and became almost addicts to it. Clare married the impressive American physicist Glenn Millikan, but tragically for her and their three sons, he, like her father, was killed mountain-climbing.

Four

Vienna

During the gap between school and Cambridge, it would have been sensible to learn typing and shorthand. But I and my parents looked down on secretarial skills as probably not leading to work at a high level (with a secretary of my own?), and a cookery course was not considered either. I wish I could claim that incipient (even if narrow-minded) feminism on my part influenced those decisions: they were simply aspects of family assumptions. If it had been feminism, it would have been on the grounds that boys did not do secretarial or cookery courses.

I do not think it was usual then for there to be even a typewriter in the house (as it is for computers nowadays), nor did I think of acquiring one and teaching myself to use it. I assumed naïvely that I would learn to cook when the need arose, as indeed I did, but in fact I could have benefited from a course, which would have given me knowledge of basic methods. The family myth was that Mother hardly knew even how to boil an egg. A few years later I learned through often-disastrous mistakes, and war-time cooking helped me and others in my generation to develop skilful methods with limited ingredients. We became economical and discovered how to use up leftovers imaginatively. I appreciated most of Simone de Beauvoir's *The Second Sex* when it appeared in England in 1953, but she poured scorn on home cooking as being uncreative. I disagreed with her on that: she wrote that there would be nothing to show for a cake a few days after a woman had baked it. That seemed to me to be a distortion of feminism.

To return to the gap between school and Cambridge, after that digression: improving my German was decided on as an occupation for some of the summer of 1935. My elder sister Prue was living in Vienna as her husband was one of the Secretaries at the British Embassy there. She had recently had her first baby, Hubert, and I would not have improved my German much if I had stayed with them. Prue chose a family where I could lodge, having been told to select one which was not too expensive. My father was much less well off than he had been before retiring, and he gave us the impression, without any details, that his investments had suffered from the world economic crisis. There was not much cash to spare. He paid the selected family for my lodging, and gave me an allowance. The plan had been for me to be in Vienna for three months, but after two of them he found he could not afford me more time there, so I had to go home. I cannot remember even considering looking for paid work, which would be the obvious thing for a girl to do now, in such circumstances.

Unfortunately for me, the family Prue had found was not only very depressing—the haggard mother was bedridden in a room which I thought smelled of death—the father was a boorish, ill-educated old soldier and as Nazi-seeming as the two repulsive sons, who I felt sure were members of a Brownshirt organisation for young people. There was certainly no question of even mild sexual attraction to them. I remember the mid-day meal as usually nothing but pasta with no sauce, and conversation was dreary as well as difficult.

I was rapidly becoming very left-wing but too cowardly, or too drilled in drawing-room-type politeness, to do more than the minimum to challenge their nationalistic and overly Germanic attitudes. I believed in the philosophy of the League of Nations, enshrined in its rules, the Covenant. The United States never joined the League, (already afraid of 'our American boys being slaughtered in the Balkans', according to a newspaper article of that time, which I have recently found), but by the early Thirties Austria and Germany had become members. I did not risk reminding my hosts of that. One of the League's central themes was *collective security*: all its member countries were to be actively concerned in dealing with aggression wherever it occurred. I could not tell them about my admiration for my father's collected lectures, *Some Aspects of the Covenant of the League of Nations.* I had learned from them that changes of all kinds had taken place through the shifting of powerful forces, especially wars, the recent one having been the worst, but all history was riddled with them, from the Ancient world onwards. The family where I lodged would have wanted Austria to follow Germany into aggressive Nazism. I found my father's theme of peaceful change an important one, and much later, in the course of my work as an analytical psychologist, I took up the subject of change and resistance to change in both patients and analysts.

My way of emulating my father at that stage in life was to use his expertise in international law as a stepping-stone to social-ism, since the impending rivalry between the democracies and the autocracies threatened the survival of the League. Inevitably he and my mother were alarmed by the bogey of Communism, and in my idealism I shut my eyes to the excesses of Stalinism in the U.S.S.R. At that time it suited me not to see its parallels with Nazidom. My terms were simple, and I was not tempted to go further left than socialism, which was still a theory for me. I had never had any personal contact either with socialist workers or with people towards whom I felt such an immediate antipathy as the Viennese family with whom I lodged. When I was in their flat I mainly kept quiet and made friends with the two maids, who I saw as representing "the workers". I went out as much as I could. The family did not make any effort to find out what I was doing, perhaps I conveyed I was visiting my sister and brother-in-law more often than I actually was. I met a few of their diplomatic friends, who were certainly different from the young people I was meeting. They seemed distinctly right-wing and uncongenial.

Looking back now, I can see that although I neither learned much German from the family I disliked nor used the time to find out anything which might have been historically valid about the bases of their dangerous views, yet it was useful to have had at least some exposure to that kind of mid-European atmosphere two years after Hitler had taken power in Germany. The group of friends I made, through playing tennis with an English friend who was living in a very congenial Viennese family, were uni-versity students and young graduates mostly studying medicine or becoming journalists. One of them, rather older, seemed especially attracted to me, which I enjoyed. Towards the end of my time there, when my parents said I must come home, he offered to lend me his flat, as he was just then going away for two weeks. My mother sent me an agitated telegram: "Living alone Vienna impossible wire plans immediately". I was in any case holding back when I discovered he was going to Germany and I sensed that the others did not fully trust him. It was worrying that they perhaps thought he had Nazi leanings, without confronting him outright, but it was useful political education. A year or so later, when several of them had come to England as refugees, they could not bear any reference to him.

Another tall young man who especially liked red-headed and blond girls of my type also took to me, but I did not reciprocate as keenly as he would have liked. I was scared of a sexual commitment and anyway did not find him attractive. Later, in England, he married the elder sister of the friend of mine mentioned above, they had many daughters and he did enterprisingly well in journalism and business. His brother, advanced in his medical studies, also took refuge in Britain and became a particularly close friend of my sister, Mariella. There seem to be sisters in many of my anecdotes, and a dearth of brothers.

The whole group of us met regularly in the popular Café Schottentor, near the University, according to what free time they had. We sat at tables out on the pavement drinking endless cups of black coffee, reading every possible newspaper and sharing our views on the world. As well as contributing to the improvement of my German, they helped me to expand on what I had learned at school from editing *The Times Explained*, especially about the history of unrest and near-terrorism under the previous Chancellor, Dollfüss. He had vainly tried to stem economic collapse, being anxious about the growing influence of the German-type National Socialists, who, my friends explained, were viciously against genuine socialism. In February 1934, having earlier suspended the democratically elected Parliament, he had ordered the bombardment of the workers' great blocks of flats, converting left-wing political aspirations into deep bitterness: thereafter they could not possibly trust him when he appeared to be taking steps against the Nazi danger, and he was assassinated by Nazi sympathisers. I am not sure how widely known it was that Hitler in Germany and Mussolini in Italy were equally dangerous to the survival of Austria, because of their current rivalries. I was only just beginning to understand the intricacies of international power politics.

My friends took me to see the huge estate, the Karl Marx Hof, and other bullet-pocked buildings. I do not know how much loss of life there had been. I was learning history in the raw. It was a serious introduction for me to some of the material damage and human agony which, throughout the rest of the century, became so dreadfully familiar, in so many parts of the world. I could no longer be a mild Liberal, and although of course I was not a participant and was ultimately safe in having a home in England, it laid the foundation for a concern for oppressed and unarmed people who cannot do anything against the immediacy of guns, and can only take long-term political action through militant leaders.

As well as those long and informative conversations in the Schottentor which were the serious part of those months, I also enjoyed walking in the hot June sun up the path along the bank of the wide and strong-flowing Danube so as to swim downstream, then mild evening flirtations in the unintellectual funfair, the Prater, and week-end expeditions out of Vienna. I remember an occasion when we were staying in a youth hostel, and one of the group was taking an exam the following week. She had not come down to the garden for breakfast with the rest of us. I thought it was obvious to start assembling coffee, rolls and butter to take up to her. I was firmly stopped from doing so because it was an unsocialist thing to do, which I thought ridiculous, and said so. They were serious, though I laughed at them, but they did not hold it against me, accepting that I was not yet socialist enough.

The café conversations led to an exciting enterprise. Someone suggested I should start writing political articles and try to get them published. The idea caught on. One of them in particular, who was himself aiming to be a journalist, and several others who had all lived through the violent times of the year before, contributed the facts as they saw them. I had no pull with the weekly magazine, *Time and Tide*, of which Lady Rhondda was

Editor then, and many of her contributing journalists were women, but I must have been fortunate in sending my article to her, rather than to the more left-wing *New Statesman*. She accepted it.

So first "Fascism against Fascism" appeared in July, coming from 'An Austrian Correspondent'. Two weeks later *Time and Tide* innocently published a letter from my sister Jenifer, she had just got her First Class degree in history, and knew I had written the article. She signed herself "J. Williams, Oxford", correcting what I had written about the Carinthian peasants' attitudes to Nazism. She wrote, among other things, 'I am afraid that the author (though undoubtedly a budding historian) has omitted to put into practice the first principle of his profession, and has generalised too freely as regards the political sympathies of the Austrian peasants'. She then gave some details, different from the ones I had acquired from my friends, who claimed to know some peasants in one or two of the provinces. She added in a pseudo-pompous style, to my amusement when I saw the letter, '. . . if not in the interests of accuracy, and only to save your correspondent from disappointment, I feel it incumbent on me to draw attention to these significant (though admittedly incomprehensible) events'. The pretence of assuming the author's maleness, and concealing her own gender by giving no first name, were typical more of her than of me.

By then my second article, entitled "A Habsburg Restoration?" had appeared, examining possible future developments. I had become '*Our* Austrian Correspondent', which was very exciting, so perhaps the sub-editor had not spotted that Jenifer's surname was the same as mine. She and I were good-humoured at that time, not caught up in the sisterly rivalry and envy which developed in our middle years. We never spoke about such uncomfortable matters. She developed successfully in her professional work long before I did, and also had many exciting times with men, which I did not. We lost the teenage banter which had been so pleasurable earlier, when we were sometimes mistaken for each other, even by people who knew us. We were quite like each other in looks but not in personality, and from then on, until recently, our lives were only minimally similar.

Establishing difference and my own individuality became increasingly important. I felt that the *Time and Tide* articles were the first steps in that direction. They would not necessarily lead to me becoming a more than occasional journalist, perhaps joining other budding women writers, but Cambridge would help me forward. Writing and being published could become both tools and a passport to stimulating company. I was keen to meet congenial people, even if what there was to talk and write about was becoming so dreadful.

Another thing which I first became aware of at that time took on increasing importance as the years went by: I had views, thoughts, feelings, concerns, about all sorts of events, but what could I *do* with them? How could they be turned into effective or influential action? That still matters to me, many years later, and in old age I have to try to accept the frustration of relative inactivity. I hardly knew then how ambitious I was and had not yet come across the slightly facile saying, "It is not what you do but what you are that matters". Perhaps it would have appealed to me, yet its simplicity conceals glibness. Doing and being are interactive, not alternatives. The account which follows, in the next chapter, of my time at Cambridge probably gives the impression that, as well as my academic work in history, I was by then actively *doing* a lot. I was, but at this distance I am mainly interested in the ideas and thoughts which were germinating and empowering those keen and idealistic activities. My doings in the mid-Thirties are the crucial background to my later career in psychology.

Later in that summer before I went to Newnham, Ka Arnold-Forster, whose wisdom and opinions I respected, asked me what I wanted to do after University, and I said, "I want to write". She sternly told me that I had to live before becoming a writer. I felt rebuffed and perhaps arrogantly considered I was already living. Yet I knew she was right. And I did get on with living. I secretly wondered whether anybody as impressive as Rupert Brooke, who had become her lover not long after their Cambridge days, when she was Ka Cox, would come my way. To be loved by a poet, an impressive one too, would indeed be exciting. But alas for him and for his friends, he died, as is well known, caught up by forces too strong for his generation of young men, whether ordinary or brilliant.

The next phase of living was the time at Cambridge: three academic years packed with friendships, both romantic and more pedestrian. They shaped all the rest of my life.

Five

Cambridge

I have a clear picture in my mind dating back to October 1935. From the open top of a London bus on the way to my first day at Newnham, I saw an ominous *Evening Standard* poster: 'Mussolini invades Abyssinia'. Although I knew that there had been dangerous wars in the Far East since 1931, I find that act of aggression stands out in my memory as a major one, and it was not far from Europe. It was part of the series of evil invasions which followed each other inexorably in the coming years. They culminated, for Westerners, in the Nazi invasion of Poland in September 1939, and thereafter that developed into the Second World War. Apart from the themes in my personal life, the sinister keynote struck by that poster was to be heard, in the background, during my Cambridge years.

Two major and deep relationships began almost at once. On the first evening I met the friend with whom I remained close until she sadly died in 1996, Tess Mayor. Very soon David Hubback, who was in his second year at King's, asked me to lunch. Clare Mallory, whom I had met climbing in Wales, was there too. They were both reading history. I got the impression that he was beginning to be in love with her, and I tried to stifle my envy: she was so obviously attractive. David's mother Eva and his sister Rachel had been on the same Hellenic cruise in the previous spring as my father and Jenifer. Eva had come to stay with my family in the summer. At her request, I went down to the beach with her to swim at dawn. She decided I was eminently suitable as a friend, and perhaps more, for her only son. Between him, Clare, me and Tess, then several friends she already had from her school days at Bedales, and ones we each made through our various interests, there developed a group of congenial people. Most of us were ripe for love. As everybody was within easy cycling distance of everybody else, we met frequently. I will write more about David later in this chapter.

Undergraduates had no telephones, but an impressive delivery service between all the colleges enabled us to send notes around quickly. In many ways life was easy, and very enjoyable. It may be that we knew how privileged we were—by the social benefits of the College system, by being well taught (on the whole) either singly or with only one other student, by the unique quality of the river, the gardens and the historical buildings—but I cannot be sure. I do not think we were a complacent batch of young people, it was rather that we could not help trying some of the time to ignore what was looming, over the horizon. On the collective side of things there were rising numbers of unemployed people, rearmament, dictatorships, and concentration camps. For us as individuals there was anxiety about what was in store: short lives, perhaps, which might or might not be merry. In the vivid present we were busy loving, hoping to be loved, fearing not to be.

Women at Newnham and Girton (the third women's college, New Hall, was founded later) were not members of the University of Cambridge until 1948. Unlike the men, we did not have to wear academic gowns, nor were we subject to the discipline of the University police, the Proctors. The women dons were much more adversely affected than we undergraduates, for whom it was mainly a theoretical state of affairs. Friends at other more enlightened Universities thought Cambridge was very backward. We ourselves certainly considered the senior men antediluvian, since on many occasions they had blocked parity for women in Senate votes. It was only after 1933, two years before I went up, that women were allowed to act on stage in University theatre productions, so that men had done the women's parts, as in ancient Greece and Shakespeare's time. When I was there Tess and several others of my women friends acted keenly and successfully.

More or less anything we wanted to do was open to us; partaking in University life and working hard were worthwhile in themselves, and not examples of crowing over any men who did less well. It was long before the days when being called Chairman was not politically correct. Chairing a committee of a University society was simply a worthwhile job to be done, by whichever person seemed the most suitable and was willing to give it time and energy. Within Newnham, in my last year, I was elected Senior Student, and that was an honour that did not call for much work. It involved chairing the students' representative committee, composed of students elected from each of the four Halls there were at that time. I do not think we met more than once a term. We negotiated with the dons, campaigning for several things that now sound almost banal, such as the time in the evening when men friends had to be out of College, and the right to have a radio or a gramophone. We could not argue that we knew a particular student who had one of those, and that a don with rooms nearby had not detected any music or noise. Live music, strings or wind, could be played, but only in the afternoon, when other students were probably not trying to write their essays.

One convention which has now gone was really good: the moveable "Engaged" sign on the door was always respected. I could do with one in my present life. Overall, many or even most of us were implicitly budding feminists. The marches and demonstrations that I can remember were political ones, not on women's issues. They were about unemployment, for example, and, during the Spanish civil war, we marched for the Republicans, the Anarchists and the International Brigade, who were fighting against General Franco's Nationalist army. Franco was being helped by Nazi and Fascist bombers.

Once, two of Oswald Mosely's followers in the National Union of Fascists came down from London to try to recruit members. They gave a dinner, which I went to out of curiosity. The violent anti-Semitic speeches brought on wild cheers and clapping: I did not join in, sitting stiffly, feeling disgusted. It was frightening, too, and the unknown man beside me asked if I was a Jew. I did not want an argument, in that atmosphere, so I enquired whether he thought I looked Jewish. I suppose I was being sarcastic to conceal from him what I was actually feeling, which was hostile and scared.

Before I come to describing more about the deep personal friendships which started soon after my arrival at Newnham, I will mention a few other political and feminist activities. During my first year I tried to strike a blow for the equality of men and women at a lecture being given by one of the elderly historians, in the imposing Great Hall of Trinity College. His implicit rule had always been known, that the Newnham and Girton women should sit at separate tables from the men. I tried going to one of the men's, and although they clapped my defiance of his authority he refused to start lecturing until I obeyed his decree, so I gave in.

I was more successful in my second year, at the Union, the Parliament-like debating society, open only to members of the University. The Italian invasion of what was then Abyssinia, now Ethiopia, had led to the emperor Haile Selassie being exiled for several years, and he was invited to speak at the Union. In those days he was, with his subjects, seen as a victim of Fascism; now that much more is known about his later life his reputation is badly stained. I wanted to hear him, so I borrowed a gown, a man's suit and shirt and tie from a friend of about the same build, and hired a man's wig from a theatre shop. With David, who was willing to risk the suspension or the loss of his membership on my behalf, I just got past the door-keeper, who was meant to stop gate-crashers. He recognised me through my disguise, but as he was a member of the University League of Nations Union committee of which I was chairman at the time, he winked and connived. Perhaps it was only a minor gesture for feminism, with no immediate results. But I had an amusingly successful time at a party afterward, in Trinity, where several of the homosexual men, including Anthony Blunt, seemed to think I was an attractive boy, and I did not disabuse them.

Important seminal strands of personal life, interests and activities, interwoven throughout the rest of the century and beyond, emerged clearly during the nine undergraduate terms at Cambridge. The previous years had been apprenticeships. To my surprise I did very well in the first-year summer exams called Mays and was awarded the Felicia Larner Prize, an internal College grant.

The long vacation was a time full of good experiences. At the beginning, a generous Newnham friend helped me financially to go to that year's International Student Service conference in Uppsala University in Sweden, where the political atmosphere was tense and electric. Feelings ran very high. At one stage, I had been roped into doing some interpreting from French into English. A voluble quick-firing speaker at the back of the hall suddenly became furious, shouting and waving his arms, alleging that I was a reactionary imperialist and a capitalist. He said I had got the sense of his contribution absolutely the wrong way round. I think someone pacified him, at least temporarily. I remembered the incident during my next year at Cambridge, when various Communist undergraduates were trying, persistently but unsuccessfully, to recruit me.

The Spanish civil war between 1936 and 1938 was of course deeply worrying to all the left-wingers of my generation. During those years almost two-and-a-half thousand young men and women fought for the Republicans against the fascist government of General Franco's armies, which had been fortified by troops and bombers from Germany and Italy. One of those who enlisted was a friend, John Cornford, a passionate Communist. His father was a Classics professor, his mother the poet Frances. He was deeply intellectual and equally deeply idealistic. I remember often reading near him in the Seeley library, where keen history students used to work. His death and the failure of the republican cause cut me and my friends deeply. His son was born posthumously. Making speeches and going on marches made us feel moral, but our government's "non-intervention" policy—standing aside from an inflammatory war—was not affected by students' protests. I wrote a poem about the bombing of Guernica, a companion to one I had written earlier about the death of an imagined young woman in the then war in the Far East. Was I, and were my friends, merely puny? We did what we could.

Paul Sinker, a classics don and his wife Ruth (sister of Jack Longland, the Everest climber), who had been at the Pen-Y-Pass climbing party, suggested I should join them in the Cuillin mountains, in Skye. It so happened that my parents and I had been invited to stay the week before, in another part of the island, in Dunvegan Castle. The Laird, the powerful chief of the clan, was perhaps surprisingly a woman. She was the widow of a friend of my father's, the journalist Hubert Walter, but she was the Macleod of Macleod by inheritance and thereby owned the Castle, a fine building on the edge of the sea. That visit provided a new angle on history for me, and it gave me a whiff of what I thought were the remains of medieval rural Scotland. Out of respect for the generous Macleod hospitality (rather than in deference to my mother's idea of how I should behave), I took part only very carefully in the conversation. From my left-wing angle, it seemed deeply conventional, and it was an amazing contrast to the often-extremist talk at the conference in Sweden. My other main memory of the visit was of going out in one of the estate's rowing boats and seeing a whale spouting, just when we happened to be looking in its direction.

Having reached the Cambridge climbers, I found that one of them, Jack Howes, was a colonial Civil Servant on leave from Kenya, where he was a District Commissioner. I did not know about ranks, so my first impression was simply that he was tall, good-looking, and immediately attractive to me. He walked with the steady, supple and loose-limbed stride that people, perhaps especially men, develop who have to keep on going for many hours, day after day. He had a deep love of country places, and knew more than I did about birds. He was probably also eager to find a congenial woman who was interested in issues and world matters. I think he was over-impressed by me, as I was quite different from the English women he had met in Kenya.

Our friendship grew rapidly; both he and I were ripe for romance. He was much less conservative than the more typical Colonial Servant, and at that time those serving in Kenya had a particularly bad name with left-wing university people. He was very keen to give me a good impression of his liberal views and his way of being with black people. He had more power over them than I had realised, in judicial as well as in administrative matters, so that with Paul and Ruth Sinker, and others of the party whom I now hardly remember, we had fascinating talk. Going up the craggy Cuillins together, in absolutely exceptional weather, sunny every day, was a sure recipe for falling in love. The usual weather in Skye, I had heard, is unmitigated mist and rain, all the year round.

Later that summer, my parents agreed to him staying a few days with us in Cornwall. The visit was not a success, as they did not take to him. His background was not what they thought right for me. That was difficult, because he had always said I was more intelligent than he was. My mother was suspicious about him and me the whole time, and had great difficulty in allowing us to be alone together. One evening, as dusk was falling, soon after supper, he suggested a short walk, so we went out. I did not consider we needed to ask permission. There was outrageous trouble over that. My poor mother must have been having wild fears for my sexual safety, which in fact was never in danger. The gap between her and me became a rift.

My father was always known as Jack by her and their friends, and that was embarrassing for me. There was something in the air which implied that for me to plan to marry a man who had the same name as his, but whom they did not like, was something really wrong. After Jack had left, there was a long family walk one day, during which it was manoeuvred that my father and I should be together, alone. With the utmost and excruciating difficulty he told me how dreadful it was to marry the wrong person. That was very moving. Yet later in the autumn I boldly, or perhaps crazily, asked him if he would give me, perhaps as a Christmas and birthday present combined, the fare to Kenya in the vacation. Of course he said he could not. It was on the grounds that it was impossible to do the equivalent for all his daughters.

The parting from Jack at Victoria station, just before my return to Newnham, was inevitably deeply painful. I felt totally lonely. The irony of that autumn was that gradually I began to feel doubtful about whether Jack himself had not in fact been really insightful when he said he was not right for me, even adding that I would be too intelligent for a Kenya wife. It had been unavailing for me to say I would switch from my history degree course to the anthropology one, so that I could work and not be "only a wife", and to try to get the well-known ethnologist Leakey to take me on as an assistant. Jack and I wrote regular letters, but the sad truth developed for me, as the term drew on, that we were not right for each other. And with a renewal of pain, I broke off the engagement. Since I had been so deeply affected by all the emotions, I rather naturally did not do so well in the summer exam as I had in my first year. And that in turn led me to work harder in my third.

By a piece of extraordinary chance, the only other time Jack and I ever met was at an exhibition of Romantic Painting in, I think, the Gallery of the Royal Academy in Piccadilly. He was alone, and so was I. It was many years since we had parted, by letter, but we recognised each other. We talked for a little while. I think both of us were happy as well as sad to have had even such a short contact.

Among the several committees of which I was a member, or held office of some kind, one was the University branch of the League of Nations Union. Towards the end of the 1937 summer term, being chairman at that time, I spoke on behalf of that branch at the annual conference, in Torquay, offering a possibly over-simple view of the dangers of Nazism, Fascism, the armaments race and appeasement, which was the policy favoured by the Conservative Government in Britain. That was my first experience of a microphone, addressing what felt like a huge audience. I was told there were perhaps nearly a thousand delegates. It was both terrifying and exhilarating to have so many people listening to what I was saying.

Liberal dons at Cambridge, such as the economist Gerald Shove, who had pacifist leanings and was a senior member of an umbrella group called the New Peace Movement, told me that both that organisation and the International Student Service were infiltrated by Communists. He was probably right to some extent, but the Party was not illegal and the energy mobilised was impressive at the time. In a personal way I benefited from getting experience of drafting petitions, manifestos and so on, getting them circulated and deciding which were the best national and international bodies to send them to. I was Honorary Treasurer, serving that role for the only time in my life, and ended up in debt. It taught me never to accept such an office again.

During the Easter vacation in my second year, I was given a small grant to research into right-wing organisations in Paris. The grant was just enough for a frugal fortnight, staying in the Cité Universitaire, students' rooms in the southern outskirts. Several of the mainly small groups were rather sinister. I expect that when France was occupied by the Germans during the War, they were the kind of people who supported the Vichy régime. Each person I visited gave me an introduction to the next. They were a mixture of mainly elderly rich men, living in hyper-elegant flats in expensive parts of Paris. Some were members of old aristocratic families, who reminded me a little of people whose children I had known when I was at school in Paris as a child: Giles de Boisgelin was my earliest boy-friend, but Isabelle de la Rochefoucault was uncomfortably proud of her rank and elegance. I probably used their names to establish that I was worth my interviewees telling me a bit about their views, though the name-dropping factor now sounds a bit shameful. I also met younger members of minor organisations, in cafés.

I do not think I made major discoveries, but it was good practice for various pieces of journalism I did later. There was enough with which to write a report for the Professor of Political Economy, Ernest Barker, who had organised the research grant and had probably been told about me by the Newnham Director of Studies in history, Miss Pybus, or by Betty Behrens, who knew France and French history very well.

The academic work at Cambridge was of increasing importance and interest to me as the months and years went by. I was lucky enough to be seen as listening closely to his lectures on medieval economic history by Professor Michael Postan—I was sitting in the front row, apparently drinking in every word, and he invited me to join a series of research seminars he was running. They were on the economics of several Eastern Counties monasteries, and involved handling original documents, learning to read them. He had imported to Cambridge, from his previous post at the London School of Economics, the new and foreign-sounding word *seminar*: it was impressive. The weekly meetings were stimulating and I perhaps naively saw them as prestigious. Perhaps I and the other students there were the professors of the future? The work has left no direct traces on me of its content, only an enjoyment of beavering away to discover a mixture of human and material facts, and discussions in a group of keen equals.

I think it was during my second year that several of us reading history founded the University History Club. It had liberal-minded Faculty members as well as undergraduates. The committee met in David Bosanquet's room in Trinity College, and soon there were over sixty members. I think he was chairman and I was secretary. We discussed anything that members brought up, chiefly about the content of the curriculum and the way it was taught. We ran a questionnaire, with wording carefully drafted, circularised it as widely as we could, received a good response, analysed the results, wrote up the report and sent it to all the History Faculty. Six of us signed the report, and out of those at least four became either professors or Heads of Colleges later.

One sentence of the report, which I have only recently re-read, is the same as my present views on the training of analytical psychologists: 'We recognise that the function of the supervisor should be primarily to elicit interest rather than to provide knowledge that the student does not possess'. During the time when I was a school teacher, I could not use that attitude as much as I would have liked. That is partly why I did not stick to teaching. The experience of the questionnaire was useful when I did, on my own, the one on married women graduates in the Nineteen Fifties, described in chapter 11.

To return to Cambridge. After I had broken away from my engagement to Jack Howes, I was of course depressed and felt I could not easily trust my judgement of people, since I had been so deeply in love and it felt as though it had come to nothing. I was taking too little account of the fact that I had had the sense to draw back before going too far forward. Being depressed contained the usual ingredient of self-deprecation. I felt bad at having caused him so much disappointment, and as we were no longer writing to each other, I did not know whether he was making a good recovery.

I managed to start concentrating on work, and though I felt lonely inside I had a good group of friends, several of whom were also having love affair troubles. By the beginning of the summer term I was seeing more and more of David, who was by then less interested in Clare Mallory than he had been. That was partly because she was falling in love with a brilliant American research physicist, Glenn Millikan, a lively and attractive man who was as keen on rock climbing as she was.

During the summer vacation between my second and last years at Cambridge, I stayed at the cottage in Snowdonia, which David's father had rented and loved so much during his Cambridge days before the First World War, and which various members of the Hubback family had managed to keep throughout the years. His mother Eva and his sister Rachel, who were also very attached to the cottage, were there, and a few other people came and went.

The cottage was just near the farm of Maes Caradoc in the Nant Ffrancon, romantic and very primitive indeed on modern standards. Many generations of slate miners had lived there, working for a pittance down the valley at Bethesda. We did not do any rock climbing but walked on the mountains, up and down those steep places where there were very few people in those days. Thousands of much less privileged young men and women than we were then are now able to discover the joys of mountains, also the mists, the rain, the snow and the wind. That summer of course we swam several times a day, where the river, two fields away, widened out into a pool, where the sheep were dipped. Further down the valley was an even more romantic narrow ravine, with rowan trees overhanging the river, which flowed swiftly there. On the nearly vertical rocks there were slate shelves fixed by the miners, where they sat while they fished. A little lower, there was a lawn-like place, where we used to light a fire and have picnics. The sound of the flowing river was a perfect accompaniment to our growing romance. It was a place where the rest of the world could easily be pushed out of mind.

From then on David and I knew that we wanted to be together, we were very happy and it was impossible to conceal our cheerful feelings from the other people in the cottage. There was a shadow, though, as Rachel felt most painfully excluded. I think she could not have wanted to be simply bracketed with her mother while David and I went off together as often as we could. Our happiness in that first flush of excitement was not something we could share with her.

David wanted to get into the Civil Service, as his father had, and having finished at Cambridge he took the entrance exam for it that summer. Failing the exam was a major disappointment to him, to me and to Eva who had always as it were dedicated him to that career, and pictured him rising very high. He fulfilled that hope towards the end of his time there, but that was a long way in the future. So he settled in to working towards taking the exam again the following year, living at home in the house where he had been brought up, on the edge of Hampstead Heath. Eva and his father, Bill, had built it when they got married in 1911, only a few years before he volunteered for the Army, and was killed.

Having returned to Cambridge for my last year, I was lucky enough to discover that one of my men tutors, who lived on the top floor of a small old house in a back street, used to be away somewhere else every week-end. Tess was deeply in love with Brian Simon, a mutual friend of ours. Brian, like David, had left Cambridge by then, and was attending the London University Institute of Education. So the two of them used to come down on Friday evenings and had the use of the flat. The arrangement suited all of us admirably. In the phrase commonly used then, we were living in sin. I forget whether Eva knew about it, and certainly Newnham did not discover it, though in fact I was not breaking any rules. We and the owner of the flat did not ask each other any awkward questions. I think we developed the theory that he had a red-headed mistress in the Midlands.

As well as working hard during that last year I continued to be concerned about political matters. A frightening experience was when I and two others took a protest, signed by many students, to the German Embassy in London, about the bombing of cities in Spain, especially Guernica. The icy-faced junior official to whom we delivered it was not impressed by our probably useless bravado. Of course nothing effective came of it, but it was satisfying to be at least trying to do something. On another occasion I spoke at a meeting in central London, at the Kingsway Hall, on the same platform as, among others, a well-known Communist, Johnny Gollan. I and many other students at that time felt the U.S.S.R. was the only country opposing Hitler and Nazi Germany. We feared the other policy, of appeasement, was too weak. Several Cambridge Communists were visiting me at intervals, trying to persuade me to join the Party, and I finally went to an early morning cell meeting. The strictness with which those taking part were meant to keep to the Party line put me off completely. It was obviously impossible to have an opinion of one's own, so once was enough.

I can interpose here that I only discovered many years later, when MI5 was investigating anybody who might have been connected with Cambridge people who either were, or might have been, spies, that that body had a file on me, my contacts and my activities. David was by then in a responsible Treasury job, having earlier worked in the Cabinet Office. He and I were questioned after Guy Burgess and Donald Maclean had fled to the U.S.S.R. The young Civil Servant sent to investigate me knew, in my opinion, almost nothing about the atmosphere among Thirties' students. He thought I had been an under-cover Communist then, and might still be one. Given all the other information about me that he could have found, had he tried, he seemed to find it difficult to understand that I was not the kind of person who would join a party in which dissenting opinions were forbidden. Nor did he play on the fact that Brian Simon, a life-long friend of David's, by then a Professor of Education, went on being an open Communist, without anyone minding. He did not follow up the interview, during which I could not resist self-righteously telling him I thought his visit was a waste of public money.

David and I and many of our close friends at Cambridge had known Anthony Blunt. He was almost devastatingly charming, to women as well as to men. But when it was discovered, to all his friends' deeply painful amazement, that he was not only the eminent expert on art history that we had believed, but was also a really dangerous spy, David and I were not re-investigated. So much for the efficiency of MI5. The old friends who were most acutely unhappy when Blunt's double life was disclosed were Tess, my closest friend, and her husband Victor, Lord Rothschild. David was much more straightforwardly patriotic than I was, and did not feel comfortable by my saying Anthony had done what he believed in, even though I thought spying was immoral.

The undergraduate years seemed to rush by. The terms at Cambridge, like those at Oxford, are too short, being only eight weeks. I know there are arguments against that point of view, but other Universities have ten-week terms. The pace of life was hectic most of the time. A Profile of me written by Brian, in the student weekly magazine, *The Granta*, describes me as, on my green bicycle, 'hurtling down King's Parade in an endeavour to save a few seconds before her next engagement'. In my third year what I enjoyed almost more than anything else was working on my special subject, Utilitarianism and Tory Democracy, in the first half of the nineteenth century. It would be one paper in the final Tripos Exam. In effect it was a minor kind of research into the political thought of that time. It included Coleridge's woolly political ideas, which were interesting but which could hardly be called theories, and to some extent it led me into wanting to find out more about the origins of socialism in France.

I spent much of many days in the University Library. It was not necessary to send for books, all the shelves were open, so I could browse and find other ones connected with the main theme for an essay. The cafeteria in the basement was good for a midday break and some talk. Working in the quiet there, with the great benefit of never being interrupted, offered an excellent contrast to other activities, which were all in company. Another good thing was that no tutor ever spurred me on or worried me by predicting (correctly, as it turned out) that I might perhaps get a First.

When the time came to decide what to do next, I was very tempted to take up the suggestion made by Professor Barker that I should stay in Cambridge to research, perhaps aiming for a further degree, though Ph.D.s were not so frequently sought then as they are now. I would have researched into the origins of socialist ideas in France. The aim would have been an academic career. Research would have suited me and would have led to work, initially, with people of student age. But I decided not to, partly because David and I were planning to stay together, and to get married. We would have to live in London, and for me that would mean leaving the pleasures, as I saw them, of University life. Also war looked more and more inevitable, and I thought I should train for work in an immediately necessary job, which would be teaching history at school level, contributing to the next generation learning to work effectively.

During the war, when living in the depths of Wiltshire, I had the opportunity of a good substitute: running discussion groups of soldiers in isolated searchlight units on Salisbury Plain. They wanted to learn about how the First World War, and its complicated results, had led to the one they found themselves in. Much later still, I did a lot of seminar work with people training to become analytical psychologists.

Six

Transition to War

During my University years I was a mixture of being in many ways grown-up, yet not feeling convincingly so. At Newnham we were called women—I believe present-day students are often called girls. The irony is that most of us were still girls, virgins, at least when we went up, in those days before the Pill. But boys and girls at school, who used to be pupils, are increasingly called students. I cannot tell whether those changes are merely due to fashion or in fact carry some kind of significance about modern and current trends. I bring them in here to illustrate and give added depth to how, at any rate for me in the Nineteen Thirties, growing up was a long drawn-out process which lacked clarity.

Being a twentieth-century person interested in general as well as in my personal history, I am reflecting on the pace of the growing-up process and that has led me to wonder how much university people in the pre-1914 generation (such as David's father, Bill, and his mother, Eva) were similar in that respect to us pre-1939 ones. At Cambridge David's parents were optimistic Fabians, with naturally no foreknowledge of the coming slaughter of so many millions of people, especially men in the trenches on the various fronts, including his father, who was one of those killed, in 1917, when David was only one year old. From what I know of them, they were much less anxious during their time as students than we were at the equivalent time in our lives. Most likely they felt they could just go ahead.

But in the late Thirties we pictured the Second World War as a combination of 1914–18 with the recent ruthless bombings in the

Far East and the ones of the Spanish civil war. We knew several men and women who went to Spain, joining the International Brigade, some of whom, such as John Cornford, were killed. Many of my Cambridge friends and I were pessimistic, since optimism or complacency seemed quite out of place. Perhaps delaying growing-up was an aspect of that complicated state of affairs. Achieving what felt to be the right amount of separateness from my original family, if possible without open or aggressive revolt, which I was frightened of, was difficult because of a mixture of personal and collective world factors. Was the approaching war going to force us to grow up too quickly, as well as preventing us from doing what we planned, unless we were going to be doctors? Would it cut our lives off short, and do that rather soon? Perhaps we should hurry to get as much into life as possible, before it was too late?

Where the economics of that time are concerned, I did not earn my living until I was over twenty-two, so I was still having to accept being supported by my parents financially, thus perpetuating one aspect of dependency or even immaturity. Out of trying to be independent of them I had not told them about having rejected the chance of doing a further degree and aiming at university work. Although they were financing me, they did not approve of my having decided to work for a diploma in education: I would qualify as a secondary school teacher, which they considered was an inferior profession for a daughter of theirs. They did not take into account that the London University Institute of Education staff were excellent both on the theory of education and in supervising practice in classroom work. I considered the diploma would complement my Cambridge degree and be valuable if I wanted to rise in the teaching profession. A girls' private school, which they might have approved of on social grounds, would not require any training. Certainly some of the staff at Downe had been far from competent. Several were "naturals", but those who were not would have benefited by doing a training.

Both my parents were also deeply unhappy at my intention of getting married, and doubly so because they did not like David as my prospective husband. They hinted that, although I as well as he had done well at Cambridge, I should hope or aim for a man who was fully worthy of me. It was a delicate business for them. There was something indefinable about him which they did not feel comfortable with. Of course I knew that many parents react in that way, but being the individual in the midst of it, without it being brought out into the open, was agonising. My mother wrote distraught letters, and my answers did not satisfy her. The likelihood of war suggested the wisdom of cautious delay, and that was not something we could tolerate. I was trying to find my way as an individual, emerging from the particular family of my childhood, yet knowing all too well that I was little more than a unit at the mercy of circumstances, the main one being the looming shadows of the coming war.

I realised with regret that I would have to give up my earlier hope of a job in the League of Nations Secretariat, working in Geneva. I can see now that anyway I had to detach myself from wanting to follow so closely in my father's footsteps, in work comparable to what he had done. Apart from that personal factor, it was obvious that I could not now take any active steps where international politics were concerned, and like many people I hated being passive at a time when so much of what we believed in was in extreme danger. David and I wanted to be the ones to make our own decisions for at least our personal lives, so we were at the mercy of the complicated tensions set up by, on the one hand, powerlessness in the public arena together with compliance with my parents' wishes, and on the other our wish to grow up fully. He and I were so strongly in love that we insisted that we were right and my parents wrong.

As a child I had frequently been criticised for being obstinate (called pig-headed) and I still was, in relation to my parents. According to an old anecdote, dating from when I could not pronounce the name Judy and was known as Du-du, I was in the kitchen garden, pottering about with my first love, Joe Hocking, the gardener, and was heard chanting to myself, "Du-du, do as you please".

I was sure David and I were absolutely different from my father and mother, and did not notice ways in which at least our situation had some aspects in common with the difficulties which had beset them during their engagement. Moreover, not only they, but also David's mother and father, had had to run the gauntlet of parental disapproval, as neither his father's Christian relatives nor the Jewish ones in his mother's family had approved of their marriage. As well as my parents not liking David (but not on anti-Semitic grounds), there was a repetition of the struggle they had had. The experiences of both earlier couples never came into the long-drawn-out letters and conversations. I only discovered the powerful if unconscious significance of such repetitions when I was training to be an analyst.

My mother's mother, steeped in rigid High Anglican beliefs, had objected to my father as a son-in-law since he was a divorced man, though his first wife was "the guilty party", in the terms of the law as it was then. I think she demonstrated her continuing disapproval by not attending their eventual wedding, which was in the only London church they could find with a vicar willing to marry them. David and I were so much in love that I did not want to point out to my father or mother that they had been right not to give in to her mother's objections. Our extreme and painful disagreement with my parents was not only ours but a version of what theirs had been.

What made us seem different from my father was that his failed first marriage had been entered into after only a brief courtship, and I did not want to remind him of that. David and I said we were not rushing, since we had known each other well for several years and had so many interests in common. Asking us to delay did not seem relevant. Like all optimistic young couples, we could not possibly anticipate how much change the war years, and the consequently different life experiences, would bring to us as individuals. At Cambridge we were two people on a level with each other, and I think he as well as I assumed naïvely that that would go on; but the war brought out irrevocably the differences between him as a man and me as a woman.

Further trouble came upon us because during the summer of 1937, soon after gaining an excellent First in history, David failed to pass the administrative Civil Service entrance exam, as I mentioned in chapter 5. The same thing happened the following year. My parents redoubled their protests. It was ironic that on one occasion he had done well in the written papers but badly in the interview, and on the other it was the opposite way round. At that time the interviewers were all untrained. It was only in the later stages of the war that the selection processes for officers in the armed forces were greatly improved, on the advice of industrial psychologists, and later still the new methods were taken up by the Civil Service, and in business. We could not know or argue with my parents that, as in fact happened, he would ultimately rise high, working in the Cabinet Office, the Treasury and the Department of Trade.

I wanted to train at the London University Institute of Education, which I considered was what I needed in terms of content and quality. My parents tried to persuade me to go to the training college in Cambridge, which would keep me a little further from David, who was living at home in London, working towards that troublesome Civil Service exam again. Then public affairs worsened: Hitler was becoming increasingly dangerous by sending his troops into Czechoslovakia, breaking yet one more international treaty. Like many other people at that time, autumn 1938, my parents thought war was imminent and I would be in danger in London. They insisted on my joining them in Cornwall, where of course they worked hard at trying again to get me to change my mind about planning to get married. During that September the British and French Prime Ministers, Chamberlain and Daladier, joined up with Mussolini to sanction the German army under Hitler to occupy most of Czechoslovakia. The infamous Munich Agreement postponed general world war, and I returned to London to take up my place at the Institute, sharing a small Bloomsbury flat with an outstandingly attractive ex-Newnham friend, much less monogamous than David and I. David's mother Eva accepted, though a little ruefully, that he was there with me more often than at home with her.

At that time I had a definite plan for the next stage of my life, which does not sound at all out of the ordinary now. I would get married, teach for about three years, so as to have experience of professional work outside home, which would be an asset later, and have three or four children. I would spend about ten years as a full-time mother, being "only a housewife". I did not want the children to have the same kind of unhappiness I had had, with a nanny, though I assumed I would make other mistakes or take some wrong decisions during their childhood.

After that I would choose between going back to teaching, or stepping forward into some other work, full or part-time, perhaps local politics, or becoming a magistrate.

It is almost certainly surprising for present-day women to hear that such planning was not only exceptional but amazing: many of them know the history of the Suffragettes' valiant struggles for the Vote, and the less militant suffragists' campaign, but they know less about the strenuous feminist efforts of the next generation, the one to which I belong. The more dramatic and famous Women's Liberation Movement is well known. From all sides I met with doubts and attempts to dissuade me: I was going to get married, and, in the general opinion, that was that. David would earn our living, I would produce children, then perhaps take up charity work and leave careers in the professions to unmarried women. It was greedy to want paid work as well as marriage.

Early in 1939, during the academic year at the Institute, I managed to get included as a translator with a group going to France: teachers, professors and lecturers in education from New Zealand, Australia, South Africa and Canada, and their wives, conducted by Dr. Schairer, a brilliant German refugee. He was head of the Department of International Studies, and he had chosen the schools to be visited. They were for various ages and kinds of pupils in several parts of France, including Burgundy, where there were good restaurants. I have fond memories of him, as he not only appreciated my work but composed the only poem anyone has ever written for me, except my father, verses in German which were romantic as well as learned. I still have them, written during dinner on the back of a brochure from the school we had visited that day. Looking now at the list of participants, I see that none of the wives in the party was credited with any professional qualification, which was no doubt typical of that period. For me, as well as it being stimulating and enjoyable at the time, it was a valuable addition to the course I was doing in comparative education.

Towards the end of the diploma course at the Institute I started looking for a teaching job. It had to be in London since David and I were determined to get married, and we were still hoping he would pass the Civil Service exam that summer. He knew that, if he did, he would work in some department for only a short time before being called up into one of the armed forces, as he would not be senior enough to be reserved; but he would have a job in his chosen career to go back to when it was over. Besides, no other kind of work appealed to him in the same way: he had always pictured himself in Whitehall. Anything else would be second best, or worse.

I would have to find a school where the Head would not object to me being married and to apply for the post before David had got into the Civil Service. Neither postponing marriage nor getting a job somewhere else and being away from each other entered into our heads. Nowadays far more men and women live together unmarried than did then, without their employer knowing, and they are not required to divulge the details of their private lives.

Two grammar schools, the City of London School for Girls, which I tried first, and Godolphin and Latymer in Hammersmith, were advertising for an assistant history mistress. I was warned, it seemed by everybody who knew anything about teaching, that it would be very difficult for me as a married woman to get such a job anywhere at all, and as good as impossible in London. It was said that there were no precedents, though some teachers who had worked for many years (beyond child-bearing age?) had not been dismissed for marrying. Of course no man would have had the same kind of trouble to get started in the teaching profession. I wish I could say for sure that I thought that at the time, though in the present climate it seems obvious as a possible grievance. From the school's point of view the interruption of a teacher having a baby is inconvenient, and at that stage in history family planning was not usually assumed, nor the present-day mothers' arrangements for child care. The interview with the elderly-seeming all-male members of the City of London Education committee was going well until the ring on the incriminating fourth finger of my left hand was noticed. At first there was a pained silence, then I was challenged, and did not get the job.

Luckily the Headmistresses of both schools were friends and I was passed on successfully to the liberal-minded Miss Joyce Bishop at Godolphin and Latymer, who understood easily what I meant when I said I was planning to teach for about three years before starting a family. So that difficulty had been overcome. Several years later she became a Dame.

With my parents, disapproval continued to hover. They were fighting a rearguard action, and I found it painful to tolerate their pain. As well as David's future being unclear, the political crises had been following each other thick and fast from the time of the Munich Agreement onward. When I look back to those months, I can sense in an almost bodily way the intensely worrying atmosphere. It seemed to colour everything grey. David and I would have liked to be pacifists, and on a damp day in May, before I had started looking for a job, we even enquired about emigrating to New Zealand. We were told very firmly that they could do with carpenters, but not intellectuals. In any case we were fully anti-Nazi, and could not really have by-passed what we felt was right, which was to confront the evils happening in Europe. David was half-Jewish, and went to Vienna to help organise the exodus of as many Jews as possible. He was still working hard for his exam in June, and felt frustrated at not being able to do more for them.

As that rainy and anxious summer drew on, my parents finally capitulated on the subject of marriage, although the results of David's exam would not be out until the middle or end of August. They tried unsuccessfully to look happy at the wedding party, in July.

So David and I went off to the Alps with our future as uncertain as everybody else's, though the sun shone on the mountains and the walks were marvellous. He had put in for a few other jobs, which he did not really want or think he was likely to get. We ran into a most uncomfortable interruption in the form of a telegram from the B.B.C. offering him an interview. He could not risk missing out on it, so he flew to London, which we could ill afford, and the people at the hotel where we were staying did not know what to make of his sudden disappearance, leaving me behind, pining. Walking alone was an awful contrast to being together. I was speechlessly anxious and too embarrassed to explain the situation to them. On his return he was sure he had not got the job. I felt we had to practice being stoic.

In contrast to all that was happening in 1939, we had had an idyllic holiday in the Alps the year before, in a chalet borrowed from a generous Oxford friend of Jenifer's, with an enjoyably old-fashioned local woman cooking for us while her little boy picked baskets of wild strawberries. Jenifer and several of her friends had looked in from time to time, which had been helpful in trying to keep up the pretence to my parents that we were not "living in sin". My mother wrote out in full the word *Mademoiselle* on letters to me, instead of the more usual *Mlle.* Although we were certainly not carefree on that earlier occasion, we suspected correctly that there would never be such days again. The resistance men of the Maquis living in it during the war were murdered by the occupying German soldiers, and the chalet was burned down.

Back in London after our official honeymoon, we took a flat near Godolphin and Latymer as David had passed into the Civil Service. He was allocated to the Mines Department. Very sadly we never moved in, since the war was getting closer all the time and the school would be evacuated. I was tantalised by being approached about a job in the Ministry of Information: someone there had heard I spoke good French, but it seemed wrong to ditch my teaching commitment, and avoid us being separated by the school's evacuation. So we stayed tensely in Eva's house, on the edge of Hampstead Heath, queued obediently to collect gas masks in cardboard boxes, to be carried all the time, and in the last two weeks of that sunny August I travelled daily to school in Hammersmith, where the staff and children practised the evacuation. According to the instructions it all sounded well planned, and we had no reason to think it would not go smoothly, though we would not be told our destination, and everybody was very apprehensive.

In the event, the day of the real thing, Friday the first of September 1939, was chaotic. The only luggage allowed was, of course, as little as possible. I used the faded rucksack which had done good service up many mountains, for several years, and as the weather was so warm, I needed no more than a cotton dress. Perhaps I took a rain-coat on the 'You never know' principle. The girls wore their school uniform, with their round straw hats. Several of their parents were there to say goodbye, mostly holding back their natural tears. All very British, and apparently competent. I cannot remember what anyone had arranged about sending on more clothes and things, but it certainly resulted in my feeling deep sympathy for all refugees ever since, leaving their homes when driven out in terrifying circumstances, with babies, grandparents, bundles of bedding and so on. My impression, after so many years, is that all of us leaving Hammersmith then were in good physical health, and we assumed nice friendly welcomes in our country billets.

Each member of staff was put in charge of twenty girls, and told to keep with them all day. As I had not yet started taking any classes, and knew little more than the names of "my" girls on that day, the responsibility felt heavier than my rucksack. The excellent Miss Bishop spoke to us briefly, we got ourselves into long crocodiles, walked through the streets to Ravenscourt Park station not far off and waited until various people in charge of the arrangements handed us each a brown paper carrier bag of food for the day and allocated us in batches to trains which pulled in to take us away into the unknown.

I ran into difficulties at once, since the number of seats in the train coaches did not fit into the school's instructions of keeping groups of twenty children together. So I lost a few of them early on. The train pottered gently through the suburbs, stopping often, and after a bit my batch were decanted into another train, then a bus, then a third train. I was seriously worried about not having been able to keep my original allocation of girls, so I settled for trying to be helpful to whoever came my way. A few of the station names were already covered over, as they all were during the rest of the war (for fear of spies being parachuted in by the enemy and discovering where they were), but from those I could see we had not travelled far. Perhaps the powers that be did not intend to send us further than the so-called Home Counties.

By mid-afternoon quite a few of us, but by no means all the school, had reached Ascot. Another bus took some of us to Sunningdale. We felt tired. Then the business began of allocating individual schoolgirls to various houses on the lists for the area. There were Billeting Officers in charge of us now, and we had to trust ourselves to them. They were more humane than the transport people had been. The group of girls with whom I now was, and a few younger brothers, were directed to a bleak church hall. The local ladies arrived. They had all had their houses inspected for spare bedrooms and had been told how many children or grown-ups they would have to accept. But by now several of them had taken in friends or relatives, real or imaginary, or said they were on the way. It was easy, but not very charitable, to feel sceptical. The houses were very large. What seemed to be happening in the church hall was that each of the hostesses chose one or more of the girls by their looks. The face of the last to be handed over, to a not very warm-hearted-looking lady, was that of a sad waif. A few weeks later I discovered the girl had cheered up and not had such a bad time as could have been predicted.

At the end of that long day I had been given a minute room, larger than the overworked term broom cupboard conveys, but there were brooms in it. I managed to telephone David to tell him where I was. Next morning I was found a larger room in the servants' quarters of a mansion, with an old iron bed, a chair, and an unpainted deal chest of drawers for my few clothes. The housekeeper told me to use the back stairs. I did not meet the owners. Three years later David, by then a Second Lieutenant in North Africa, was talking about pre-war life with the driver of his Jeep. It turned out that the driver had been chauffeur to that particular Surrey family, and said my story was typical of them.

Following the few days in that unwelcoming house, I was taken in by two kind elderly spinsters, who immediately said David could come down every evening from his office. In their kitchen there was a spotless roller towel with another one under it: they told me only to use the under-one. I complied, of course, and did not show my amusement.

Miss Bishop was energetically trying to discover where all the four hundred girls were, and the staff, in that part of the country dedicated to large houses half-hiding at the end of long drives. Her task was immense: she had to be forceful, persistent and as polite as possible with the various members of whichever Ministry had not realised that simply getting as many children as possible out of London was not all they had to do: there had to be an actual school with a Head willing to make room for the Londoners, in an area with enough billets. After about three weeks she had successfully negotiated with Newbury Girls' Grammar School, at the edge of the pleasant and compact country town that it was then. The billeting officers saw to the children and the staff found themselves lodgings or, in our case, a house to rent.

Seven

The Second World War

The story of the opening hours of the Second World War, with the German army's invasion of Poland on Friday, 1 September 1939, has often been told, and this is not the place to repeat the history books' accounts of public events. But it is worth giving a personal impression of how those days unrolled. It was a strange mixture of what I, like so many other people, had by then been certain was going to be the future, and what had now become the actual present. The uneasy interlude, the dress rehearsal of the year following the Munich Agreement, was now irrevocably in the past. In a confusing way, past, present and future were all happening at the same time. Writing now, so long after those events, I remember that only three years before, I had bought the first of T. S. Eliot's *Four Quartets, Burnt Norton,* with its opening lines:

> Time present and time past
> Are both perhaps present in time future,
> And time future contained in time past.

I felt as confused as that.

During the two tense days between the invasion of Poland on Friday on the first of September and Neville Chamberlain's broadcast of our declaration of war against Germany, major events were happening on the mainland of Europe. Everybody knew they were only the beginning, and that Britain was going to be involved sooner rather than later. Britain was a country, but Britain was even more truly its people.

Almost immediately after Chamberlain had spoken, the air raid sirens went off in London. I did not hear them, out in the depths of elegant Surrey. Though there was no raid, the news that the sirens had sounded acted as a direct warning of the reality of war. The evacuation of school-children had evidently been necessary, which was perhaps only a minor satisfaction to those of us involved in it, but I and other equally ordinary people were taking part in what were going to be large events. Everybody assumed that bombing would start at once, which turned out to be wrong. At Cambridge we history students were known as Historians, which sounded important. Yet history had been, in my mind, the past: I saw it as the people and events in the time before I was born. Suddenly history had become what was happening now, to me and to countless other ordinary people: what we do and what is done to us. It was not only the activities of outstanding people, famous or infamous, their successes and their crimes.

At the time I am describing "Social History", the many aspects of how people lived, was relatively new, at university level. Traditional specialists mostly looked down on it as an easy option, not really scholarly. The Cambridge Regius Professor of History, George Trevelyan, was its best-known pioneer, and the "general reader" was captivated in the Nineteen Twenties by his *History of England* and by his later *English Social History*, being able to identify with the people in those books.

Although his knowledge of literature as well as of history was broad and deep, Trevelyan was not fashionable with several of his colleagues, and unpopular as a lecturer by the time I was at Cambridge. In conversation he was brusque, but as his wife Janet was my godmother, I was often invited to their dinner parties in Cambridge, and had stayed with them twice in their austere Northumberland house. There, as I was not the only visitor to notice, the food was of the unimaginative kind provided by many intellectual women in pre-war days, the "hot" water was lukewarm, and there was lino on the floors. Janet was a teetotaller, so there were not even the minute glasses of sherry which were usual then. It would be an anachronism to criticise those things: they are simply worth recording as items of social history. The Trevelyans had an aristocratic aura round them which came both from the eminence of their minds and from their rootedness in the country. Rather puritanical people such as they were, did not seem to need luxurious meals for there to be good conversation.

During those visits I had been on long walks with George over the moors, and to get him talking I had discovered the technique of asking him leading questions, which he answered in an interesting but always undidactic way, so I was not bothered by his rather off-putting manner. With an archeological historian also staying there, we went not only to the Roman Wall but also to several ancient houses, examining the stones for evidence with which to date them accurately: Trevelyan was not a crudely unscientific historian. I also greatly enjoyed getting him talking about poetry, and about the works of various writers in their historical setting. Recapturing some of the atmosphere of those days and of conversations with George Trevelyan links me with several aspects of the intellectual richness of life on offer then, much of which I lost during the coming war.

At the beginning of the evacuation period David and I were separated by only relatively few miles, but we minded desperately, without being able to talk about it much. We hardly ever had times alone together. Being stoic and brave was required for many days, months and years to come. And being brave meant not complaining, since so many people in Europe had been having a dreadful time for several years, and obviously there would be more, and worse, deadly tribulations to come. Poland was already invaded: Polish people were in immediate danger. So the sad fact that David and I were not able to set up home in what had promised to be the pleasant flat we had taken, in St. Peter's Square in Hammersmith, had to be accepted as a small part of it all.

I knew my calmness about it was only superficial. Apparent reasonableness had to cover up acute disappointment. It was a kind of acting in the drama of the double life which had started when I was a child, and which still today disturbs my peace of mind. In my experience, it is impossible to organise not to have the feelings, or emotions, that actually are there. They are experienced and more or less tolerated, or they are pushed aside, suppressed with the help of will-power, but not always repressed into unconsciousness. Denying them is usually not more than temporarily helpful, unless it becomes deeply ingrained.

A few years ago a psychoanalyst friend asked me which kind of defence against anxiety I found the most frequent among my men patients, as compared with women. He and I both agreed, as an admittedly big generalisation, that it was denial. That mechanism included fending off, by-passing and keeping a stiff upper lip. Women, he and I said, tend to mix being anxious in with being depressed. We help ourselves by being busy, doing things. But in the first two or three weeks of the war, it was difficult to be active in that way.

As I mentioned in the previous chapter, Miss Bishop and her close helpers were pushing all the relevant authorities into understanding that the school was an entity, that the girls and staff, scattered around in five different areas, had to be reassembled in some place where they could both live and carry on with their education. Newbury, in Berkshire, turned out to be a pleasant place. The Head of the girls' grammar school accepted that Godolphin and Latymer should share its buildings: the Newbury girls had the morning shift, while the London staff taught small groups in miscellaneous places, or the girls did their homework in their billets. Some of the older pupils, preparing for university entrance in subjects which did not need apparatus, were taught in the homes where the staff had settled. And the proper school day started at 1 p.m.

David and I soon found a small suburban house to rent, with a garden, not too far from the school and the railway station. He could get to and from his office in London as the train service was good. We were near the fields where the seventeenth-century Civil War battle of Newbury had taken place, between Royalists and Parliamentarians. The local pub was called the Gun. One Sunday two of the Godolphin staff saw David and me coming out of the pub, and told me off the next day, saying it would be bad for my reputation if any of the girls had seen us. The social atmosphere of suburbia seemed at first a sad come-down from what we had pictured it would be in St. Peter's Square, which had the reputation of being a favourite place for intellectuals to live. That is a small and, perhaps snobbish, vignette of the adjustments that the War was going to require of us.

Two of the other staff came to live in our house, the portly biology mistress, called Miss Richards, and the slimmer, more agile one who taught games, gym and dancing, Miss Samways. They were known as Dick and Sam. Dick shared my love of birds and we also shared the housekeeping, the first of several war-time experiences of difficult give-and-take in a joint kitchen.

During the first year of teaching I found it all very exacting, preparing lessons and correcting essays. I liked the two youngest classes, they were still eager to learn, and the two eldest were interested in history for itself. The ones round about fifteen years old were the most difficult, and with them in particular I disliked having to keep close to the text books. I thought that perhaps a more flexible approach might have suited them. Miss Scott, the senior history mistress, was tolerant of my inexperience. I tried out some of the progressive ideas I had acquired at the Institute of Education, such as suggesting to the geography mistress that her subject and mine might be combined. That was not successful, because it could not be fitted in to the syllabus as laid down for us, and I soon discovered that it was not going to be possible to make newfangled changes when the rest of the staff had much more experience than I had. The only married teacher was much older than I, well past child-bearing age, and I felt my presence might be a little difficult for some of the young unmarried ones, who were quite likely envious of me.

Having told Miss Bishop that David and I were planning not to start a family for several years, it was embarrassing a few months later to admit to her, and to the staff, that we had changed our minds. Getting pregnant was intentional. We took the decision because our apparently sensible earlier plan of waiting a few years, in the interests of my career, would not hold out against the biological drive. Rationalising that, we told ourselves that it would be tragic for David if he had no child and were killed in the war. Our reasoning was that he had been deprived of having a father by the First World War, and if we had had no child that would have deprived him of fatherhood. His mother had been splendid, and it was always said that she was successfully father-as-well-as-mother to her three children. In retrospect it can be seen that we were falling unwittingly into perhaps repeating for a child the far from ideal experience he had had of being brought up by a war widow. We were considering him and not the child. Nor did we give any thought to how I would manage on my own. I am perturbed now that we did not reflect carefully about what we were undertaking, but fate treated us well, as he was not killed, or wounded at all, although he was in many dangerous campaigns. The emotional wound to him and me, and our elder daughter, Cassandra, through being separated for much of the first five years of marriage and her childhood, is another matter, and more difficult to evaluate.

We had always known that David would be called up. His papers came through in June 1940, just at the time of the dramatic evacuation of the British Army from Dunkirk. We also understood, though it was not admitted openly, that the army was badly disintegrated and the specialist units hardly existed, for a while. He had hoped to go into Intelligence, which several of his friends had already succeeded in joining, but had to become just an ordinary private, until he was selected to serve in Signals and to train to get a commission. Basic khaki uniform was horrid, ugly, stiff and harsh. He felt just competent enough in maths, and learned to manage radios only with reluctance. If they would not work, hitting them usually solved the problem. He may have underestimated his ability to adapt to the double difficulties which army life presented him with: the loss of privacy in barrack conditions, and Signals technicalities. But certainly the first summer in uniform was utterly uncongenial to both of us, given the particular people we were. After the fall of France the danger of invasion was very ominous to everybody. David was posted to various places, several of them difficult to reach from Newbury, but somehow or other we had occasional week-ends together. There was very little leave.

During that grim summer, when I was pregnant, we had to face the problem of what might happen if the Nazis successfully invaded England, since David was half-Jewish. We had taken no notice of that, before those anxious months. The baby was due in December, and there was a sharp edge to what we had perhaps let ourselves in for: should I try to get onto one of the ships taking mothers and children to America? As I remember it, we realised that we had to give a lot of thought to the question, the many arguments for and against. It was difficult to keep rational, which would be to go over there, but we had somehow to allow full weight to our emotions as well. Feeling, as compared with thinking, was on the side of staying in Britain and facing in the same country as each other whatever was perhaps going to happen to anyone with Jewish connections. German invasion was possible, but was it probable? The consequences of it were almost too difficult to think about. In fact, I suspect we could not really face them, they were simply too frightening.

While the air Battle of Britain was on the edge of breaking out, David's unit was stationed in what had been a holiday camp, on the edge of Prestatyn, a sprawling town of bungalows and caravans, on the chilly coast of North Wales. In the school holidays I took rooms there, to be near him, and had to spend all day-time on my own. There seemed to be no-one congenial to get to know, and it was tantalising to see the foothills of the Snowdonia mountains just to the south, where we had often walked, but which now were out of reach. I was not good at occupying myself and could think of nothing more enterprising than reading, and knitting garments for the baby. The landlady and I did not make friends, having very little in common. She objected to the noise of David's army boots on the stairs when he left in the early morning and came back most evenings. Neither she nor I was able to get him to comply with her request to him to take them off in the hall. I secretly agreed with her, but I realised that for him she fitted with his inner picture of a "bossy mother". Also I suppose he had to demonstrate both his maleness and how much he hated having to be in uniform. The war brought on that kind of tension and friction very easily and I was too deeply anxious about it all to cope adequately. I had not yet got into practice about the kind of adaptations the war was going to demand of me, and I was far from enjoying my pregnancy.

One experience etched itself miserably in my mind. It was a Sunday afternoon. David and I went to the local, crowded, uninspiring park. I thought, not enviously but perhaps mistakenly, that all the Prestatyn family parties were enjoying themselves, the many children fooling around, eating messy cream buns and shouting as loud as they could, without being told off. Conversation did not flow between us. Suddenly, out of the blue, I "saw" that he was now simply a male, a soldier, and I was equally simply a female, pregnant. I told him what I had "seen", those crude contrasts. Then I tried to explain more: the difference from when we had been two *people* at Cambridge. I was wrong, since we had of course always been a man and a woman. Perhaps he felt I was reproaching him for being a male, which I did not mean to. I simply wanted it all to be discussable, but it was too difficult. A painful gap had opened up between us.

In the autumn of 1940, Sam and Dick found a place of their own. My elder sister Prue, having fled from Sweden, came to share the Newbury house with us, bringing her son of six and her new baby daughter. They had had to leave Stockholm, by a circuitous route including travelling through the U.S.S.R., which was not yet at war with Germany. Her husband was working in the British Embassy in Stockholm: Norway had already fallen and Sweden might also have been invaded. For a short time they took refuge with my parents in Cornwall.

Then we found a nanny to look after her children and our own baby, who was to be born in December. We all fitted in somehow. Prue went to London daily to work in the Admiralty as a temporary Civil Servant. David was stationed at Aldershot by then, and had become a Second Lieutenant. Cassandra, to be known as Sandra, was born not long before the school Christmas holidays. The next term I was able to go on feeding her myself as Miss Bishop was very helpful about rearranging my working hours. The girls in the top form, away from their own families, enjoyed pushing the pram at week-ends.

I think the combination of several people's needs worked well, during that very anxious winter of 1940–41. Various London friends came for week-ends, resting from the nightly air raids, and David occasionally had a short leave. Once, we managed a whole week in Cornwall. In some ways, we were getting used to the war, the over-full trains, the blackout, rationing, cooking economically, using up scraps and so on. In Newbury there were hardly ever air raids, only the heavy bombers with throbbing engines as they went over in the evening. We were not in danger, as many of our friends and families were. We knew that the time would come for David's division to go over-seas, and that there would be no information as to which cam-paign it would be.

During 1941 quite a few of the Godolphin and Latymer chil-dren had gone back to London, and some of the original school was re-opened. All the staff had to take turns to go there to teach, and I had not enough enthusiasm to be cheerful about the journey on Tuesdays and Thursdays. Leaving Sandra behind was painful, though she was developing enough to benefit from the company of her cousins. Some time in the summer our shared nanny had to leave, as she was called up into the Army. Prue decided to take her children to go to school in Oxford, liv-ing in our parents' house there, since they in turn were spending the war in Cornwall.

I was getting restless, partly from being separated from David for an indefinite time. He was contributing, presumably, to the ultimate defeat of Nazi Germany. Being a school teacher did not interest me deeply and it did not feel like real war work. We thought that perhaps having another baby before David went overseas would be a good solution to my feeling rather useless. I would give up teaching and look after two small children. So we started the second. If I shared a house with another mother, I thought I might be able to combine motherhood with some kind of writing, though I had nothing definite in mind.

After protracted and complicated negotiations, my sister-in-law Diana Hopkinson and I took an attractive house, Ivy Cottage, facing the Green in the small Wiltshire village of Ham. It had a room suitable to be a study for me, and a large vegetable gar-den. Jesse, a part-time gardener, discharged from the Air Force for unexplained reasons, came with the house, so to speak, as well as his portly, warm-hearted wife, Winnie, who helped us in many ways. There was a village post office and shop, and a bus once a week to Newbury. The friendly driver bought unrationed fish for us and threw it over the garden wall on his return. I did some of the shopping in Hungerford, about four miles away, on my bike. I had a basket seat fixed to it, and could take Sandra around that way. Diana's husband, another David, was in the Army Education Corps in Egypt, and she had a son, Thomas, only a few months older than Sandra. In many ways it was successful, but the two children did not really play together much: they each adopted a corner of the nursery to be their own favoured area. Diana already suffered from serious deafness, so confiding in each other was not easy and we were both lonely.

In 1942, David got embarkation leave, and inevitably disappeared into the blue: neither he nor his men knew where they were being sent. Our main hope was that it was not going to be India, or even further East. On the way, as he was only able to tell me later, they stopped at various ports, such as Freetown and Capetown, and they were issued with a stock of condoms. Many of them had only recently left their wives or girlfriends, so they cheerfully blew most of them up into balloons. After a while he wrote that he was in North Africa.

In England it was very hot. I was anxious, in a general way, and even fell into superstitiously imagining our days were sunny in sympathy with the climate where he was. The German army under Rommel was advancing towards Egypt, so the Middle East was in danger of being lost, where the British were concerned. Letters arrived irregularly and they could not contain any censorable information. They were small print-outs of microfilm, which saved transport space. David wrote as often as he could, his letters were for his mother, Eva, as well as for me. He hated having to read his men's letters to their wives, and his own were read by an officer senior to him.

Twice before the war I had had serious outbreaks of urticaria (nettle-rash) and had noticed that such skin troubles happened at times of emotional stress combined with physical exertion. On one of those earlier occasions the doctor at Cambridge had recommended Freud's *Psychopathology of Everyday Life*. That introduced me to psychosomatic ideas, and how the mind and body interact.

But dry knowledge did not prevent what happened next. I was worrying about David and had moved house as well as suffering from the heat. Those things together led to disaster: I ran a fever and miscarried. I had to go to the cottage hospital in Marlborough, for a few days; I was in a minute room, my bed about one foot away from another woman's and next to a large ward where sick children were crying all the time. That was ironic and tantalising. I cried and cried. Eva kindly travelled to see me, and did her best to comfort me: I felt inconsolable. What added to my distress was that, in the notes at the bottom of the bed, I saw that the diagnosis was "abortion". That was no doubt the correct medical term, but I felt insulted, as I ignorantly thought it meant I had brought about the miscarriage intentionally.

Sandra and I were able to have some time at the family house in Cornwall, before the autumn set in, and the cold winter. My sense of proportion was to some extent set straight, as two friends of my parents were staying there, the exiled Dutch politician, Dr. van Kleffens, and his wife, who would not see their country again until it was liberated from the occupying Germans. So I realised it was a time for trying to think up some occupation to use my mind and to complement being "only" a single mother of one small child, in a remote country village.

My own mother was energetically growing a lot of vegetables, and selling the surplus in the village and the local town. It was very satisfying "war-work" for her. But she did not have much company, and, in spite of not complaining openly, she often felt lonely, especially when the winter winds howled mercilessly round the house for days on end. In the evening she and my father perseveringly read long Victorian novels, and poetic dramas by Robert Browning, out loud to each other. I did not know how to be sympathetic enough to her: selfishly I said to myself that she had her husband. But there was a cloud hovering just perceptibly round my father, who had, up to then, been enjoying his new work as a magistrate: it was becoming clear that he had Parkinson's disease. There was little effective treatment for it then, though their youngest daughter, Mariella, studying medicine in Edinburgh, was keen to advise and collaborate with the local doctor. So there was the prospect of a long period of deterioration before an inevitably sad death. The retired family gardener, Joe Hocking, my friend from childhood, living nearby, also had it. My mother found that painful and ironic. She confided to me later that she had felt Joe and her husband should not have the same illness as each other. She was still imbued with out-dated attitudes. She had hated meeting him, when the two old men were out on tottering walks, up and down the familiar lanes, with nothing to talk about.

Back at Ivy Cottage, Diana and I, with Thomas and Sandra, settled down to another winter of carrying on. There was a ration of food for chickens and we kept a few, including a bantam, called Henrietta, especially for Sandra, in the hope of getting her to eat eggs. She had a favourite children's book about a hen with that name and remembers that she enjoyed "owning" the bantam. She fairly soon gave up her dislike of eating eggs.

Since we never suffered from real food shortages, and had no extra-hungry teenagers to feed, it amuses me to remember some of the economical habits or devices in use during the war. When the hens were laying well, we preserved the eggs in a mysterious translucent liquid called waterglass, in a large brown earthenware crock. We had packets of concentrated dried eggs, which saved on shipping space in the cargo ships crossing the dangerous Atlantic. There were no bananas. Sugar was rationed, and flour. Expectant mothers and children had free concentrated orange juice; wild rose-hip syrup also was full of vitamin C. The ration of butcher's meat, such as joints or cuts of beef, pork and lamb, was small. We enjoyed several sorts of unrationed offal (a word some classy people hated), liver, kidneys and hearts. As in most homes, there was a meat-mincing machine which we screwed to the wooden kitchen table; it was fiddly to wash, but shepherd's pie was easy to produce. Freshly killed rabbit was nearly as good as chicken, with lots of garden herbs. Tins of baby food had not yet been invented, nor electric liquidisers, but I had some perhaps surprising satisfaction in pushing the home-cooked vegetables, with a large wooden "mushroom", through a capacious hair sieve. We preserved our green runner beans in earthenware crocks, with layers of salt. We bottled fruit, dried apple rings and made our own jam. As Ivy Cottage was not wired for power, there was no refrigerator. Home freezers did not exist yet. There was a large walk-in larder, with cold slate shelves.

The oil cooker was temperamental, especially on windy days, when one or all of its three hideous enamelled burners flared up and filled the kitchen with smelly black smoke. The oven was balanced on two of them. There was no detergent for washing up, we used up old scraps of soap in special little wire containers. Biscuits were sold loose, not packaged as they are today;

the grocer weighed them out into strong re-usable blue paper bags. Crumbly broken biscuits were cheaper than whole ones. We had real baskets for shopping in those pre-plastic bag days. Most of my generation of women responsible for looking after even a small family in war-time became extremely economical with anything which had to be imported over the dangerous Atlantic: food, paper and so on. A modified form of that habit survived me being teased, in a kindly way, for many years, by younger people. And it is now environmentally virtuous.

That autumn I discovered that only a mile away, at the end of an avenue of tall trees, lived two members of the Bloomsbury Group of writers and artists, Ralph and Frances Partridge. The house, Ham Spray, had been the historian Lytton Strachey's, when the painter Dora Carrington was also there, and Ralph. It looked south, towards the calm line of the Berkshire Downs. Frances had been intrigued to see Sandra and me gleaning corn as extra food for our chickens, in the field beyond their fence, after the harvest. It was tantalising that we had been so near them already for quite a while, without knowing them, but friendship developed quickly.

Their son Burgo was about six or seven at that time, having some kind of education, but not in the village school, as Ralph and Frances were pacifists. The local people, all very patriotic, were not comfortable about that. They did not credit Ralph for the fact that he had fought valiantly in the First World War, gaining the British Military Cross twice and the Italian equivalent, and his experiences then were the origin and basis of his pacifism in the Second. Frances found out that I knew French well, and Burgo, an energetic and brilliant boy, came for French lessons with me.

In her book *A Pacifist's War* (1978), Frances wrote about having lunch with me one day. She had wondered 'if there was any special reason (that I had invited her) but there didn't appear to be' . . . until I told her about having, innocently as I thought, mentioned the lessons to a certain Mrs. Hill in the village ('The queen among the gentry'), whereupon Mrs. Hill almost fell over backwards and said, "I simply can't believe it! *You*, a serving soldier's wife teaching the child of a Conscientious Objector! I'm going to have nothing more to do with them now, I'm going to boycott them absolutely". Frances wondered how she would pass off an unexpected meeting with Mrs. Hill, and I thought that, logically, I should be the one to be boycotted. She told me recently (as I write in the twenty-first century and she is over 100) that she and Ralph had visited several of the battlefields and he had remembered just where various horrors had taken place.

On another occasion, after reporting, in her book, a spell of appalling winter weather and "a tussle of wills" with Burgo who was ill, she had been supported and helped by Ralph and wrote that she 'couldn't get on for a week without him. Meanwhile Judy Hubback *has* to get on without her David and had said (turning a little pink) that it had become an obsession with her to imagine him coming round the corner of the house'. She certainly was a most empathic friend at a time when I was especially lonely. She was intuitive and always responded in a straight and simple way. For example, after I had told her that I had felt quite mad that week, her answer was: "In your position I think you would be mad if you did *not* sometimes feel mad".

Lunches and dinners at Ham Spray, where there were often Bloomsbury friends of theirs, were times for really good-quality conversation, always stimulating and refreshing. Anything and everything could be talked about. Lytton Strachey's brother, James, had translated Freud's writings, and Frances had done the index of most of the volumes. They had a small swimming pool, which somehow or other they managed to keep going, so the following summer we enjoyed that too. I don't think Mrs. Hill discovered that we bathed nude.

David was in Egypt, recovering from jaundice which had kept him out of the grim battle of Alamein. It was a relief to hear that, as there had been a worrying gap in letters. Once the battle for North Africa had been won, the army was being prepared for further action. Exactly what that would be could only be guessed. From my point of view, and indeed his, it was certainly better than if he had been sent to the Far East, to fight against Japan and perhaps be taken prisoner. The news from there was always very grim. He enjoyed sightseeing in Egypt, during his convalescence, and wrote regularly to me, and story letters to Sandra. I think we more or less realised that an invasion of the mainland of Europe would have to be attempted soon. It seemed likely that the war on land and at sea would go on for several years still, although by then both the U.S.S.R. and the U.S.A. were on the Allied side. Anyway, Italy was still under Mussolini and would have to be invaded, via Sicily.

Giving Burgo French lessons was worthwhile but not enough to occupy my mind. By some chance, of which I now forget the details, I found more part-time work in the form of giving talks and running discussions with groups of seven or eight soldiers working the searchlights and anti-aircraft guns, at various remote sites on Salisbury Plain. The work was organised by the Army Educational Corps who allowed me a strict ration of petrol, just enough for the mileage travelled: a friend in the Navy lent me his Morris Minor. I used to ask the soldiers at each meeting what subject they wanted as the focus of the discussion, and most often they chose the years and events which led up to the outbreak of the war: why they were fighting. It was interesting and stimulating. Rather more difficult was an evening lecture at a Women's Air Force camp: all the large audience looked both tired and bored, asked no questions when invited to do so, filed out obediently, with relief, at the end of the prescribed time. I felt I had had to be unkind, speaking at a compulsory lecture, and only did it once. Small groups of individuals suited me better, at that time and later.

I tried my hand at writing children's stories for Thomas and Sandra, but they quite rightly thought the printed and illustrated ones were better. Then I started working on a book, which I planned to be suitable for general history in the top forms of English schools and the first year of American universities. There were to be ten chapters, each for a different stage of world history and about particular significant events or phases in various countries. Each chapter would consist of as many passages as I could find, written by different historians, of various nationalities, illustrating the many possible angles and interpretations of apparently identical events. Later in life, when I had become an analyst, I found that in a clinical setting it is wise to allow that there can be more than one plausible interpretation of a patient's mood. Categorical views are usually dangerous, perhaps including this one. I did not progress further than the overall planning of that history book and the chapter on Napoleon. There were practical aspects of life which could not be altered much to produce time for writing: as well as the kitchen being far from labour-saving (though it was picturesque, with a well in the middle and a long stone sink under the window), there was of course no washing machine. After pegging up the clean clothes to blow in the garden, if it was not raining, we went for walks or bike rides every day. Winters were much colder than they are now, and the only room available for writing had no heating in it and faced north. So that although Diana and I shared much of the child care, there never seemed to be enough time for writing.

Once we knew that David's division had successfully landed in Sicily, our spirits rose. There were in fact some quite dangerous battles in the process of driving the Italians and Germans out of that island and onto the mainland of Italy, but I do not remember feeling the same kind of anxiety which had beset me earlier. His letters were more cheerful than they had been up to then. Perhaps there was something simple, emotional more than rational, in knowing he and I and Sandra were again on the same continent.

In letters it was impossible for him to say anything much about the campaign, except that the British were advancing, but evidently it went reasonably well. He glossed over the details, conveying only indirectly that, as he was in Signals, he was not normally on the front line. He told me later that on one occasion he and several of his men were swimming off a beach about a mile long and they could see, at the far end, German soldiers also enjoying themselves. Once he had reached Taormina, he and other officers were stationed in what had been a monastery, until recently the headquarters of the Germans who were now driven up into mainland Italy. He brought back a watercolour of the monastery, and another of an attractive olive grove. He and several others had time to climb Mount Etna, which was only steaming in a mild way at the time. Guns were more dangerous than volcanic magma.

After some delay, and another gap in letters, his division was back in England, and he was with us at Ivy Cottage for a short leave. Sandra can remember the excitement of his arrival there. I had told him in letters about getting to know the Partridges and had been looking forward to introducing him to them. I had not realised that he, being forced to be a soldier, would not appreciate their views on the war. It seemed to me that they as well as I were careful to avoid that subject when we had dinner at Ham Spray. Frances noticed 'a reluctance in both of them [David and myself] to plunge below superficialities, or discuss how the war affected those taking part in it'. I felt that we had got through the awkwardness fairly well, but it was another example of how the war was sending him and me along distinctly different paths. My activities inevitably seemed rather small, but we did share the fact that each of us was having to live a life we disliked.

We had discussed whether we should try to have a second child while there was still the next phase of war to be got through: he might be in a dangerous campaign. We had come to the same decision as before the miscarriage, to go ahead and hope all would be well. He was going to be stationed in the attractive village of Long Melford in Suffolk, and likely to be there for a while. He set about looking for somewhere near him for Sandra and me to lodge. Many Army wives were becoming camp-followers.

David found us two rooms in the house of some kindly people: in the larger one we had a small coal fire on which we cooked, and he and I slept there. Sandra had a small bedroom, and adapted remarkably well to a major change of circumstances. One of my main memories is of how cold it was that winter: the house where we lodged was up a hill, and the wind was almost always blowing hard from the East. Long Melford was in a valley; it was damp as well as cold. But it was really good to be together quite a lot.

Sandra and I were there for only a few weeks though, because there were all too soon the signs of a probable miscarriage. It may be that the advice I was given, to travel home to Wiltshire and to be in the care of my own doctor there, was the only thing possible, since the alternative of going into the local Suffolk hospital posed the problem of who would look after Sandra. Perhaps I should anyway have left her at Ivy Cottage, but I could not know in advance that I might get ill again. She was enjoying and benefiting from seeing her father, in the

My father, John Fischer Williams,
in about 1910

My mother, Marjorie Murray,
in about 1910

My father (centre) with his four younger daughters
(left to right): Prue, Mariella, Jenifer, Judith, 1928

Jardin d'Enfants, Lycée Molière, Paris, 1921–1922
(Judith is the third child from the left in the third row, standing)

23826

H. Courte & McPetitin

Lamledra, above the Vault Beach in Cornwall, Judith's holiday home in childhood and in her teens

Judith, around age 12

David and Judith,
at the 1940 "Looking into the Future" Exhibition

Central Office of Information, London

David at work in the Treasury
(left of centre, the tallest person), 1956

Lettice Ramsey

Lettice Ramsey

Judith, around 1957

Ramsey & Muspratt

Judith, around 1965

Children of Judith and David Hubback:
Cassandra (Phillips),

Camilla (Lambert),   *Christopher (Hubback)*

Judith, at Newnham, July 1998

evening and early morning. It was urgent to decide what to do, so she and I took the complicated cross-country train journey of the return. It was certainly good to be home again, in many ways, but fate was hard on us a second time, and the miscarriage took its course. My sister Prue and her small daughter were living at Ivy Cottage by then. Prue looked after me most sensitively, while the children played. We hoped they were unaware of how unhappy we had all become.

I worried a lot about not being a good container for a new life to develop in. It was an undermining anxiety, and I felt more discouraged and depressed than angry; certainly not brave, which Prue said I was. Trying to keep hold of a sense of proportion was just possible, but only just—one couple's bad luck as compared with the unimaginable number of people almost all over the world at risk of death, or major injury, at any moment. Allowing myself to be angry might have helped: but angry with whom? There was no answer. It did not make sense to think that an unbelievable Old Testament kind of God was punishing me for something mysterious. Perhaps I had committed one of the Seven Deadly Sins—and would compound it with anger, which anyway was one of them? Or would it have been overweening ambition, attempting something which was mysteriously forbidden to me, or that I was fated not to succeed in doing? Unwittingly I hid my anger and my speculations behind depression.

When Voltaire wrote: *Il faut cultiver son jardin,* I think he meant that you *must* till your garden, get it to be as good as possible, and not that the only thing to do is to resort to gardening.

In the early spring of 1944, there was a heightened expectation of an invasion by the Allies of the mainland of Europe. David's division moved to Southern England, and it became possible for him to use his Jeep to drive up to see us. We had already discussed the question of whether we would risk trying yet again to have a second child. The local doctor thought we could, since the cause of the recent miscarriage was not known, and there would not necessarily be a repeat. I expect he sensed how determined we were to try to put the past behind us, even if that was rash. There was an old saying that the will to life is especially strong when many people, women as well as men, are being killed. Anyway, perhaps something of that kind got hold of us. Before David and his division went off to Normandy, I was again pregnant, and again hopeful.

March, April and May ticked by, and the first four days of June. By then David could not visit us, so we guessed that big events were on the edge of happening. The fine weather was being closely watched. Would it hold? Would the sea be too rough for the landing craft? On the fifth day a great windy storm blew up. Was it malign? In a curious way, I found myself remembering the tense days of September 1939, when the weather had been benign, at least for evacuating children from cities. And in all the years, ever since, if there is stormy weather in early June, my mind flips back to 1944.

Some time on the 6th of June we heard on the radio news of what had happened early that morning: the Allied troops had landed through the waves on many Normandy beaches. They had scrambled up the low dunes, thousands of men and masses of equipment, strongly opposed by the Germans. Surprisingly soon, on the 7th, a letter arrived from David saying that he was among them. It was an amazing time, partly exciting but mostly anxious. A few letters later, he was able to tell me that he and a sergeant (both in Signals) had been sent at once in to the nearest town, Bayeaux, to see if the main post office was booby-trapped. Since he could tell me the story, they had obviously not been blown up. I think that was the only incident of extreme danger, in his whole time in the army, that he told me about: he was rightly feeling proud, I should think.

The other emotion he reported was not so much of having to face danger as of disgust: within a few days there were many once beautiful Normandy cows lying dead and bloated in the ruined apple orchards. He did not mention the dead soldiers. But later he said many of the peasant farmers were angry at being disturbed, and the cows killed, though they were very willing to sell creamy Camembert cheese to a new batch of soldiers. The local girls with closely shaven heads were those who had fallen for comforting the German soldiers, in bed or anywhere convenient, probably cheering themselves up also, while their men were away.

The campaign progressed at first slowly, round Caen, then the speed of it accelerated, and letter after letter was about the many famous cathedral towns through which he passed. They were ones my mother had drawn, painted or etched, so I knew them, in a way. It was only through the radio and newspapers that I got a picture of the grim, fearful or sad days of war, but I remember that in one letter he was able to refer to interviewing (through an interpreter) prisoners of war from western parts of the U.S.S.R., who had been forced to serve in the German army, and were relieved to be out of it now. There were others from more distant eastern parts, for whom an interpreter could not be found. They were in a bad way, hungry, lonely and depressed.

In the towns David's keenness for sightseeing was fully satisfied. I got the impression that he and his men were some of the very first to enter Paris triumphantly, driving in their camouflaged Jeeps down the Champs Elysées, lined with cheering crowds, and then on, pursuing the Germans towards the East. Only a few days before, Resistance fighters were still ambushing the straggling Germans in the suburbs and several of them were killed. I heard later, from an old friend, Professor Paul Mantoux, that his son Etienne, a brilliant young economist, who I had known at Cambridge, was among them. After Paris, there were still more cathedrals, as the Army sped towards Belgium.

But back in peaceful Wiltshire, during that successful forward drive of the Allied armies, I was feeling deeply miserable, having lost a baby a third time. It might be thought that the cause of the loss was stress, psychosomatic again, my body reacting to tenseness about David's safety, but that could not be proved scientifically.

The background was that during the landings period and the battle to break out of Normandy the Germans had been defending themselves staunchly, so casualties on both sides were serious. Compared with how it had been in the North African campaign over terrain which was much more suitable for modern battles, the Allies in France were now fighting their way forward over thickly inhabited country, farms, villages and small towns. All that time I was naturally anxious for all men and women in uniform, but for David especially. It was not a daily subject of conversation with Diana, simply constant tense fear.

Some time in July, being five months' pregnant, I started sensing that all was not well inside me, in my already thickening body. When the local doctor, who knew about the earlier mis-carriages, examined me, he immediately looked grave, but tried to prevent me being too worried and sent me to Newbury hospital. By some kind of irony I found myself there in the care of Dr. Tom Scott, who had delivered Sandra. He broke the news to me that he would have to terminate the pregnancy, explaining that the placenta and the future baby were wrongly positioned, and that if I went on until the eighth month either the baby or I would be in grave danger. It was obviously a sensible decision, and I did not protest. I trusted his professional knowledge.

When I came round from the anaesthetic, I could feel that I was bleeding profusely, though attached to a presumably helpful blood drip. There seemed to be "someone" with me all the time, or perhaps it was that I hoped there was: I "knew" I was sinking, going to die gently, but it was not an unpleasant or frightening experience. I can clearly remember that with my mind I said to myself that I was dying, and with my feelings I said, death will be all right. No action was required, no fighting. I was accepting, not being passive. Later, I was grateful that the drip continued to restore life to me.

The day after my not dying, I asked Dr. Scott if he could apply for David to be given compassionate leave. I am afraid he thought I was unbalanced, and certainly not patriotic. He did not say so openly, but was obviously surprised that I had the cheek to make such a request, which of course he did not grant. But we remained friends.

So again there was a return to Ivy Cottage, on my own, without the prospect of a much wanted live, healthy baby. I tried a few pseudo-philosophical thoughts: perhaps it was "all for the best"; perhaps one child was all my "allowance"; and, even crazier, perhaps it was "meant". Rather more sensibly I thought I could move on after the war towards doing something more important than bearing babies and rearing new people—it was not a good world for them, it was a voracious Moloch demanding cannon-fodder every generation. Ruminating like that was almost useless, merely an ineffective way of trying to shake off a renewal of depressive moods.

One sunny afternoon, as I was lying on the front lawn under the large cedar tree, Frances Partridge looked in and we talked. I told her I had thought I had nearly died, and was ashamed that that was self-centred and important—to me. I had not seen it in quite such a simple light before, but something clarifying and moving happened between her and me, which had made the confession possible. Frances was sensitive and wise. I guessed she knew that denying, contradicting, or saying anything banal such as "You'll be over it soon", or "It's not the end of the world", would be useless and unreal. Instead, she said that feeling as I did was absolutely natural, and appropriate. I had had a really life-shaking experience, and of course it was important. Our friendship immediately increased in depth. She had made it possible for me to trust and respect my feelings, without in any way denying my right to think about them. I knew that Frances played the violin beautifully. From then on I was quite a lot more in tune with myself than I had been for a long time.

During the summer, the Ivy Cottage arrangement came to an end. Diana and I each decided that we would soon move back to London. Sandra and I went down to stay with my father and mother in Cornwall, where Prue also was with her daughter, Fidelity; the two children were good friends. Still trying to recover, I spent a few days with Will Arnold-Forster in his house near St. Ives, Eagle's Nest. I had adored him from afar at the age of fourteen, the first man I had ever found attractive, with his piercing bright blue eyes and quick responses. And his wife, Ka, now sadly dead, had been more of a role model for me than my own mother. We talked about his and my favourite interests, international affairs and Cornish ones, gardening and, where he was concerned, painting. He tried to take my mind off my despondency.

From there I went up to London, stayed with Paul Sinker, my old friend from Cambridge and climbing days, and found a small early eighteenth-century house in Highgate, charming but very unpractical, which I rented. It had a garden and was near a congenial school for Sandra. Being alone with Paul soon after staying with Will, made me realise clearly how sexually deprived I had been during the war. He was apparently light-hearted about sleeping with other women than his wife, which I was not used to, nor had I realised that at Cambridge he had found me very attractive. After an emotional struggle, I decided not to enjoy myself. It was not the right time. Years later, I regretted my scruples.

Where public things were concerned, was the world now approaching the satisfactory endgame, so-called, of an indescribably awful war? Or were our hopes merely specious?

Eight

Transition to Peace

During that autumn of 1944 it looked at first as though the war would be over soon. My thoughts were beamed on moving towards the next stage, and I was tired of celibacy. So much so, that I think I was in danger of idealising the future. David would be demobilised, even if not at once; we would have another baby, perhaps two; our family life would start up, satisfyingly; and I would, sooner or later, find some congenial and worthwhile work.

It was a false dawn. The war in the Far East was still fearfully grim. The armies on the Western Front which had been driving ahead so rapidly were held up, and casualties became serious again. Southern England was now being targeted by V-2s, the unmanned rockets, which arrived without any warning at all, so they were more dangerous than the recent V-1s, scornfully or cheerfully nicknamed Doodlebugs. I had just got myself and Sandra settled into the new house, and had started casting around for work. But, looking at the situation clearly, I realised it would be crazy to put her and myself at risk when I had spent the war keeping her out of obvious danger. So it meant looking for somewhere to live out of London, and another period of waiting.

We were offered a room in Oxford by Phyllis, the wife of Francis Hicks, a cousin of David's. Francis had been a prisoner of war for over four years, having been captured at Dunkirk. Phyllis was doing his work, running a house for boarders at the Dragon School, including their own two children, and teaching. She was glad of some adult company unconnected with the staff-room, and we made friends through talking about our views on all sorts of things. I had met her superficially, with Francis, in North Wales before the war. Francis had been much of the way up Everest, and Phyllis saw herself in a too lowly light as "only a wife and mother". The war had shown how she was much more than that, without her needing to climb mountains or carry arms. I told her so, and added that I was beginning to be interested in practical psychology. I felt I was the more likely of the two of us to slip downhill into Milton's mood, described in a sonnet when he was irreversibly blind, unable to do much more than 'stand and wait'.

I had not yet regained my strength after the third miscarriage and felt that I was not doing more than just keeping going. It was the old frustrated, powerless and depressed mood that I knew all too well. But one day the legend of the ancient Scottish king, Bruce, came to my aid. In his despondency when sheltering alone in a cave after losing a battle, his attention was caught by the sight of a spider which fell down each time it climbed up the wall, but regularly tried again. So even a story from a children's over-simple history book was of some use. I was not good at being alone, and needed to link up with someone congenial. Everything felt temporary.

One bleak December day a message came from David. He was a Captain by then, on General Montgomery's staff, in Brussels. It happened that the Secretary to the Cabinet in London needed a Private Secretary. The person to be appointed had to be of the right, fairly junior, rank in the administrative Civil Service, to be currently serving in one of the armed forces, and to be within reach. David fitted the bill exactly. He was asked to go for an interview and got the job. It was tremendously exciting. Within very few days he was out of uniform and had achieved a position of unparalleled interest and importance. From then on he was going to know, I gathered, all the secrets at the highest level of national and international policy. It was not going to include going to Cabinet meetings, but he would see all the relevant papers and work closely with the Cabinet Secretary, Sir Edward Bridges. It was just before Christmas, so all three of us, together at last, went down once more to my parents' house in Cornwall, to celebrate, with others in the family.

David's life was in the process of being altered in a very major way. He had suddenly moved from being a conscripted soldier to being able to look forward to just the kind of career that it would have been foolhardy even to dream of. I felt very pleased for him. On active service in the Army he had never mentioned substantial matters of any kind. Now he was going to have to be even more scrupulous about not revealing anything of what was going on at Cabinet level. We used the phrase typed on office letters, "Top Secret Hush", in family talk, as though it were a joke, in capitals and red ink. It was some time before I saw that the change in his life was going to affect me as much as I feared it might.

One of the first decisions we had to take was about where Sandra and I would each live, until the danger of the V-2s was over. David and I wanted to be together as much as possible, and since we had the house in Highgate I could be there with him. We arranged that Sandra should stay in Cornwall, where Prue was living and could look after her, in safety, combined with her own daughter, Fidelity. There was a small nursery school in the village, Gorran Haven, which they could both attend. The two girls were already good friends, and the family house by the sea provided an excellent material environment, with her aunt and grandparents in charge. It was further experience for her with members of the extended family.

With hindsight, David and I took the rational but wrong decision for Sandra: we gave more weight to her physical safety, than to her psychological need to be with us both. She was excluded as a result of her father returning from active service, and at risk of feeling I had abandoned her and favoured her father. David and I went to Cornwall one week-end and there was such thick fog and mist that the sea was invisible all the time. The damage to her only became clear when, many months later, the war in Europe being over, she was back in London and the second baby, Camilla, had been born. In the local school there Sandra was happy, but at home she was miserable every evening, clearly depressed. When I tried unskilfully to get her to explain what was wrong, she could only answer: "Everything". She developed pneumonia and was delirious all one night. I still regret deeply that I had not trusted my intuition and done more to protect her from the strain we had unwittingly imposed on her. If I could re-live that time I would manage somehow or other to find the fare to go down more week-ends.

Where my marriage was concerned and in relation to how the next stage of my life developed, with a lot of emphasis on activity, and on aiming to combine professional work with married life and motherhood, I now see that I was caught up in a version of the competitiveness that had coloured my childhood in my original family. Being female still seemed inferior to being male. I think I valued evident achievements more than inner ones.

The way in which David's life and career were developing was not only impressive but also, alas for me, enviable. His need for maleness was met by his having been a soldier, and being a father. Now his mind was going to be satisfied as well. He was in Whitehall, not just a famous street but shorthand for central government and administration, an elite position which was then still largely male. Until I had achieved having at any rate one more child, I was engrossed in that aspect of femaleness. Without success in that part of life, I thought my confidence would remain low. So other ambitions would have to wait, before they could be achieved. David was just as keen as I was that we should have a larger family, before I did anything more.

Over the next few years my ideas and thoughts were taking shape. I made the discomforting observation that, as compared with living lovingly over many years, for a husband and wife to continue to be "in love" was rare. We were not among those rarities. We had been separated much of the time for the first five years of marriage, the foundation ones, during which intimate companionship could have developed. We had not joked together over the trivialities of daily life or been to parties, or cinemas. We had not danced. There had not been frequent enough opportunities for airing our feelings and reflections during the times of major danger to ourselves and to the wider world. And when David returned to the Civil Service I was deprived of discussing political matters. It was all too easy to slip into nostalgia for the free-minded and free-living Cambridge days.

The background for David's and my difficulties was personal but also part of twentieth-century social history. It used to be said, I think fallaciously, that the higher education of women was the reason for the many marriage problems among professional people, since the whole of the century was a time of major transitions in many other ways as well. When I was young, there was more difference than there was later, between the demands made by society in Western Europe on a woman and the ones made on a man: 'Biology is destiny', Freud had written, simplistically, about women.

Yet one of the benefits of the social changes of that century, especially in "the West", is that there is much more respect shown now to women's all round needs than there used to be. That is the positive result of the Women's Liberation Movement, whose members took up, in the Sixties and Seventies, where the Suffragettes had left off earlier in the century. It was sad that both groups' strident campaigns put defensively minded men into a reactive mood. I did not become a Women's Lib person, since I considered their demand for simple equality was crude, though understandable and even necessary as part of historical development. I was like the Russian Mensheviks, who were gradualists and defeated, as compared with Lenin's much more aggressive Bolsheviks, who founded the U.S.S.R. on millions of corpses. I worked, in the Nineteen Fifties, on the preliminaries necessary for progress, described below, in chapter 11.

From observation and from my own experience, I had come to see that both partners viewing the sexes as having equivalent needs rather than identical ones would be the best basis for relating during the rest of their lives. Present-day young couples may think that is banal, and hardly needs saying. Many of them have had little opportunity to get to know about the quiet work done by women, and some men, two and three generations before theirs, from which they now benefit. If the husband has a far more satisfying life than his wife, some kind of discontent may be sown in her, unless she is either a saint, has good luck, or makes a positive effort to come to terms with the situation. I got through my difficulties only very slowly. And I recognise that it has not been at all easy for the general run of men fully to accept the consequences of the basic changes in women's demands, which stem from their needs.

In spite of stresses, David and I regained a great deal of what marriage is about. I still wished to do more, and to take an active part in more than only domestic life, as soon as it became possible. Also I wanted conversation and opportunities to develop views and opinions, scope for discussing what was happening in the world outside domestic life.

When the war in the West was over, Sandra could come back to London and we had another baby on the way. I had given up the temporary teaching job I had found in London. Medical research on what can go wrong during pregnancy was concentrating on the situation where one of the partners was classified as rhesus negative, which was a danger to the survival of the foetus, and this was found to apply to us. I was told that the rhesus factor does not affect first pregnancies.

I doubt if I fully understood or trusted the scientific facts, and mostly felt fatalistic. I was told to be very careful. At one stage before Camilla was born, there was the predicted major scare and I bled profusely. I might have lost her and was kept in bed. Just then Sandra had both appendicitis and measles and was taken to hospital in Plymouth. I was not allowed to travel, and I am not sure if anyone explained to her why I could not come. Prue was one of the first women to insist successfully that she should stay with her in hospital. My memory is of simply gritting my teeth and leaning on tenuous hopes that both Sandra and the unborn baby would be all right. When Camilla was born she had come into the world as a result of her parents' insistence on persevering, and we wondered whether that would be part of her personality.

The major public event in the summer of 1945 was the dropping of the atom bombs on Hiroshima and Nagasaki. The news of them, the descriptions, the photographs, were absolutely appalling. They were rapidly followed by the surrender of Japan. I think that in countless families like ours there must have been a lot of agonised discussion. The old, but not outworn, theme rearose sharply: does a good end justify such awful means? We discussed whether the Allies should have warned Japan, either verbally or by dropping a bomb somewhere in the Pacific Ocean (what a name for it!) to demonstrate its huge power, but they wanted to defeat the enemy in the East quickly, before the U.S.S.R. came in. It was clear that the war was shortened, but the tortured deaths of millions of people, the long-term sinister health problems and the destruction of two large cities, were appalling.

What followed was the risk of nuclear war between the most powerful nations, the U.S.A. and the U.S.S.R. In only four years after Hiroshima the U.S.S.R. developed nuclear arms, and had the hydrogen bomb by 1953. The nuclear arms race, which brought in several other nations as allies in the two camps, led to what became the Cold War, dominating the world for over forty years. Ordinary men and women of all ages over almost the whole world ran various protest movements.

Many professional and amateur historians consider the twentieth century as the most murderous there ever was. David and I used to discuss that, he mostly saying there always had been wars, and me saying that modern weapons and technology make basic aggression even more evil. Any attitude at all complacent used to worry me, and still does. How I was thinking then led me gradually towards one of the major problems of psychology, the tension between opposite inborn forces in all of us, whatever aspects we consider or names we choose to give them.

On the material side of personal life, there were many practical difficulties during the immediate post-war time. Since there were five years between our first and second daughters, then nearly two years before our son Christopher was born, and David was working very long hours, my contribution to it all was to try to see that each individual member of the family was responded to in the most suitable way. To some extent it was a juggling job, and an unremitting one. I had to be a kind of chameleon, inside which there was the next potential version of me. I discovered that I had committed myself to a far more demanding and complicated series of tasks, and pleasures, than I had imagined beforehand. Also, I could not have anticipated how outside events were going to affect me. Many women must have found the same things happening to them.

Immediately after birth, a baby breathes instinctively or is helped to do so, and thereby starts the long process of relating and responding to the world, taking something from outside into its body, its self. For me one aspect of becoming a mother was how, from the first moment of extra-uterine life, each of the babies seemed to display, in a simplified and partial form, one of the characteristics which turned out later to be typical of them. The satisfactory thing was that they were themselves, individual people, immediately. The small seeds of more developed relating were just perceptible. Of course I did not know that many years later that would be my experience when a new patient came into the room: something particular to that person could be noticed at once and would become the basis of a way of relating which, when understood, could be of major use to them.

Where David's and my new babies were concerned, I thought Sandra looked calm, confident and serene. Camilla was born before the doctor arrived, and the nurse was out of the room for a few minutes, so she and I managed without professional help. She looked around, seemed to take in what she could see and (I imagined) said to herself "It looks interesting". Christopher was in a great hurry, apparently trying in vain, through yelling hard, to reconcile himself to such a major change of circumstances. The abominable nurse took him off, without asking my permission, to spend his first night away from home. In the morning she brought him in and added to her starched, heartless and unimaginative behaviour by announcing to me: "Well, Mrs. Hubback, your baby kept everybody awake all night with his screaming". I was not strong enough to answer her with a suitable counter-attack. It was one of those events in which I wish that I had asserted myself more. Christopher had much to protest about, then and later. Well before becoming an analyst I both felt and knew in my bones that such an angry experience could have long-term bad consequences. That nurse evidently knew nothing about how despairing an infant, a very young person, can feel in the process of adjusting to life outside the womb. He was an anxious baby for several months.

If I had come from a working-class background, no doubt I would have managed without any help. But I might have had my mother close by, or other members of an extended family. As it was, on David's not yet sizeable salary, we could nearly but not easily afford live-in help, and we found a young Irish girl, full of energy and humour. She had one of the small attic bedrooms. A student, the daughter of a Finnish friend, came to live in the other. At intervals the bank manager sent for me, since David was always at work, to complain that we were indulging in an overdraft which we had not negotiated. Once, when I was tired, he drove me to tears. He could not know that I minded not contributing to the family budget. Banks then closed at three in the afternoon, and were not open on Saturdays. David, like all Civil Servants, worked then. He slept every other night in the Cabinet Office basement—on an austere iron bed. One way and another, it was a hard-working time, for both of us, far from luxurious. Many foods were still severely rationed.

If I mentioned difficulties (as compared to actually complaining, which was taboo, and David's mother disapproved of what she called self-pity), his favourite and annoying phrase was, "Worse before it's better". That referred to the world at large, as well as to how it was for us with young children. Perhaps it was fortunate, at that time, that the war had trained us into assuming and accepting rather narrow lives. We were not living in want, or being persecuted, as were so many millions of other people all over the globe, then and later. It was, I now see, very good that we were well aware of dire world events and conditions beyond the pleasantness of Highgate, and Sunday walks on Hampstead Heath. We could not be complacent about social conditions, nor could we mind the absence of as yet unknown inventions, which are now ordinary.

London life was interrupted by nearly two years in Paris. For me it worked out that that was the beginning of being able to see quite a lot more clearly the possible steps forward into the combination of several years of full-time motherhood with doing or observing some of the things that I would then be able to write about. I did not see that aspect of it at once, but I can clearly remember the excitement I felt one sunny day in August 1947, when we were on holiday, and the large headline on the front of the *Manchester Guardian* (as it then was) announced the offer by the U.S.A. of major economic help to war-damaged Europe. It was soon to be known as the Marshall Plan. After months of international discussions and negotiations about how it would be put into action, David was moved from the Cabinet Office into a new job on the British staff of the O.E.E.C., the

Organisation for European Economic Cooperation, set up in Paris to administer the workings of the Plan.

For him it was fascinating work, and in the course of it he developed a deep interest in international economic affairs and, broadly speaking, in how countries should be run, the minutiae and the pitfalls, the interactions between the would-be cooperative politicians who were also pushing their own ambitions, and the administrators trying to serve them dispassionately. The subject of the machinery of government became his most important interest. His career in Whitehall advanced satisfactorily for most of the rest of his professional life, though he never reached the highest rank in the Civil Service that his mother had believed was possible.

In Paris David's work was partly similar to that of full-blown diplomats, with lunches, parties in the early evening and dinners for visiting politicians. It was expected of me that I should go with him to those functions. I tried not to appear to be "only a wife", but that had to be done skilfully, not assertively, or showing off that I was not a total ignoramus, since in fact I knew quite a lot about current matters and the background of them. If I had been a man, I might have been doing similar work, but I do not think that I would have enjoyed the tortuous office politics. A few months later I discovered about the sexual affairs which flourished in tense late-night work, while people were drafting communiqués which concealed as much as they revealed. Unattached secretaries could find temporary partners easily during those long negotiations, typing and re-typing until the text was satisfactory to the delegates. My experiences during the war had not inducted me into that world. I was in the grip of a naïvete which got punctured, painfully, all too soon.

Much to my regret, taking part even as only a wife, meant employing a nanny, as I was not always at home for the children's bedtime. My own experience as a child, also in Paris, had caused me to dislike having to entrust children to someone other than myself, and to try not to make the same mistakes as my mother had. Friends of my generation who were happy with their childhood Nanny think my views are fixed and generalised. Some of them say they would definitely not have liked to be looked after by their mother.

I was inexperienced about finding a suitable nanny and re-alised too late that I should have looked for one before leaving London to go out to Paris with us, to replace the Irish girl who we all liked. She had just then had a baby. She had asserted that she knew nothing about how she had become pregnant, and I could not face the responsibility of her travelling with us. We had at least three different nannies for the children during the time we were in Paris, each unsatisfactory in one way or an-other. One was too young and inexperienced, as indeed I was in many ways. The next was rather rough and mainly interested in making boyfriends. The third was a war widow, who had had to park her own three children in a Home. She was a really nice woman, and of course she pined for them. The flat was too small for us all, so personalities mattered a great deal.

I was not, as so many mothers are now, out all day, but all the same I do not know how much damage the children suf-fered from the less good nannies. I have only recently been told a few anecdotes, about things that one or other of them said or did, unknown to me at the time. They confirm my view that, even in mainly 'good' circumstances, small children may have to cope with far too many difficult emotional experiences. They ei-ther do not, or cannot, tell whether such things will go on for ever. They live in the present. When I look back to my own early years, I am sure I had no concept of time, apart from meal-times and bedtime. The present was the obvious fact. I made a great scene, once, age four or five, when someone used the phrase, 'Before you were born'. I insisted there was no time be-fore me. I was inevitably labelled pig-headed. But perhaps that characteristic helped me later to persevere, in the face of setbacks.

These reminiscences lead me to wonder whether it was possi-ble that I had not yet fully emerged from the difficulties of the war and the immediate post-war time, which included becoming responsible for three children. The present was very present, but the past was still there. I was perhaps unconsciously caught in a regression to the childhood assumption that current things, whether pleasant or unpleasant, would go on, and on, and on, for ever. In fact I was lucky that a few years later I was able to apply my experiences to life beyond my own family and to dispute the then commonly held idea that the Housewife role would go on all through a woman's life. That role can be a lonely one—I had found it so.

I had given up, even before the war, all dreams of working in a powerful international setting. They had been based on my wish to use what I had inherited from my father. Circumstances made them impossible, and anyway they were grandiose. During the next phase I converted them into the kind of work which did become possible, combined with family life: journalism, broadcasting, social research and psychology.

During the course of my adult life there were three major phases. They have in common that they were all about struggles. In the first, history included the study of *past* conflicts between nations and classes, wars and revolutions. I could not have any influence over them. The second phase became the study of the *contemporary* problematic relations between men and highly educated women, where I did make my mark (see chapter 11). The third was the study of *internal* conflicts, conscious and unconscious, both in me and in the minds and lives of my patients. I moved step by step from very outer to very inner matters.

My life developed in very different ways from David's. I had originally pictured us as travelling on two parallel and close lines, but from then on they diverged in many significant ways, like the branches of a tree. But our tree was well rooted.

Nine

New Opportunities

Living in Paris in the late Nineteen Forties and meeting people there made it possible for me to emerge from an amount of domesticity that I had found very demanding. I did not see myself as good at responding well to it, and was bothered by having in mind an unrealistic picture of a wife, mother and housekeeper who tolerated cheerfully being always on duty. That imagined perfect woman did not see that, actually, she was basking in being a martyr. The husband who went with the scenario would not only, for example, take the children off while his wife fell asleep during an afternoon rest, but also discover how to protect her from them rushing in and waking her over-enthusiastically to tell her all about it, when they came back. David enjoyed doing things with them, but he did not realise that for me duty seemed to begin again the moment they were under the same roof. That kind of incident illustrates how a man and a woman could differ in their views of each other's needs, and what convention assumed were their duties. The children's liveliness was a boon, but I, perhaps greedily, wanted some less limited free time. During the months in Paris I had more freedom from domesticity and child care than before, so I was able to build on what had been only tenuously possible in the difficult war years and the immediate post-war ones.

The first occasion when David's work came in useful to me, and gave me an opportunity I had not foreseen, was when he and I were hosting one of the duty sherry parties. Among the guests was the Paris correspondent on *The Times*. He seemed bored, looking beyond me, as people do while sipping their drink, trying to see someone more worth talking to. I took a risk, plunging unconventionally into conversation, and asked him what he had done that day. "Oh", he answered gloomily, "London rang up to ask me to do a piece on some sort of educational subject". I thought, "It's not about politics, he thinks it's beneath his dignity, but it's not beneath mine". To his surprise I offered to do it. My credentials were adequate. He accepted. The article was to be about an experimental year which was being set up for young people between school and university. During that time they would be filtered, so as to stem the too-great flow of those wanting to exert their automatic right to go to university straight after the Baccalauréat examination, since many of them were likely to drop out before graduating. I am grateful to the *Times* man, since he enabled me to get started on combining some journalism with being "only" a wife and mother. The opportunity was there, waiting to be picked up. The sherry had presumably helped me to be bold, at a time when I mostly felt insignificant. It was an example of building on past experiences: a childhood in Paris schools, a tour of several institutions in French provinces while at the Institute of Education, and a time in teaching.

The first piece appeared in *The Times* itself, early in February 1949. At about the same time I wrote one for *The Lady*, on housekeeping in Paris, describing the many elements I had noticed which were different from how things were in England.

In preparing that second article, I met several non-diplomatic wives and heard about French women's difficulties over how to limit the number of pregnancies. They were mostly Catholics and took the opportunity of confiding in me, a neutral outsider. They were reasonably happy, but made it clear that they felt they were sexual objects, and that was not enough. They were trying to get round the total lack of proper quality birth control advice or medical facilities, and several of them said their husbands were not backing them up. As there were anyway not yet enough Family Planning Clinics in England, apart from the problems for Catholics, I merely commented, in the article, on many young married women having larger families than they wanted. That was a different matter from the Baby Boom stage of the post-war years.

Towards the end of our time in Paris I started planning an enquiry into the subject of professional women in France. It got interrupted by our return to London, but I was able to take the idea forward later, in a rather different form (chapter 11).

The Spectator took an article on certain new trends I had observed in French education, especially the demand from liberal-minded parents for a better balance between sheer intellectual instruction, to which all pupils in the *lycées* (grammar schools), had to submit, and new methods for attending to each individual's abilities and needs. It was recognised that many school leavers were unduly exhausted and unimaginative. The Ministry of Education was sponsoring and encouraging experimentation, and there were said to be over 800 *Classes Nouvelles* running all over France. Each of those classes was limited to twenty-five pupils, and time was made for art, music, handwork and expeditions. The teachers there found that it was possible to deviate from the rigid official syllabuses and that every piece of work did not have to be marked, so many competitive attitudes were reformed.

I was told it all seemed cranky and revolutionary. Apologists for the experimental classes said there was nothing new in such an approach, citing the enlightened views of eminent men in earlier centuries, such as Rabelais, Montaigne and Rousseau, to prove their point. To some extent they were right, about "nothing new": the traditional rigidity in the classroom had often been unavailingly pilloried. I then expanded the *Spectator* article into three detailed ones for *The Times Educational Supplement.* I had much enjoyed the small-scale research which had been the basis of beginning to write again.

There were a few private schools near where we lived, for young children, run on similar liberal lines to the one Sandra had attended in Highgate, but as she was already seven years old and well up to doing solid work, we decided that in the long run she would benefit more by going to the local state junior school. For the first term she was really miserable (as she had been in the little school in Oxford), was puzzled by everything and of course needed a lot of support. There could be no concession, in the classroom, to her not speaking French. It was a great relief to her, and to us, that immediately after the

Christmas break she found she could understand it all, and I think she fitted in well enough. At the end of the term she came out top.

Camilla was too young to go to any kind of school, but she picked up quite a lot of French through buying the bread and the milk, getting the change right and joining other children in traditional songs and games in the small dusty playground nearby.

The flat we rented was unsuitably elegant for small children and suffered from them ignorantly ill-treating it. There were pink satin curtains, glass-topped black lacquer tables, and would-be-Japanese screens—we wondered whether the pseudo-elegant and brash owner had been a high-class prostitute who had entertained German officers there. It was too small for us, so we went out at week-ends as often as possible.

On one of our Sunday drives and walks in the country round Paris, our attention was attracted by the shouts of children. Peering over a wall, we saw groups of young people playing in the courtyard of an old Chateau. They had all lost either one or more limbs, and were enthusiastically dashing about on crutches; at least, most of them were. On enquiry we were told that they were war orphans, as well as having had amputations. That chance sight led to a full-page illustrated article. *The Times* sent out a photographer from London. Later I heard the cook had reported to the nanny that the telephone arrangements about meeting him were part of an affair I was having. The woman in the porter's lodge was said to know all about it. At the time I did not think that was funny. Now I can say, "No such luck".

In August we rented a villa in Brittany and the near-by holiday camp provided good material for another big article, also in *The Times Educational Supplement*. The extension of the holiday camp movement had been accelerated by the need for short-term evacuation from endangered cities during the war. Camps had previously been almost only for children from poor industrial districts, who particularly needed to get into the country. Now they were used by families of other social classes. The minimum stay was a month, and I was told the children did not mind the discipline and the austere way of life, as they were used to them. At the same time the camps were said to contribute an important element in the liberalisation of main-line education, since the children painted enthusiastically, could do other kinds of handwork, swam, composed dramas and sang on every possible occasion. Some ran a newsletter. I was told they discovered about team work and even the benefits of being considerate towards other people. Very little of all that happened in most schools.

Summer camps were much more numerous than their English equivalents were then, and have since become, adapting ideas from the U.S.A. For English readers in the Forties they were rarities, and that made them worthwhile for me to write about, when I was cutting my teeth as a journalist.

The holiday in Brittany also led to two articles published in the *Western Morning News*, a paper I knew from my days in Cornwall. I described several aspects of Brittany and Breton life, both for themselves and to illustrate differences and similarities with Cornwall, and the various islands off the coasts of both those promontories. It would have been good to have time to do much more thorough research about, for example, tunny fishing, which was conducted then from broad-in-the-beam special boats, with tall rods in the stern looking like great antennae. Each rod carried up to seven lines; in earlier days, I was told, every one of them had a bell with its individual note, so that each tunny fish announced its capture and imminent death. Dolphins and porpoises were not at risk, as they are now from nets.

Some articles gave me scope for a different, freer, kind of writing than I had had before. I have preserved two such pieces, and though their style is much more mannered and flowery than is fashionable now, the *Manchester Guardian* accepted them for a slot which they kept for such essays.

In the first of them, I modelled myself on Henry James' "A Little Tour of France", which, with its dated title, was written in the 1880s. I described many beautiful places he did not visit, which were still uncrowded when we went there. They included the Cave at Lascaux, discovered only in 1940 by a boy and his dog digging for rabbits. Its existence was known during the war to only a few people. When we went there it was still open to be visited and its amazing character had not yet been exploited for tourism. It was thrilling to gaze at such early artistic success, with only two or three other people who happened to be there. Those wall paintings were deeply moving: the energetic-looking cows, oxen, ponies, deer and a few people, such as the man keenly displaying his erect penis. They still looked fresh, and it was tempting to try to get an imaginative glimpse into the minds of the painters.

In the second article I followed my literary interests again, using my vestigial memory of Thomas Gray's "Ode on the Death of a Favourite Cat Drowned in a Tub of Goldfishes" (originally written in 1747) to describe elaborately the death of one of our goldfish. Our children buried it in a matchbox, in the public garden, by gaslight, having composed a pagan service for the occasion. My style in those essays certainly needed editorial pruning, but the *Manchester Guardian*'s leniency gave me courage, kept to myself, to hope that one day I would be up to writing poetry of better quality than the juvenilia of my school and Cambridge days. It would have been good to have more scope to develop in that direction, but fortunately I was well aware of not being more than slightly gifted for it. No delusions of grandeur, but pleasure, decades later, when a first line "came" at times of leisure or simple reflection. There were phases of that kind of experience, and longer phases of it lying fallow.

David's mother, Eva, died in 1949. It was agreed between him and his sisters, Diana and Rachel, that he would acquire, as part of his share of her estate, the house in Hampstead Garden Suburb, which their parents had built before the First World War. So he and I and our children moved into the house where he had been brought up, on the edge of the Hampstead Heath Extension. That part of the Heath consisted mainly of fields, so it felt almost country-ish. From my point of view that was its best feature, and Camilla made a large collection of wild flowers found on the Heath, pressed and organised into albums.

The younger children went at first to a morning class along the road, in a nursery nurses' training college, and Sandra to the junior school in the Garden Suburb. Camilla followed her there and both in turn went on to North London Collegiate School in Edgware. It had a good academic reputation, though much of the teaching was still, I thought, rather old-fashioned. The disadvantage was the distance from home and the shortage of out-of-school activities, since the girls had to get home before dark. I think I bored them when I talked about the advantages of the clubs and societies I had so much enjoyed at my country boarding school. Sandra went on to Somerville College at Oxford, and Camilla to New Hall at Cambridge. Neither of them liked the look of Newnham. It was important to them to choose different colleges from mine.

On the whole, the girls' education seemed to go well, but Christopher had a less satisfactory time. He hated the nursery class, and it was a mistake on my part to think that the company of other children there was better than being alone at home with me. The junior school was better, but, perhaps characteristically for a boy who had two older sisters who read a lot, he did not take to reading easily, preferring activity. When he went on to the prep school where David had been, the Hall School in Hampstead, he flourished, but the system there was to move boys on to higher classes (called forms then) during the year, if they were getting good marks. So he made friends and then lost them when he did well, especially at maths. There was an excessive attention paid to marks by the Head and the teaching staff: the mothers were meant to go to hear every pupil's marks read out to the whole school each Friday morning. The fathers of course were all at work. I was not a keen attender at the ceremony, which was aimed at encouraging the boys to get into a good Public School. There was a pack of Cubs, which Christopher enjoyed, and he did well at games and on the sports days.

From there he could have gone either to Westminster School, which would have been David's preference, as it was his old school, and he could have been a weekly boarder, or to Bryanston in Dorset, which was run on much less traditional lines. He had offers of places at both. David happened to be working in Japan at the time a decision had to be taken, quickly. It was difficult to discuss it fully, as there was much less intercontinental telephoning in those days than now. Bryanston, being in the country, was chosen. It was good in many ways, but too far from London for easy visits. The other disadvantage was that, owing to David's work, it was always I who saw

Christopher onto the train at the beginning of term. In his teens, it would have been good if there had been more possibilities for the two men in the family to do things together, especially as David had had no father since babyhood, and was very close to his mother.

Ten

Moving On

We lived for sixteen years in the house which had been David's home more or less all his life until our marriage. For each of us in different ways, including our children, it was full of memories of his powerful mother, Eva, and her personality lingered like an aura in every room, and in the garden. For a while it felt to me as though it was not quite our place, and I had to be careful when we were settling in not to suggest too many changes. I even dreamed, one night, that she and I were in the kitchen and she was complaining that I should not be there. I managed to realise that the Eva in the dream was not the actual Eva but was a figure personifying my over-harsh conscience about being in "her house". And I dreamed a few nights later that she said it was all right: I had permission to be there.

We could not afford the several changes which would have helped me professionally through making it more labour-saving, so we concentrated at first on trying to improve the heating. Eva did not mind the cold, that was well known. Her daughter Diana wrote an impressive biography of her, in which she gave a full account of Eva's many contributions to public affairs (*Family Inheritance*, 1954). She was not afraid of making rueful but friendly references to how her mother usually dressed with no reference to elegance, and was hardly bothered by any conventions she felt were unnecessary. During the war years most houses were cold, but she remained stoic: the house was considered cold by everybody except her.

Eva was very warm emotionally and always willing to help people if at all possible, even if they wanted something rather different from what she proposed. Her intellectual energy was exceptional. She was a pioneer: she saw a social problem looming, examined it and did something about it. She and her many friends were some of the most important thinkers and activists who laid the foundations of the Welfare State. Their names used to be well known in connection with education, citizenship, population, women's and children's issues, family allowances and other progressive matters. To mention only a few, they included such people as Dorothy Layton, Eleanor Rathbone, Mary Stocks, Ernest and Shena Simon and Ellen Wilkinson. Although they all, I think, had resident housekeepers, they knew that most women had to manage in really difficult home conditions. At first I found living in the house where countless worthwhile enterprises had been conceived and developed was something to be seriously reckoned with. But so many people were taking those matters forward that I soon realised, with relief, that I was not the allotted heiress.

Eva was a widow and David was her only son. He had not "replaced" her husband, but his position in the family was unique. He told me that he had slept in her bedroom until the age of eight and then moved into what had been his father's dressing room, the other side of a communicating door. And naturally it mattered enormously to her who he married. She was open about the fact that she favoured either me or the daughter of one of her close friends as suitable to become his wife, so I had known she approved of me. And apart from the slightly uncomfortable impression that she felt I had taken him from her, she was always extremely kind to me. She was interested in what I did and conveyed that I was living up to her wishes for him.

Before her death, Eva had started writing a book about women in England, which was going to include a chapter about their views on matters connected with work and personal life. She was at that time Principal of Morley College for Working Men and Women, in Lambeth, and a member of the London County Council. She had contacts with many working women's organisations country-wide, and with their help she had organised a questionnaire to which almost a thousand women responded. The results were waiting to be worked over, and

David and his sisters agreed that I should do that. The *Manchester Guardian* took an article about it, with the sub-headline: "Many Grievances and Much Contentment".

After describing the contents of the answers I summed them up, far too optimistically in view of how much more has had to be done since then, saying: 'Thanks to the early pioneers [of girls' education] and the success of the movement for political and social equality, the cause of reasonable feminism has been won. These developments have had the effect of glossing over the differences between the sexes. For biological reasons there is division of labour; but culturally women have the same needs and desires as men'. I included my own mild view that the home life and education of girls ought to be such that women who wanted to emerge in middle age might be able to 'find life worth living outside the immediate family circle'. Many of the women had conveyed that general opinion objectively, but I was voicing my own view in a clearly subjective way. Doing that article sowed the seeds in me for the research I did from 1953 for two years, into the lives and some of the contentments and dissatisfactions of married women university graduates. Those seeds did not germinate at once.

Where writing is concerned, I mostly lay fallow for a while after our return from Paris. It was a new phase of life for both David and me. In term-time the children got off to school, Camilla and Christopher going at first with one of the au pair girls who lived with us, and I was going to be more or less free until collecting them in the afternoon. In his teens David had travelled to Westminster from Golders Green, the nearest underground station to our house, and he was once again in that part of London every day. I often used to walk up the hill with him to the top of the Heath, for him to get the train at Hampstead. There were few people about at that time of day and it felt almost like being in the country, throughout the changing seasons.

I can say, nostalgically but accurately, that there were more birds singing then and more flowers to be enjoyed than there are now. The walks were a great pleasure before cycling several times a week to Golders Green to do the shopping and spending more time than I wanted with the series of Swiss girls who were keen to find out from me, during lunch, as much as they could about England and the English. The hours that David had to work, first in the Cabinet Office and then in the Treasury, were long and strenuous, but intensely interesting. He was in congenial company, and what he did was, much of the time, momentous. He got home, very hungry, too late for supper with me and the children.

After a while I was lucky enough to be put in touch with the producers of two series of B.B.C. programmes. The first was the French equivalent of *Woman's Hour*. The producer became a kindly and useful contact for me to get going on freelance and part-time work. At first I was interviewed, then I wrote scripts in not quite idiomatic enough French. For the next two years I composed about a dozen talks in English and read the professionally translated version. I was encouraged to choose the subjects, which included descriptions connected with family life, toys and games, a friend who was a woman doctor with five daughters working in the wilds of North Wales, the adoption of a baby girl by a single woman, and the controversy about imported American children's horror comics. Many parents feared they would drive out the much less violent English ones. One of the talks was about how a woman can feel she is leading a double life, having a complicated sense of self, a theme to which I was beginning to turn my attention.

The other series of programmes was in the then European Service, and it consisted of unscripted fifteen-minute conversations between four speakers, the second half of weekly English lessons to Sweden, the first part having been grammar. The other speakers were experienced, congenial and well-informed men, and I enjoyed their company. We were allowed to select and discuss any topic which appealed to us that week, talking about it among ourselves for a few minutes before going on air. Two subjects were banned: the Royal Family and birth control.

Another B.B.C. opening also came my way, in 1952. It was writing a play for the History section of Schools programmes, in the then Home Service. The outlook was good for that line of writing, and I was optimistic, as the producer said he would offer me more if the script was accepted and was broadcast. The play was about the origins of the Red Cross, constructed round the grim experiences of Henri Dunant, the Swiss businessman who found himself (in both senses of those words) travelling in the middle of the battle of Solferino between the armies of the Italians, French and Austrians, in 1859. I described how appalled he was by the cries, the wounds, the nearly severed and bleeding limbs, but that he did not panic. He started organising people. Men were rushing about, the dragoons waving their sabres, the footsoldiers firing off grenades, shells and bullets. The play included dialogue as well as violent action and strong emotions, developed from the available records and fortified with remarks attributed to Dunant such as 'Wounds feel the same whatever uniform you wear. We are all brothers today'. It brought out the effect on the course of Dunant's life, especially the devoted work he put into his creation, the international Red Cross. Establishing it ruined him financially but his efforts culminated in many Western European Governments signing its founding document.

At my request the producer arranged for me to sit in on a class of young teenage boys, and he chose a school in the tough East London area of Dagenham, where I could watch their reactions. The feedback reports were good: in one of them the teacher even said that the boys were morally better for listening to the play! I was disappointed to receive no further requests for history Schools programmes: I had not realised that the girlfriend of the producer was one of the regular writers. It was salutary to discover that I could not hope for an easy ride in that competitive world.

My continuing interest in history was not used again in such a direct way, apart from filling in time a few years later, in a tutoring establishment for girls who wanted to get in to one or other of the older Universities. Several of their parents were eminent left-wing politicians who did not think their schools had supplied good enough history teachers. One of those girls later became a Soviet spy, a fact which was unconnected with me, or, as far as I know, with her subsequent Oxford tutor, my sister Jenifer.

The idea of embarking on research into various aspects of the lives and views of married women graduates came to me in a flash, one evening, in the bath. It has given me pleasure ever since to come across accounts of other people's comparable experiences. Those writers tend to be people who are research-ing in one of the hard sciences, such as branches of chemistry, physics or mathematics, as compared with literary or sociological ones. That is perhaps why they are surprised when they make an intuitive leap of imagination which leads on to something valuable to their specialism, but to themselves also. It is usually after someone has been thinking hard, beavering away for a long time, seeming not to get anywhere and even almost giving up, having not yet seen some potential connection. Suddenly, perhaps during the night, intuition from the creative underlayer of their mind enables them to "see" something fresh, a way for-ward, an idea, a link, a new angle, and great joy comes to them. In fact the new thing has been germinating slowly, most likely generated by a variety of factors. Frequently such people are men. Intuition used to be, and indeed often still is, too often rel-egated to women, sex-linked, and underestimated as a way of relating to one's material, as well as to other people.

I had been observing and thinking in a reflective way, over many years, about a variety of topics connected with women and men, but when the idea of the enquiry crystallised it had a feeling of rightness about it. It was worth doing. I would be tap-ping in to a subject of general interest to many women and their partners, but I also knew that I would be working towards find-ing out more about my own dissatisfactions, under cover of re-searching in a sociologically respectable way.

There were four interrelated aims behind the project, which are now part of social history. The first was to collect a large number of facts about the occupations of married women gradu-ates in the U.K. At that time the subject was controversial: on the one hand, were the talents of some of these women misem-ployed, and did others know they were underemployed? Or, in contrast, were highly educated married women trying "to have it both ways", if they wanted other opportunities as well as family life? Were they taking work away from unmarried ones, hypo-thetically unemployed as a result of the married ones' selfish-ness? To quote *The Economist* of 17 April 1954, 'On the subject of women graduates there is a rich assortment of folk unwis-dom'. I hoped that through collecting a large number of facts I might contribute towards breaking down prejudices, or at least get those who held them to examine the bases of their simplistic opinions.

The second aim was to be in a position to study the views of those who took part in the enquiry. Many, or perhaps most, intelligent married women recognised the importance of domestic life, "home-making", as it began to be called in the newly fashionable Americanism of those days, especially while their children were still young. But they also saw that they need not be only home-makers, for the rest of their lives, if they had other capabilities and wishes. Their families would not necessarily benefit from them being restricted to home.

Several of the questions were about the kinds of professional or voluntary work the women were doing, which contributed to my third aim of finding out more about part-time work. It had already become clear, from preliminary enquiries, that far less of that was available than was wanted by suitable women. In fact, one of the major changes to have happened since the Fifties is that the managers in the professions especially favoured by women have discovered that they can drop their ingrained certainty that only full-time work is on offer. Several women with similar views to mine set up agencies, at about that time, for professional women seeking part-time work, which had to be not too far from home. Job-sharing came in; I think it had been rare before that.

The fourth aim was to contribute to the discussion, which was getting going in a big way at that time, about the form and content that the education of very able girls should take. It was seen to be a particular part of what was the best education for all girls, as distinct from that of boys. The subject quite likely has a sexist sound to the ears of enlightened people nowadays. But it has to be seen and understood in its historical context.

In the Forties and Fifties the memory was still fresh of the nineteenth-century heydays of the famous women headmistresses, Miss Beale and Miss Buss. Both had championed the academic education of teenage girls, closely based on that of boys in Public Schools. The girls' uniforms included shirts and ties, like the ones their brothers wore, and many schools still follow that example. Those great headmistresses contributed impressively to intelligent girls' minds being fully respected, but by the mid-twentieth century a critic such as Mary Stocks (who had been Principal of Westfield College, all-women at that time) voiced the opinion that the Beale-Buss pattern was all wrong. It was too narrowly based on girls' intellectual needs during their teens. The suggestion of education for the whole of a woman's life might be too idealistic, but it was beginning to be launched. Mary Stocks had to stand up to such views on women as that of John Newsom, who wrote, in 1948, in his book *The Education of Girls*, 'Home making and the early nurture of children is a dominant theme in their lives'.

I found that statement by a male writer, respected and influential at the time, both complacent and narrow-minded. Even if home and children are major themes for some women, and for several years, there are many important secondary ones. What a monotonous symphony it would be if the other themes were only subsidiary ones. Of course it is still the case that, during the years when there are one, two or more young children, the struggle to combine motherhood and either a career or a job is a hard one. Those years may look short when viewed later, but at the time they feel very long, especially if there is no energetic grandmother within reach.

I was keen to take part, through the research, in the debate about how much contribution educated and married women with children can make to society. It was almost as though I felt the enquiry had to be justifiable in the eyes of the world. With hindsight, I think that I also needed that aim, or motive, since my work for a degree in history did not count directly as training in academic sociology, and it was important to me not to be, or seem to be, a mere amateur.

The other and more person-centred aim was to find facts which might substantiate or refute anecdotal information and the complaints that friends and acquaintances frequently voiced. Many of them at the time felt, and indeed knew, that they were not using their abilities to the full. Some of them said that they were anxious lest their minds, not being fully stretched, would gradually dry up or run to seed. They did not want to become boring, while their husbands were forging ahead, doing interesting work. For example, one evening two husbands and wives came to dinner with us. A few days later, I met one of the women in the street and she said to me, sadly, "I enjoyed being at your house last week, but I did feel a fool, having nothing to say. All I could do was sit and listen. When I was at University, before the war, there was always so much to discuss. Now all I seem to know about is my house and children, and I don't think other people want to hear about them in the evening".

I was well aware that the women, whose lives and views I was planning to investigate, formed at that time only a small portion of all women, so that the results would most likely be of only limited value. But I was not going to pretend that it was otherwise. Moreover, the clinching and practical reason for working with information from University graduates was that the sample was easy to collect and clearly defined. I was going to be doing it at home, on a shoe-string, without the backing of an established organisation.

When I wrote the account of my thoughts and considerations about married women graduates, based on the results of the re-search, at first in a pamphlet published in 1954, then in a book, in 1957, the participation of most husbands in the care of small children was far in the future. So what would be obvious for many couples now, where the man mitigates or even almost fully shares the near-slavery that babies and toddlers impose— broken nights, tiredness, messy meals and so on—those things get no mention in what I wrote in the Fifties. I had asked about the husband's approval, or otherwise, of his wife's paid or vol-untary work, but did not think of including a question about practical help or cooperation from him. At that time in history there was a much more definite assumption of division of labour between most men and women than there usually is now. Kindly husbands spoke about *helping*; more or less grateful wives wished they would *share*. To ask too much or too often was called nagging.

Eleven

Wives Who Went to College

The research which led to the book, *Wives Who Went to College*, is an aspect of social history which contemporary sociologists may find interesting, as there have been so many advances in methods and conditions of research since the early Nineteen Fifties. For feminists, both the content of the questions and the main lines of the replies show what a long time ago those days were, not only chronologically but also in terms of how far we have come since then, in Britain. Moreover they throw light on certain other perennial aspects of women's lives, and their feelings about them, especially those connected with having children.

The information given in the answers to the factual questions was straightforward; the attitudes were more complex and perhaps a few present-day women may look back, indignantly or with sympathy, at a situation where many of my generation felt we were second-class citizens. Yet feelings are facts, psychological ones. For many women a large amount of what emerges here does not add up to grievances. The enterprise as a whole features in the history of Women's Studies in the relevant university syllabuses. The present chapter includes personal ideas, but since it is also historical I am recounting as many details as possible about how the enquiry was organised and conducted. It is part of what I observed and did during some of the years fairly soon after the end of the Second World War. That war altered the course of the lives of millions of women. And, as it had been for their mothers after 1918, the position of women took a great stride forward.

I was in the fortunate position of being in a stable marriage in which I did not have more paid work than the commissions for free-lance work which came my way occasionally; mainly I was looking after the family. David had inherited his mother's freehold house, and we had no mortgage to worry about. His salary was by then adequate for our ordinary expenses. Our three children were at day schools, and not yet teenagers. They had got through pneumonia, croup, tonsillectomy, chicken pox and measles some years earlier. Sandra and Camilla were both great readers, Christopher won running races. They swam well and walked well up mountains. Adolescent identity crises were still in the future. We could have more or less free holidays, in August, in my parents' house in Cornwall, and in a cottage his sister Rachel owned. There was another, very primitive, mountain cottage, in North Wales, where we usually went at Easter. Cousins and friends came too. Cooking was on primus stoves (not easy); there were oil lamps, candles and an outside lavatory—difficult on rainy nights. David really did get satisfaction from digging a hole in the slaty soil and burying the contents of the bucket when we left.

I could not afford to do the research without some kind of grant, especially as I would have liked not to have to call on my share of what David's salary contributed to our joint income. So I worked out the lowest limits within which I could do it and combed through the Directory of grant-giving bodies. I narrowed down my chances of success to just a few. The most likely seemed to be the Leche Charity, about which I knew no more than what was in the Directory. Filling in grant applications has become one of the skills that graduates have to learn, if they want to go into their chosen field. They often have to work on them for a long time, while struggling to live on scraps of short-term and poorly paid employment, backed by their tutors who may themselves be doing the same at a more advanced level. I was an innocent in that process. I had no tutor or prescribed application form, so I simply went ahead, applying to the Trustees of the Leche Charity.

The sum I asked for may look very small on modern prices, even allowing for inflation: it was for stationery, postage, those parts of the secretarial work which I could not do myself, and, at some unknown time in the future, technical assistance in working over the answers. From the meeting with the gentlemanly and encouraging Trustees I emerged the proud receiver of £50 and a request for a report in due course.

I found drafting the questions very interesting indeed. I thought it important to keep the thing to a length which I considered sensible: that was the number of questions I would myself be willing to answer, if I received a request of that kind, coming from someone unknown to me. Rather more than half of the questions were about facts, and others were designed to reveal attitudes and reactions while being as unobtrusive as possible. The text of the questionnaire was published in the book, *Wives Who Went to College*.

Considering the plan historically and in detail showed me that a comparison between women who were at University before 1939 with those who were there during and after the war would probably reveal interesting differences. I did not go back earlier than a graduation date of 1930, since graduates before that would probably have got going in married life, and perhaps founded a family, at a time when poorly paid domestic help was plentiful, if they wanted it, giving them spare time; also, taxation was lighter than it was to be later. I thought that more of them than of the later ones would have been able to combine having children with continuing their careers. I wanted to include those whose families were no longer very young, so as to find out if, by the Nineteen Fifties, many of them were doing work, paid or voluntary, as well as being wives and mothers. The last graduation date was 1952. As I am writing in the twenty-first century, I notice that the people in the questionnaire who would now be called *partners*, whether male or female, were then all called husbands.

I knew that the accepted method of organising research of the type I had in mind included a pilot survey. It had been emphasised to me at school that if I thought clearly my ideas would express themselves clearly. The questions must be objective, not loaded. A skilled statistician, Claus Moser (later Sir Claus), who was a friend through David and his Civil Service contacts, showed me how to reorganise my rough draft, and between us we produced the final wording of the questions and their layout.

I sent them to a hundred London University married graduates, all of them unknown to me, with a covering and personally signed letter. The pilot results would indicate the number of answers I could expect. That was crucial, since, without the hallmark of a college address or of a research institute, the questionnaire would have to make its way through its inherent qualities, and tap the graduates' interest. I was told not to expect more than about one-third of the forms to return filled in. So the first gratifying thing was that out of the hundred, sixty came back. I had determined to get at least one thousand answers to work on, so I would have to send out two thousand of the forms. At this stage, and at later ones, Sandra, Camilla and Chris helped with filling envelopes. They were aged thirteen, eight and six.

The method of collecting names and addresses took into account the fact that the married names had somehow to be available. Not all universities and colleges could supply what I needed, though the ones which could were very willing to co-operate. For those which did not have lists of old students it was necessary to use the parliamentary registers: before 1948, as well as having a residence vote, M.A.'s of Cambridge, the Combined English universities, Oxford and the Scottish universities elected nine Members of Parliament between them. In the end two thousand graduates from eleven colleges and universities were circularised: Aberdeen, Birmingham, Cambridge (Girton and Newnham Colleges), Durham (St. Hilda's College), the University College of Hull, London (Bedford and Westfield Colleges), Nottingham, Oxford (Lady Margaret Hall and Somerville College), Reading, St. Andrews and the University of Wales.

A ten per cent sample of those who did not answer showed that the main practical cause of that was a change of address. That might or might not have been due to separation or divorce, and it was only possible to speculate about other reasons, such as a dislike of questionnaires. At this distance in time it strikes me, with amusement, that doing that test sample illustrates my perfectionist effort to be as professional as possible.

As well as the first stage, the pilot survey, and the second stage, which was the main list, I had to have a control group. That was constructed, after the women in the main sample had filled in their forms, from married women who had not been to

University, but were from the same social background as the graduate ones. I circularised the first thousand women who had answered, except those who were abroad, and asked them to get one non-graduate married sister, cousin, sister-in-law, cousin-in-law or friend, to answer an almost identical set of questions. They were of about the same age-group and had been to school until at least the age of sixteen. Four hundred and twenty of them answered. Most of them had done a one- or two-year training. Those facts seem to indicate that very many women of the kinds being researched wanted to get some sort of re-spectable qualification so that they would not be "only" wives and mothers. And they might be doing work in which having children was an asset.

Of the two thousand sets of questions sent out (with signed covering letters) fifty-eight per cent were returned. I had 1,165 answers to work on, from which valid generalisations could be made. Many letters were enclosed with the filled-in forms, every one of them interesting. I wish I had kept them all, but I have some selected passages from the ones which were especially striking.

The tasks of analysing the answers, with as many details as possible, seemed at first utterly daunting. And unfortunately my records of that time do not include any indication as to whether I had, in advance, been realistic about how to organise the next stage. It was early in the development of computers, let alone the kinds which are familiar now in all offices and many homes. John Madge, a friend of ours working in the sociological organi-sation, Mass Observation, which had been founded and run by Tom Harrisson, came to my rescue. Tom, and I think John, had originally been anthropologists, researching academically outside Britain. During the War they had turned to applying their skills to investigations within Britain. Their wall-length Hollerith machine—I remember there being about seven or eight feet of it—is perhaps now in a museum of such early machines. It had been devised by a certain Hermann Hollerith, for one of the late nineteenth-century population censuses in the U.S.A. It could do every necessary calculation of the answers, with a card-punching and sorting mechanism.

John was interested in my project and with great generosity

he offered to do all the preliminary classifying for a nominal fee. I could then ask him to work out as many cross references as I needed. The machine used to eject small cards into slots along the front of it, and count them. Perhaps a mechanically educated person would not have found all that as intriguing and exciting as I did.

The answers confirmed what was becoming known at that time anyway: that the marriage rate among highly educated women was not far below what it was for the rest of the population. The nineteenth-century pioneers of university education for women had thought of themselves as being future salary-earners who would join men in the professions and perhaps compete with them. They sometimes seemed to me to have overstressed the incompatibility between the biological and the intellectual sides of women's lives, and to be aggressive about not needing to listen to their emotional needs. Freud's sententious 'Biology is destiny' was too easily adopted as an unquestionable truth by those men who wanted to keep women away from their all-male college high tables.

And it was not only men who tried to confine women to traditional roles, if Winifred Peck can be believed when she wrote, in *A Little Learning* (1952), that the Principal of Lady Margaret Hall at Oxford just before the First World War had said sarcastically to one of the students: 'I really don't know what all you girls are up here reading for. You should be at home learning to be good plain cooks; any man would value you then!' Perhaps she herself was unmarried, perhaps the young woman was especially unacademic, and the Principal spoke sharply because she regretted that she had been a party to accepting her to study there. My impression in the Nineteen Fifties was that there seemed to be fewer men than in the past who preferred their wives to be less intelligent than themselves, or at any rate less intellectual. I feared that more women than men were prepared to marry someone much more intelligent than themselves, and run the risk of possibly being looked down on, or arrogantly stigmatised as boring, some time in the future.

An interesting fact which emerged from the rather meticulous examination of answers about family size is that many of the women who obtained First Class degrees each had more children than the others. That seemed to indicate that all-round high ability and academic success had not necessarily discouraged motherhood. They were energetic as well as able.

Among the questions and answers about family life there were several which could not simply or easily be dealt with as statistics, since they were about attitudes. The results of the one about husbands' views were only partly satisfactory, and I could perhaps have found out more by face-to-face interviews. But it would have been difficult to do enough of them. In general, more than half the women in the sample said that their husbands backed them in what they were doing. I felt sad for the rest of them. I think now that even asking that question was a sign of the social atmosphere of the early Fifties. It would probably not be worth inquiring about now.

The women were asked about their attitudes to domestic work, and many of them wrote that the question was too general. They included in their answers such remarks as: 'I like cooking, I dislike cleaning'; 'I only like domestic occupations because I am in a job and they provide a contrast to my usual work'; and 'I dislike domestic work except for the care of my children'. It has to be remembered too that most of us then had fewer electrical appliances than we, our children and grandchildren now have. One of my aims with that question was to test whether the idea, or the picture, of a Blue-Stocking was still around to a significant extent. I think the answers more or less indicated that it was already out of date.

One of the features of domestic work is that it is varied and calls for many implicit abilities. But it does not essentially require the power to concentrate and to work single-mindedly, which good-quality study does. When we work domestically we have to discover how to combine various skills and do several things at once, especially when young children need us urgently. I do not think I am exceptional now in having to call on a lot of patience to overcome irritation if I am frequently interrupted when I am writing, since I cannot escape into a college or university library. My nostalgia for the protected Cambridge stage of life is even more acute if the interruption is my fault because I have forgotten to switch on the answerphone, that perfect mechanical secretary who says, truthfully or not, 'I'm sorry, she's in a meeting, she can't talk to you now'. I recognise that people in many office jobs have to learn to tolerate interruptions. But temperamentally I sympathise more with Jane Austen than with them: she is said to have had to hide her manuscript between two pages of blotting paper when a neighbour dropped in.

The question on whether the woman working domestically at home ever has any real free time aroused interest at a period in history when it was frequently said that 'a woman's work is never done', and when it was conveyed to her that she should not complain about it. It was her lot, or her fate. Could it even have been an unconscious remnant of a medieval belief in the long-term punishment of Eve, that mythical ancestress and once archetypal woman, the female who dared to challenge the male God's omnipotence? My intention was to question the assumption that having no fully free time is inherent in home life (breast feeding is in a class of its own), and to suggest indirectly that the problem is capable of being faced, and solved.

Another reason behind my including the question about real free time was that, although normally healthy babies and young children need the sense of security that they get from the constant and reliable presence of their mother (or a regular alternative person of either sex), the ever-tied woman may come to exaggerate her importance, turn into a kind of martyr and revel in that role. The growing child does not then gradually discover the need to respect 'the other' as being a person, rather than a thing. Where the mother is concerned, it is best if she is little by little able to think and talk about other matters than her adorable, precocious and unrivalled offspring. Real and definitely free time, when the children have other people in their lives as well as her, enables her to emerge from the most intense stage of devotion.

A section in the final question, which was about income and earnings, enquired how much the woman minded if she had no income of her own from any source. It applied to one-third of the graduate wives, and to three-quarters of the non-graduate ones, which was a noticeable difference when considered sociologically. But only a small proportion of them minded very much. So it did not turn out to be a burning issue, and I realised that including it among the questions pointed to something I myself minded about. Also it was before the Women's Liberation Movement had got going.

The other question which I considered important was about overtiredness: 'Do you rarely, often, or usually, feel overtired? To what cause, or causes, do you attribute your answer?' It was not about ordinary tiredness, and I thought those answering would notice that. It was impossible to measure the answers scientifically. I assumed that someone is overtired when she enjoys life much less than she usually does, wakes up tired, gets irritable easily, and looks older than she is, in spite of skilful make-up. There are other indications, and many women wrote about the subject, giving various opinions on it. I could not find a contemporary report of a study of overtiredness among women, let alone men, though Margery Spring-Rice's pre-1939 book, *Working Class Wives, Their Health and Conditions*, was very revealing about those subjects and had made a deep impact among concerned people.

One of my interests in the Fifties was that educated women should, ideally, contribute to society the best they could. That may sound moralistic, but tiredness reduces our effectiveness, and I knew many women who agreed with me in deploring the varied and obvious causes and effects of overtiredness. Another motive in enquiring about it was to rebut the objectionable saying that university education is wasted on women who marry. When the research organisation, Political and Economic Planning, undertook to publish a summary account of my findings, those who ran it did not want me to include the material on overtiredness, as they thought it did not belong in a sociological study. But when I came to write the book, I gave it a whole chapter.

At that time I commented that the standards of meal planning, cooking and child care had gone up so much that many women were straining themselves to reach them, which included the regrettable attitude of "keeping up with the neighbours", or at least doing better than the feckless ones. The same applied to the pace of life and expectations of maintaining the companionship with husbands which had been enjoyed before the birth of children. In spite of more domestic machinery than had previously been available, many women did not have as much of that as they wanted, or as is usual now. Disposable nappies had not been invented. Many clothes still needed ironing, even without doing that excessively. Machinery does not, in itself, look after babies, who often cause sleepless nights. It was unusual, even in homes where there was a TV, to park children in front of it.

Some women also thought that much of their overtiredness was due to frustration caused by not using their abilities in a way they considered suitable, or appropriate, compounded by guilt, since they criticised themselves for being discontented. They believed they ought to be energetic, self-disciplined and full of what one woman called zest for life. They were all too easily labelled self-pitying. And when one is overtired it is difficult to remember that it will not go on for ever.

The answers about overtiredness lent themselves to elaborate tabulations according to age, numbers of children and income. On the most simple of overall classifications, almost half of those answering, forty-eight per cent, said that they often felt overtired, and thirty-seven per cent that they rarely did. By and large, the younger women and those whose children were still young could be expected to be less well off than the older ones, and therefore perhaps more of them would say they were overtired. But it did not work out that way, which suggests that non-material factors are relevant. Many women gave several reasons for often being, or not being, overtired. The most common factors, as might be expected, were lack of leisure, overwork, too many claims on her time, lack of help and domestic worries. Pregnancy, feeding the baby at night, her own health problems, frustration and boredom all featured high on the scale of causes. But the main reasons for not feeling overtired were correspondingly predictable: good health was top of the list, adequate help and the right balance of time spent in and outside the home, general contentment and a supportive husband all contributed to a more cheerful picture.

Among the letters I received, many were simply but beautifully accurate on the matters being considered. One woman wrote: 'I certainly feel that I would be in much better physical and mental health if I had someone to help me even half a day a week. Or somebody to take the children (both are under three) off my hands for a couple of hours a week. That would apply if I had relatives living near. I feel I am "rotting away on a Kentish hillside", though I admit it is a very lovely one'. Another wrote: 'I have filled in your form as adequately as I am able in my present state of mental decay. My husband has discussed with me this eternal problem of the overworked housewife (and husband—mine assists magnificently and ungrudgingly) and we have come to the conclusion that a lifting of the endless financial worries would work wonders. Mental exhaustion is worse in my case than the physical'.

The next letter is worth quoting at length, while remembering when it was written: 'The hardest of my tasks is attending to young children at night and in the early morning; my husband will not help because he is sure he needs more sleep than I do, and I think that is only part of the general attitude of "the children are the woman's concern"' and "a wife is there to look after others, not to be looked after herself". And I get annoyed with those who say, "You can't afford to be ill". It seems to me that a woman needs (a) a strong constitution, (b) very firm views about looking after herself and (c) not to be *too* sympathetic to the rest of the family if she is to be healthy and happy under the present regime'.

At the end of the chapter about overtiredness, I wrote what was then considered more sophisticated psychologically than it is now, and was disliked by several of my men friends: 'In understanding each other, men need to develop intuitive sympathy and women the power to think clearly. They would both benefit by an interchange of the qualities which have for too long been considered to be the special reserves of one sex or the other'. That generalisation was easy to make, in the mid-twentieth century. But it could not be said too often, since it was difficult to achieve.

Some time in the Fifties I heard, on the B.B.C.'s *Woman's Hour*, a woman from one of the West African countries boldly defending the custom of polygamy on the grounds that two women are needed to run the average family. Instead of the second woman being an employed servant she is, said the speaker, rewarded for her essential work by what amounts to equality of rights and privileges with the first wife. That is a solution to the problem which is rarely, if ever, successful in our ostensibly monogamous society. Sexual affairs with the au pair girl, or the nanny, are not as open as the second-wife arrangement reported from West Africa.

Twelve

The Fifties: A Kind of Wilderness

After running the questionnaire described in the last chapter, I was at first not sure what to do with it. Various people who were interested in feminist issues suggested that it would be worth offering an outline of the results to the research institution Political and Economic Planning, PEP. It published occasional pamphlets 'to give a clear and accurate presentation of the facts' on matters which could benefit by 'public thought and discussion'. The research behind PEP's usual productions, and the writing, were normally done by its own staff.

PEP was interested to have the material for one of its series of broadsheets, but told me that its publications appeared anonymously. Since I had had the idea myself and carried it out without much backing, I was firm that I should be credited with the authorship. I look back now with amusement when I remember that my insistence felt like a triumph of assertiveness. At that stage of life I was more used to being tentative than forthright. David's Civil Service work had to be anonymous, but his was not my world. I accepted PEP's offer to insert a footnote on the front page of the pamphlet, informing the reader that it contained 'the results of an inquiry initiated and organised by Mrs. Judith Hubback M.A. (Cantab) and made available to PEP for this broadsheet'.

It appeared in April 1954 under the title of *Graduate Wives*. I had not yet thought of writing a full book about it, and it was helpful to be linked with PEP, since the publication of my material did satisfy its aim of instigating discussion on matters of public interest. In addition, having my name acknowledged seemed to signify that I represented the figure of the emergent individual having a place in an Establishment organisation. Mine was more a personal than a politically minded feminism. In a female kind of way, *Graduate Wives* was *my* baby, and I would have felt side-lined if it had appeared anonymously, with no author/parent—not even a struggling single mother. I did not want a chip on my shoulder. As it turned out, the pamphlet made such a stir, that a few months later the idea of a full-scale book was conceived. It took nearly two years to write, fitting it in with the rest of daily living. But by the time it was finished, and generously typed by my mother on her ancient and clattering Corona machine, it did not take long to find a publisher. My not very adequate thanks were to dedicate the book to her and to the memory of my father, who had died by then.

Graduate Wives was reported fully and at once in *The London Times* and the then *Manchester Guardian*. In the Fifties, before Rupert Murdoch had bought the first of those, David and I used to read both of them. On the day of publication it was exciting, and surprising, to find that the pamphlet was the subject of the second leading article in *The Times*. The sub-editor had not resisted the obvious title, 'Blue Stockings as now worn', but I was comforted by the opening sentence: 'Political and Economic Planning in their broadsheet, published today, on graduate wives, lend no support to the old-fashioned view that

A Ministering Angel in woman, we see,
And an angel need covet no other degree'.

That article started off a series of over fifty letters to the editor, which he finally closed nearly three months later. The *Manchester Guardian* readers were also keen letter-writers. I think there was no overwhelming other news to fill the letter columns at the time, but they certainly showed that the subject was timely and appealing. And it was new. Personal and typical life experiences were the writers' most frequent subjects, but there were also well-informed views on social issues and meaningful observations on the contemporary position of women. One of them was close to what I myself had believed and done, before the War, at a time when it was unusual to have a plan: 'The crux of the matter lies in whether a woman graduate has become established in her profession before she marries. Where she has, she will by hook or by crook generally keep it up in what way she can till her children are old enough to be left without anxiety. When she marries straight from university she is less likely to do so'.

None of the letter-writers mentioned contraception of any kind. It was many years before that had become an assumed part of any woman's life, let alone unmarried teenage girls (horror of horrors). For the women in my sample, had there been easily available contraception it would have made planning the phases of motherhood and the return to a profession possible, or at any rate much easier. Out of historical interest it is worth mentioning that for those not included in my sample, namely working-class women, family planning clinics hardly existed until the end of the Nineteen Fifties. By the mid-Sixties their number had increased and the Pill had become available through them since 1961, but it was not mandatory for them to provide family planning irrespective of marital status until 1970.

For most of the women who wrote to me in the Fifties I think it would have been impossible to get advice and help about contraception, except with a private doctor, willing to do so. Such a one could be found, for example through a friend or the grapevine, but many women could not afford the fee. Moreover, it is impossible so long after to do more than guess as to whether a woman would try to get the man to equip himself with a condom. They were still usually called French letters, and certainly not on sale at the front of the pharmasists' displays, as now, along with pastilles for sore throats, and from slot machines in pubs. Perhaps many married women found them what Dr. Joan Malleson, my helpful gynaecologist, called unaesthetic. It was only the very liberated doctor who did not make a great palaver about whether the woman was married, or soon to be married, when she was consulted for advice on contraception. I remember it feeling rather clandestine when I kept an appointment to see Dr. Malleson. As far as I know, just a few gynaecologists with liberal attitudes were working in London, and in other large cities, at the time of my survey. In country places I think there must have been a total lack of the various kinds of contraception which suit women.

This letter appealed to me: 'Women who give up salaries in order to become mothers are not saints—they are following their natural instincts. But I do not think Dr. Schweitzer would be angry if I used his life as an analogy. Do our feminists really think that he has buried his talents in Lambaréné, and that his theological and musical training has been wasted on the sufferings of a handful of backward people? Someone once said that all movements went through three stages: the first generation was holy, the second learned, and the third worldly. It will indeed be unfortunate if this is true of feminism in this country'.

Of course most letter writers were women, but there was a sprinkling of men. One of them, using the cliché of being "a mere man" tetchily asked: 'Is this long correspondence making any sense?' Over half a century later he might be surprised to hear that one of the on-going consequences of feminism is that many men, after the first reactive backlash, are now painfully evaluating themselves in new ways. They are actually applying their minds to sexuality and difficult relationships. I can borrow that man's words, using them differently from how he meant them to be heard, and say that men are trying to "make sense" of how they relate to other people, thinking and reflecting, emerging from outworn attitudes. The psychology of gender differences became clearer to me when, later, I had become an analytical psychologist.

Other quality newspapers reported and commented sensibly on the results of the survey. For example, in *The Economist*, there was the following: 'On the subject of women graduates there is a rich assortment of folk unwisdom . . . The old battleaxes who regarded marriage and motherhood as betrayal of The Cause are probably all dead by now, but their influence still shows itself in a tendency among teachers and dons to tut-tut over every promising professional who gives her domestic concerns priority; while the same "wastage" is quoted by anti-feminists to prove that the higher education of women is mostly down the drain'.

The writer of one letter to *The Times* thought 'we should distinguish between "making use" of an academic education and "making money" out of it—the two are often confused. In bringing up four children, I make far more use of my philosophy, politics and economics than my husband does of his Latin and Greek in the British Civil Service'. And the following extract from an elderly correspondent, who had been at Cambridge in the early years of the twentieth century, is even now worth quoting: '[the university] prepared me, mind, soul and body, as nothing else could have done to face life, marriage, two wars with anxiety and exacting voluntary war work in both, 30 years of county council and other local government work with an adaptability of mind and body that I should not otherwise possess. It enables me now to share as fully as possible in the varying interests of four daughters and a son'.

In contrast to those two letters, the popular newspapers almost all picked up the economic wastage theme in their headlines, repeating monotonously (it seemed to me) what they presumably thought would catch their readers' attention. But, where practical matters were concerned, the content of most of the articles was fair and accurate. One of the best was the Liberal *News Chronicle*, and it reported 'a flood of letters', from which it published many extracts, offering a wide variety of views. The pamphlet was noticed at some length in over thirty English papers, in eight South African ones, six in New Zealand, several in Kenya, Rhodesia (as Zimbabwe was called then), Australia, India, Pakistan and Bermuda, presumably using their London reporters. The *Daily Worker* columnist wrote disparagingly and sarcastically, under the headline of "Educated Wives—But They're So Silly". I knew her indirectly and thought that some of the points she made were ones with which I whole-heartedly agreed, but in her criticisms she fell for the temptation of bringing up themes which were not in the pamphlet. She held strong Women's Liberation views, before that movement had been named and launched, and her opinions were plausible.

My work was a preface to the spate of books by soon-to-be famous women. It played the part of a preliminary skirmish, and a few years later, when the pace hotted up, the main fighters had had time to get mobilised and to vie with each other for publicity and fame. Some younger women, just graduating, read and warmed to what I wrote, as they knew what their hopes and fears were. Over the years I chanced at intervals to meet people who had read the book that I later wrote based on

Graduate Wives at that stage of life, and who told me it had encouraged them to think about their futures clearly.

When I had written the book, and been offered a contract by Heinemann through one of their directors, Alan Hill, they and I decided that it had to have its own title. So it became *Wives Who Went to College*. I like a title which tells the potential buyer what the book is about. It was pleasing that it was reviewed by well-known women at the time, who all wrote at length and favourably. Among them were Marghanita Laski in *The Observer*, Mary Scrutton in *The New Statesman*, Geoffrey Gorer in *The Medical World*, Lady Ogilvie (then at Leeds University) in *The Sunday Times* and Janet Adam Smith in *The Hindu*. It is to celebrate rather than to parade them that it seems worth giving their names, which are still remembered in literary circles. And my local paper, the *Hampstead and Highgate Express*, reviewed it well.

An amusing incident happened when I spoke live, one Saturday evening, on the B.B.C. Radio programme, *In Town Tonight*. The interviewer started off by saying: "Well, Judith Hubback, so you are married?" "Yes", I answered cheerfully, "I have a child and three husbands". One of my women friends rang up to congratulate me on my unintentional description of Hubback family life. Since then, and especially since I have been an analyst, if I feel the audience is friendly when I am giving a paper or speaking at a meeting, I warn them that I might possibly make a slip. Alas, I often do. Or perhaps it is not "alas". Never to do so would be falling into the trap, that the prophet Isaiah warned against a long time ago, of trying to be "holier than thou". In more modern terms, I would add that at least some layers of unconsciousness often show up in otherwise ordinary talk.

Between *Graduate Wives* and writing the book, I wanted to research into the subject of part-time work. Not many of the women in the enquiry had achieved paid part-time work in their previous profession. Voluntary work was easier to find. Many of them would have liked to find suitable paid work in their own field, preferably not full-time. The ones who were especially keen for it were the members of the Medical Women's Federation. There were many letters written by prominent doctors to *The British Medical Journal*, *The Lancet* and *The Medical Press*.

The President of the Federation at the time, Dr. Annis Gillie, was energetic on the subject. She saw women as wholes, body and psyche combined, whether they were colleagues or patients. She became a great ally. Inevitably some senior men medicals were not keen on the theme and several of the major professions were still inflexible. The achievement of opening them up to part-time work or time-share arrangements was still in the future.

When I began looking into the subject, I found that other women as well as myself were taking up the theme and working to decrease the difficulties. One or two agencies in the Greater London area were getting going about then, filling an obvious gap on behalf of educated women. I tried to get a grant at one or the other of what seemed to be the obvious research bodies to finance me to work on it all, and was disappointed not to succeed.

On several occasions I was asked to speak at meetings about the position of educated women. I thought my daughter Camilla was right when she pointed out that I did not know much about the general run of women, who mostly had a far harder time than I and my kind, and which she could see needed publicising. But I had not had access to scientific ways of finding out about them or to membership of an organisation of professional sociologists.

About twenty years later I took part in a series of discussions between five professional women, and the husband of one of them, leading to a book edited by Beatrice Musgrave and Zoe Herzov (*Women at the Top—Achievement and Family Life*), on women's ways of combining family and career, and the consequent difficulties, especially when children are young. We explored the social and psychological implications of working outside the home, which may sound utterly out of date now to many people, but it was still well worth thinking about in the late Nineteen Seventies. And, in the twenty-first century, it is still discussed by sociologists and even in government departments, where it is seen in mostly economic terms.

My impression from conversations nowadays with women who belong to two generations later than mine, is that the emotional issues for them are hardly at all different from what I experienced. One of my memories of the years when my children were young was the taunting and boringly repeated phrase, "Never get done, never get done": there always seemed to be another insistent task, and I was incapable of leaving it undone. I am reminded that when my sisters and I were young, our nanny had a "nursery maid" to do the chores for her. And as children we were expected to be tidy as well as obedient. Those qualities on our part were convenient for grown-ups. That said, cynically, I have to admit that I became methodical in an anxious and obsessional way. Women now who want to do something else as well as being mothers while their children are young have benefited from the diffusion of studies of child psychology. There are many labour-saving products and mechanical aids, though the environment may suffer from them. And the faces of buggy-pushing mothers often show ingrained lines of strain or irritation. If single mothers or young couples are lucky enough to live within easy reach of a grandparent who is congenial and not otherwise committed, such as being dependent on paid work, the young parents are relieved of a lot of worry, and the grandchildren benefit.

The social atmosphere, or the theory about the atmosphere, round the subject of women and work outside home, is now much more rational and liberal than it used to be. Many men discover that they get rich rewards from genuinely sharing the hard work and difficulties as well as the pleasures of parenthood, at all stages. Yet virtue is not all on the woman's side: at an unconscious level, some mothers don't easily share what they can't prevent themselves from feeling is their intrinsic and archetypal role. The internalised image of Mary the (virgin?) mother of Jesus is still a powerful one: the Joseph figure in art and on Christmas cards has to yield the limelight to her and to the Holy Spirit who fathered the baby.

The credit for the improvements round the lives of women in many Western countries goes of course to the valiant Women's Liberation people of the Nineteen Sixties and Seventies, and there have been times when I have regretted that I was not in the thick of that movement. Later, as the twentieth century progressed and became the present one, the tempo of wars went up in so many parts of the world, with reports of countless, repeated, rapes of women and the dreadful consequences for them and the children who resulted, I have felt bad about how impossible it is to be of any practical use. Making donations to various charities is a sop to that guilt. In this early part of the twenty-first century rape is the fate of millions of people world-wide, which is a more serious cause of concern and conscience than the position of women in the "western" world.

The situation for me has often been comparable to how it was in the Nineteen Thirties, when I was a fully anti-Nazi socialist but had not fallen for the commitment required for being a communist. The simplistic style of the best-known Women's Lib activists in the Sixties and Seventies did not appeal to me, and I could not go in with the bellicose political atmosphere of that movement. It did not fit with the kind of person I had become: still aiming to find the right way to harness my early idealistic interest in what could be done about the many evils in the world, and to redirect my energy to what it would be realistic for me to achieve. I had taken the path of inner change, initially for myself, then for those I worked with, accepting its limitations as well as trusting to its possibilities. I concentrated more on issues necessary for individuals than on the need for social reform on a broad spectrum. When I took into account my life with David, his love for our children, and theirs for him, it was possible to channel my earlier political ambitions into being an analyst. I think David and I would have been too painfully at loggerheads if I had become a full-blown activist in the Women's Lib movement.

For a while after the main work and thoughts on women, I gradually became a free-lance journalist in a few dailies, weeklies and journals, writing not only about women. For example, the *New Statesman* commissioned a series of three articles on secondary education in Modern Schools, in various parts of England. About two-thirds of children between 11 and 15 were taught in them. The then current phrase, which grew out of popular reactions to the 1944 Education Act, was that they had "failed the 11+". Although education officials professed not to judge them like that, most of the children and their parents saw themselves in the negative light of not being allowed to attend an academically oriented grammar school, which was more prestigious. The word "Modern" could not modify deep-seated feelings of inferiority. My aims were to improve the image of the children and to help their parents to feel more positive; to raise appreciation of the Heads and class teachers, who struggled to work well in difficult circumstances; to draw attention to the need for much better school buildings and playing fields; to fortify the hard-pressed local authorities' efforts to help with housing provision for teachers, which was already an issue at the time; and to open up the subject of not good enough training colleges. 'Many heads', I wrote, 'say that young people now entering the profession have not the calibre, guts, stamina, character or sense of vocation that they had themselves'. Much of that type of criticism could probably have been discounted, and anyone aiming at a State school, who had been trained, could get at least his or her first job.

I found visiting them and thinking about their problems very engrossing, and suggested that 'an attitude survey should be undertaken on a national scale to discover what deters many of the best young people from going into the teaching profession . . . why they change jobs so often . . . frustrating relations with the education authorities . . . and any aspect of the subject which would immediately occur to any trained industrial psychologist'. Seeing many schools and talking to educationalists reminded me of my parents' disappointment and disapproval when I trained to become a teacher after Cambridge, though I chose the Grammar school level. And, looking forward to my later career as an analytical psychologist, I can see that my interests were turning in a psychological direction.

During those mid-Fifties I perhaps appeared successful to people who could not see that behind the front I presented there was a deeply unsatisfied person, struggling with self-doubts and frustration. I had not yet defined my difficulties clearly or fully. I was always interested in whatever my children told me about their lives, since all three were active within their own range. But where fully adult conversation was concerned at home I felt isolated because David and I could not talk about politics or foreign affairs. Those were matters he was dealing with in his office and he knew the crucial aspects of them which were subject to the Official Secrets Act, not available to the public or to journalists. It was almost impossible for me to express my opinion on matters reported and commented on in the newspapers: he invariably said that I "had not seen the Papers"—the official ones, of course.

At the non-rational, emotional, level I remembered with sadness how we had been able to talk about all our views on world issues in the now idealised Cambridge days, and yearned for the intimacy we had then. I knew vaguely that I had probably slipped into the category of being in a mid-life crisis, but it was no easier for having a name. Already in the Fifties many of us were likely to live longer than the Old Testament's assumption of three score years and ten, so none of us could know when mid-life had been reached. An acute concern about identity would be a better way of naming my troubled state, combined with being depressed. I had known those states at intervals much of my life, and now they were combined with being anxious about my future. I was far from knowing in what direction I should try to go. Several of my earlier ideas recurred to me, but they were unsatisfactory.

For example, when we had come back from Paris and settled into the comfortable house at the edge of Hampstead Heath, the combination of personal professional ambition and social conscience had pricked me into thinking of various possible next steps. I did quite a lot of private examination of how to combine what I knew of my capabilities and interests with available openings. It was already too late to aim for the academic level of work, though something connected with a combination of teaching and historical research would, I thought then, have been suitable. I had not enjoyed teaching history at the school, or didactic, end of the spectrum, caught in the constraint of exam syllabuses. I would have liked a setting in which I could enable older students to develop their potential in their chosen field, and do my own research. That was an idealistic view of the possibilities for me. They were unreachable, since I had not entered university life at the senior level early enough. I envied Jenifer for living in Oxford, where there were many friends to be made, and where congenial work might be more achievable than I thought it would be in any College or University within reach. Long-distance commuting was still far in the future. I did not see myself as having the potential to break into the world of graduate research in academic history.

Another thought had been to try to become a magistrate, preferably in the children's courts. Then I heard that over the age of forty I could not start the process of qualifying for the Bench in one of them, and that I would have to be proposed to the Lord Chancellor from some sort of party political basis. That may have been inaccurate information, but I did not pursue the idea, as anyway I felt uncomfortable with the prospect of legal power over people, tending vaguely in the direction of wanting to find out why they broke the law, rather than how they should be punished. Also I saw it might be a form of misguidedly trying to follow in my father's footsteps.

Those deliberations had been before I had set up the research, and to some extent that had postponed further thought about a definite way forward. Not being able to follow it up with investigating the subject of part-time work left me in another gap. I reconsidered some of my earlier inclinations and again there did not seem to be an obvious way forward. I saw that the research into women whose stage of life was similar to mine had carried the meaning of self-examination. I was really one of my own guinea-pigs. I went on with free-lance journalism, intermittent talks on the radio and waiting to see whether something appeared from somewhere, but that all felt directionless. The "something" did not necessarily have to be prestigious, but it had to be better than what felt like drifting.

At that stage of my life, feeling frustrated was not a new experience. On many occasions, of which perhaps the most significant had been the three miscarriages during the war, handling frustration had been very difficult. *My* wishes, or plans, were being held up by some *Other* unidentified enemy force. What was it? I was not yet analytically sophisticated enough to put the question better: is it a power working from the outside—a harsh God, a cruel Devil, or Fate?—or was it an enemy inside me, one for which I had to accept responsibility? I had sometimes wondered whether there was a psychological cause for those miscarriages and not only one that physicians could name. Was it that I was somehow not yet ready in myself to have a second baby? Or, worse, was I rejecting a potential new person? It was worrying that they had all been males. Did that have a meaning? Was I saying NO to the life inside me? That had been frightening. Being frustrated and powerless were emotions I could hardly bear. Grumbling, complaining, moaning, were all considered wrong in my original family, and in David's. I had not yet dared to question their somewhat puritanical views. The simple thing was that I longed to be happy—a different person.

Then my discontent began painfully to focus round envy of David's work and the satisfactory position he had already reached in the Civil Service. He had always wanted to be a Civil Servant, on the administrative level. He had served his country, as he certainly saw he had been called upon to do, during the war, but had not enjoyed it more than minimally. He only found one or two men in the Army congenial, they did not become friends after the war. He did not have the lowbrow or even middlebrow personality which might have made Army life easier. Many of his friends who were slightly older had been in reserved occupations, and had gone forward in their careers without the interruption of being in uniform. He had envied them, ruefully, but without guilt. Then he had been lucky to be demobilised early when he was moved from the Army into the Cabinet Office at a very important time, and after that there was the Paris job; then the Treasury. By the mid-Fifties he was happy, doing important work. All the extended family knew he was. His earlier envy had melted, he was fully stretched intellectually and had achieved what he wanted.

Envy is nasty. It is psychologically correct that it should be one of the Seven Deadly Sins, chosen from a long list of common human frailties by the medieval Church, since it is a killer of happiness. I was very unhappy finding I was in its grip, and felt guilty about it. It was especially painful in relation to David, since we were married. In the eyes of the family I was meant to be impressed by his success like the rest of them, with no ambivalence to complicate it. My inbuilt standards told me that how I felt was morally wrong. I concealed my state from them but could not conceal it from myself. And my discomfort in relation to David was added to by having known for quite a while that I envied Jenifer with her academic and social opportunities. My feelings could not be discussed, with either of them. I was fairly sure that if I told David he would feel I was reproaching him, and I was cowardly about that. I found out later that envy only decreases effectively if one is able to work on it very thoroughly indeed, and that has to be combined with getting for oneself something equivalent to what had been envied. I owe that psychological progress to my analysis and to becoming an analyst.

The fact of being so unhappy became clear to me one morning when I had walked down to Golders Green underground station with David, who was going off to a particularly interesting and important meeting abroad. As I turned back up the hill, to go into the empty house, I saw that I simply must get help. I realised I was severely depressed, that seemed to be the word for my trouble. I also knew there was something important in my life, which used to be there, but was no more. I did not know if that mysterious "something" could be re-found, or revived. Perhaps it was irrevocably lost.

I wrote to an old Cambridge contact, Catherine Storr. I thought she had read English when we were both at Newnham, knew vaguely that she had followed that with becoming a doctor, and some kind of psychologist. I described my plight to her, my general state and the idea that something lost needed to be found, if at all possible. I was ignorant about the varieties of work done by qualified people in any profession of which the name began with the three letters PSY. But I had chosen well in turning to her. We were acquaintances rather than close friends, so she was able to get a reasonably objective picture of how I might be helped.

I could see that Catherine was thinking carefully. Her opinion was that, on balance, I would do better with a therapist trained on modern and progressive Jungian lines than with a Freudian of any kind, but I gathered it was a near thing. I liked the way she was not being categorical. She gave me the name of a colleague, Dr. Robert Hobson, who saw National Health Service patients at the Middlesex Hospital. It is slightly surprising to me now that that did not sound alarming. Making contact with him turned out to be a major decision, with consequences for the rest of my life. It was not so much a change of direction, as a step towards a new horizon. Moreover, the first advantage of being referred to a doctor, in a hospital, was that I was going to benefit from the double meaning of the word "patient". As a noun, it comes from *patior*, latin for "I suffer". As an adjective, for example, a patient person, was what I needed to become.

Writing today, so many years later, I can see that the various turnings—up the hill, to Catherine, and to Dr. Hobson—are images or verbal ways of pointing to the turning back I had to do in psychotherapy and deeper analysis, before I could turn towards the next stage of life, a new one. The image of the way, the path, the road, or the route, is an old one, a powerful one, expressed in numerous languages. It is a word about a material or an actual thing, but it also has inner and psychological reality. It carries an archetypal quality. It is one of those attractive words with meanings which overlap each other, and step over banal boundaries. It has been used world-wide and all through recorded history, by a great number of thinkers as well as spiritual people. There could hardly be a better word, image or symbol for what I am aiming to convey about the next stage of my life. Uphill, downhill, straight and narrow, winding, stony, long, hard, impossible—but, just sometimes, not too difficult. Many and varied poets knew the image well, such as John Milton and Walt Whitman, Henry Vaughan and George Seferis, to pick just a few, at random, out of many possibles. The two Emilies, Brontë and Dickinson, only knew the hard and tragic ways of tense unhappiness.

Thirteen

A Possible Way Forward

Beginning psychotherapy, in the autumn of 1956, was a very new experience. There had been no opportunity to find out what was likely to happen from any friend or acquaintance, as I knew no-one who had had therapy, let alone full analysis. Or perhaps I should say no-one had ever told me they had. I had lived in "a different world".

In many ways I was a good subject for it, since I came with no preconceptions, let alone scepticism, prejudices or fears. I had read no text books, unless dipping a little, many years earlier, into easy Freud should be counted. At that time the title had been heavy and off-putting, as I hardly knew what it meant: *The Psychopathology of Everyday Life*. In chapter 7 I mentioned that it had been recommended to me when I was at Cambridge by a general practitioner who had seen that the urticaria (nettle-rash) I had developed was a psychosomatic reaction to a combination of physical and emotional stresses. I had found the book mildly interesting, but not enough to whet my appetite into reading more, as I was deep into history and contemporary international politics at that time. Now I wanted, and indeed needed help so much that passively, naïvely and somewhat optimistically, I assumed help would be granted. Catherine had conveyed I was suitable for therapy.

Since then I have often thought about what the notion of help involves and includes, in a variety of settings, both the concept in itself and how it operates. The proverbial saying that 'God helps those who help themselves' contains one aspect of the many interactions in therapy. As a Jungian analyst I have preferred to see myself as an enabler who finds ways of accompanying people into and through their own ways of struggling, as compared with being a helper. I try to work towards them finding their own inner helper.

Dr. Hobson had a pleasant manner, correctly non-committal rather than what would have been too cordial, too warm. He had a slight stammer, so I formed the impression that he had not got everything sorted out; that would help me to find him congenial. His room was a small one, almost hidden somewhere at the back of an annexe to the main building of the Middlesex Hospital. To describe what it was not, I can say that it had no Harley Street aura, there was no grand waiting room, and that was all to the good.

Although I can remember a great many details of atmosphere and facts about quite a few past events in my life, I am not sure how that first session started. Did he say or ask anything to get the talk going? Or did he, the medical psychotherapist, follow one of the well-tried ways, simply waiting to hear what I, the patient, would say, or perhaps even what I might do? He certainly did not request me to lie down on the couch and direct me to say whatever came into my head, as the traditionally cartooned Freudian psychoanalyst (bearded, out of sight and notebook in hand), is thought to tell the typical patient. I believe my not being able to recall much about the beginning of my first encounter with an analyst of any kind indicates that making and keeping an appointment were more important than the details of what was said. As I wrote in the previous chapter, it turned out later to have been a small step on a long road, and an approach to a turning point. The work of many years had begun, and, with another image, the river with its source in the small room in the Middlesex has not yet reached the sea. Putting it that way reminds me of a remark someone made on the radio recently: 'the sea is large, my boat is small'. Not a bad motto for a therapist's consulting room, to be invisibly inscribed above the door, and remembered privately.

(For the sake of clarity, and in outline, it is worth mentioning that the general term **psychotherapist** means any trained person who conducts therapy of the patient's psyche using his or her own psyche. The medium is talk. He or she works towards the patient discovering unconscious forces and motivations. The **psychiatrist** has done a medical degree. The **psychologist** has a university degree in psychology. The **psychoanalyst** has been trained to work with Freudian concepts and methods. The **analytical psychologist** has done the same with the Jungian approach. That last term is admittedly a bit anomalous, since a degree in psychology is not essential, but the early Jungians, especially in Britain, could not call themselves Freudian as they had not been trained at the Institute of Psychoanalysis. I use the term **analyst** for either of those last two kinds of professionals.)

The reader who has not experienced psychotherapy of any kind may find it odd that there is much for a professional to think is significant in connection with just how a consultation starts. Many years later, having progressed enough to be supervising the work of trainee analysts, I used to get them to examine closely the exact way in which their first meeting with their prospective patient had come about. What was the expression on their face, their way of dressing, walking, sitting, general demeanour and so on; with what words had that first hour started? Later, we could go back to the notes of that encounter and see whether they had had a prospective quality. There are pros and cons of knowing things in advance of meeting a patient. We are usually in the hands of the referring colleague or agency, so wanting to form our own untainted impression is often impossible: it is an ideal. I also found with trainees, as well as with myself, that it was worthwhile examining carefully what had contributed to a therapy not getting started. It is sometimes obvious, but it can be subtle. I remember reading a very perceptive book by Pittenger, Hockett and Danehy called *The First Five Minutes*. Perhaps the beginning of a therapy is like the important first few words of a poem, for example: 'My heart aches . . .' in Keats' *Ode to a Nightingale*; or: 'Go and open the door . . .' in Miroslav Holub's *The Door*.

I have to interrupt this account of some aspects of my psychotherapy and subsequent full analysis, to insert a mention of a remarkable book, *The Door of Serenity,* by the Australian psychiatrist, Dr. Ainslie Meares. It was published in 1958 and I bought it five years later, just about at the time when I was being accepted to train as an analytical psychologist. Holub's poem has reminded me of it. The book is the account of a most remarkable treatment over seven years, during which a profoundly ill young woman was enabled to emerge into life through bringing Dr. Meares what he called her 'weird paintings' and slowly finding she could talk about them with him. She changed from being 'tense, furtive, quivering like a frightened animal', into what he described as 'a person of great insight and sensitivity'. He also wrote that she was one of 'those whose minds have been burnished in the fire of insanity, and who have come through the ordeal'. Her painting, his listening, their talking and their way of relating, worked together to save her after insulin coma, electric shock treatment and group therapy had all failed.

The book is personal and impressively sincere, illustrating how much the sensitive therapist learned during the hours when he and the patient were striving to communicate with each other. He accompanied her while she was finding serenity, health she had never had. I realised that neither was I as ill as she had been, nor did I ever, later, have patients who were similarly ill: she was schizophrenic, he wrote of her being 'mad', but her doctor's use of himself, his fully extended self, helped me to glimpse what a lot is involved in discovering how it is possible to get in touch with the amazing and unique symbolism in another person's inner world, and how that symbolism is expressed in imagery. There are individual images as well as collective ones.

Later, when I was working as an analyst myself, it turned out particularly valuable to be in the Jungian world which does not interpret a patient's images as being merely examples of stereotypes (e.g. snake = penis) which they may perhaps be, but keeps in mind the collective/archetypal meaning while searching for the meaning to the individual's person. Getting the "feel" of each patient's kinds of images is always more valuable than jumping quickly to their typical origin or connection. The individual first, then the archetype: both need acknowledging.

Apart from whatever Dr. Hobson said, or asked me to tell him, I think my first communication put a lot into a small nutshell: I said I was depressed, and that I realised depression was ordinary, a common state to be in. A few months later, by which time Dr. Hobson knew that poetry was one of my loves, I was much affected by him revealing that he also was very fond of poetry, through recommending a poem of Blake's that he thought I would appreciate, *The Marriage of Heaven and Hell.* Those analysts who are more austere than he was, and especially those who are conducting a full analytical therapy, refrain from revealing their likes and dislikes, having found from experience that it is better practice for patients' curiosity not to be gratified directly. The mutual dependency can become too great. Once I was qualified, I found that such talk was suitable near the end of a long analysis, if it felt right, but of doubtful benefit to short-term therapy. For me at that stage, feeling lonely and hungry for significant communication, his revelation was helpful. And I certainly benefited from reading that poem. It was superb. Looking it up now, I find it still is.

I realise that my view on the questionable value of the analyst revealing his or her personal views or experiences is a controversial one. Whenever the subject has come up in a discussion group to which I belong, all of us members of the London Society of Analytical Psychology, it becomes clear that feelings run strongly on the matter. And there are innumerable examples to fit any number of situations. I am mentioning it here because it was one factor which I experienced first in that once-a-week therapy with Dr. Hobson. My sessions were on Monday mornings. One Sunday evening he called. "I'm sorry but I can't see you tomorrow", he said. "My mother has just died". The regressed young me was furious—but I was too used to being polite to say that. I then became, inside, so guilty at my self-centered reaction that that also became unmentionable. Some years later I remembered the incident and that I had not been the grown-up I thought I was, but a regressed little girl whose "parent" had needs more urgent than hers. She must have been very frightened of the nasty and ungenerous side of her being discovered. It had to remain out of sight: she wanted to be liked, even admired. Perhaps she was laying one of the foundations of a later Jungian understanding of the opposite forces both at work simultaneously: the bad and the possibly good. By my silence I had deprived Dr. Hobson of an interpretation. But what the patient discovers is, in the long run, more valuable than what the therapist might say.

During my main analysis my innocence about much to do with therapy showed up in another way early in my analysis with Dr. Jackson, who I saw after Dr. Hobson. It was connected with his children, the real ones, not the transference ones. Something must have occurred which conveyed that he had a daughter: I innocently asked her name. Perhaps he could not think of how to interpret my curiosity and there was a pause: then with much embarrassment he said: "She's called Judith". The other occasion, not much later, was when I had somehow heard he was going to attend a conference and would be reading a paper. In innocence again, I asked him what it was about. When he said it was to do with chairs, I was very puzzled indeed, and was far too cowardly to ask. I was an absolute beginner and "saw" in my mind a straight upright kitchen chair. How could that be an analytical theme? I did not know that it was probably about whether the patient should lie on the couch, as did those who were seeing Freud, or sitting on a chair, as Jung preferred.

So I have to admit to the misdemeanour of generalising from my own experience, first as a patient, then as an analyst. I can think of occasions when details about my troubles would have been a burden to my patients: but one major event, my husband's sudden death, when there could have been no advance indications, was certainly not hidden from those in my practice at the time. I do not remember any of them finding condolences difficult or unreal. They were able to understand that I had not "abandoned" them crudely or callously. But it was fortunate that on that occasion I had no patients in a regressed or primitive state.

I had started by presenting myself as being one particular person, but it was defensive to generalise about depression. I suppose I wanted to be seen as able to name the core trouble, but I was also concealing how severe it was by trying to put it in context, which intellectualised it and kept at bay my anxiety about it. Dr. Hobson probably saw that. When he brought in Blake he was humanising sensitively. My trying not to exaggerate was an important element in complying with one of the precepts of my upbringing, so it was easy for me to minimise my difficulties. But with another part of me I hoped to make an impact. I also needed to convey how complicated it was to feel something while believing it was not allowable to feel that way.

Some years later, when my further analysis had progressed enough for me to be allowed to train with the Society, I noticed something which it took me a long time to be clear about, and to be able to formulate without in any way colouring it with a value-judgement. It was that listening to a patient's trouble usually activates in the purely medical mind the reaction of wanting to name it, to provide a diagnosis, the correct one if possible. That is scientifically right and I think it most likely helps the doctor to feel safe, since such knowledge gives power. By analogy, in another area of life, I like being able to name a bird or a plant. My impression is that where a patient is not in a psychotic state, even a therapist who qualified in medicine before taking the further training to become an analyst does not invariably need to be satisfied by naming the trouble, and is then more likely to consider carefully how the patient is hampered by blocks against relating, both in therapy and in the rest of life. Since my background before becoming an analytical psychologist was in the arts, I have not the same kind of specialist knowledge as a psychiatrist has, but enough to discern when a patient should be seen by one or admitted to hospital.

I discovered by experience that analysis has a particular kind of listening as its basis, listening with what can be called the Third Ear, and noticing with the Third Eye. Comment or skilful interpretation may or may not be suitable straight away. That kind of listening and noticing are the ground out of which therapeutic relating grows. And, if all goes reasonably well, the patient's insight develops gradually, with ups and downs, spurts and doldrums, while he or she is learning to value inside voices. Dr. Hobson was a good and sophisticated listener.

There was a time when analysts who qualified after doing a university degree in one or other of the arts subjects, as compared with a medical one, were known as lay analysts, especially in medical circles. I remember feeling touchy about that, during my training, as I considered "lay" made me sound inferior, lower in the hierarchy. And I was touchy because secretly I did feel inferior, and did not want that to be discovered. The word "lay" defined me and others like me in negative terms, as being not fully professional. It took too little account of the valid differences. In that matter there was a personal dimension for me, since my younger sister, Mariella, was a doctor, a neurologist. And when I told her that I had decided to train she had been taken aback, almost shocked, and declared at once that I could not be an analyst: I was not a doctor. I realised later that we were each envious of the other.

I have attempted to outline some of the ways of describing the two kinds of minds to be found among professional psychotherapists. If put in that way, their minds may sound rather crudely and simplistically contrasted. And they are much less so in the present climate, so long after I started becoming a therapist, which was via myself being a patient. There is a far less rigid frontier between the physician and the psychotherapist now than was usual then, in the middle of the twentieth century. And I may be typical of the hybrid members of what have come to be called the helping professions, in that the overlap between body and mind is increasingly well understood. It is what I am interested in, more than invariably giving priority to the one or the other. The Cambridge doctor had been right in his view of my nettle-rash. Without my realising it at the time, I must have benefited from contact with him and taken in what he offered. Later, I had to learn to detect another important thing: estimating if a patient is likely to be physically as well as verbally aggressive, dangerously so, to themselves or to someone else. That is not always easy, even to very experienced practitioners. If there are even small hints of suicide, the fear of it lurks in the wings.

Psychotherapy once a week continued with Dr. Hobson for six or seven months, into the summer of 1957. At that point, he took up an appointment at the Maudsley Hospital, a long way from where I was living. He and I discussed whether I should continue seeing him, in the new venue, or bring the arrangement to an end. I asked whether he thought I could move on to a full analysis, which would be with someone else. In good-quality analysis, several times a week, it is not so difficult to work effectively through the blocks and resistances as it is in psychotherapy or counselling. He considered the idea carefully, but said he did not think I was suitable. In spite of deep disappointment, I accepted his opinion. At the same time I had a nagging feeling that I should not have been so compliant. Being a good girl was no longer quite right: perhaps "Daddy" did not know best? During the time I had been in therapy with him I had come to see that the research into the lives of the women I had written about in *Wives Who Went to College* was a way of preparing myself for examining my own life and my views on it. I had shown him the proof copy of the book, and he had been impressed as well as interested to hear about it. But he had had no time to read it and to see its extra personal dimension and meaning. So it was up to me to help myself forward, if at all possible. I had probably not voiced to him my growing under-standing that having the sessions in a hospital out-patients' de-partment had led to my insight that I was one of the unhappy half-alive people who frequented the waiting rooms there. I wanted to be fully alive. Several months passed, with no plans and no action taken.

The great advantage of stopping seeing Dr. Hobson was that David was relieved. He had always hated me being in therapy, even to the extent of having asserted, when I first told him about it, that I was not depressed. He said I had a good hus-band, a good home and three nice children. They were doing well academically and in various school sports. His denial, of what seemed to me to be the straight fact of my being de-pressed, was absolute. He took the usual rationalistic view that it was self-indulgent to spend so much time on myself, and could not see that I needed his backing, since being in therapy, or analysis, is not easy. He felt no need for it himself. I saw I had made him very anxious and that he possibly felt criticised, with-out being able to voice that. My trying to talk it through got us nowhere. That was a deeply sad aspect of how we were then.

It was a pity that he had forgotten two short episodes when he had felt powerless to understand his reaction to a troubling situation and had not wanted to talk about it, though the first time that would have been impossible. That had been a panic attack, during the war, when he realised that his Unit was going to play a crucial part in the liberation of France through the at-tack on the Normandy coast, heavily defended by the Germans. The Army doctor as good as told him to pull himself together. He did. As it turned out, he and his Unit landed on the first morning, under heavy fire. And the following morning, he and one other man were sent to see if the Post Office in the nearest town, Bayeux, had been booby-trapped: fortunately, it had not been.

The other panic was later, when we were living in Paris in connection with his work. One evening, ten minutes before we were due at a dinner party, he absolutely could not come with me. The French couple who had invited us had been long-term friends of my parents. I simply had to call them, to make our excuses, and of course they were very annoyed indeed.

Returning to the difficulties which arose when I started therapy, it became clear that a major disagreement had opened up between David and me. We were once again turning out to be far more different from each other than either of us had realised when we got married in the fateful summer of 1939. We could not see then how much we were going to be affected by our lives being forced to go in different directions. But it would have been facile, in the mid-Fifties, to think of our difficulties as caused only by the frequent separations during the war years and my fears for his safety in battles. They were trials of our commitment to each other, and I thought we had got through them. I discovered later that Jung wrote a great deal about the stages of life and considered the middle years crucially significant: there could be major changes of meaning and purpose. I was the right age for a mid-life crisis. It was difficult for David to tolerate it.

I hoped that the success of the *Wives* book, the appreciative reviews and the many requests for articles, for speaking at meetings and so on, would be enough to satisfy me and to counteract the depression. I had attempted to get a grant of some sort, to follow the earlier research by exploring how much part-time work was available for the kinds of married women I now knew about, but my efforts yielded no results. I had no intention at all of trying to become an analytical psychologist, but I knew I needed better-quality peace of mind. Certainly David would have been relieved about his painful disagreement with me if I could have settled satisfactorily into continuing the combination of family life, sociological research, coaching girls who wanted to go to University, other bits and pieces of teaching or lecturing, and free-lance journalism, all of which was going fairly well. That would have been convenient, for him, and therefore to some extent, for me. He would not have minded his colleagues knowing what I was doing, as, in terms of Establishment Civil Service people, I would have been a more suitable wife, and perhaps an easier one for him.

The change from being in once-a-week psychotherapy with Dr. Hobson happened later that year, in 1957. Although he had told me he did not see me as suitable for full analysis, I think he must in fact have mentioned me to a colleague, Dr. Murray Jackson, also a member at that time of the Jungian Society of Analytical Psychology. Dr. Jackson took the initiative in contacting me, saying he had heard I was considering analysis. An appointment was made. That was the first of a number of slightly unconventional, or at least individual, aspects of my analysis, since more often the patient is given the name of a therapist and is the one to ask for an appointment. However, the day came, and the next thing was that he was late for the initial consultation. It is fairly usual in general practice for the doctor to be running late and to keep a patient waiting, but not in analysis, though I did not know that. After what felt quite a long wait, I was nearly going home to cook the supper when he turned up. Later in my career, I found that it was useful to notice and comment on details and to try to examine all sorts of conscious and unconscious motives for, in reverse, a patient being late. Given that analysis is different from ordinary socialising, I might even have had the persecutory idea that he did not want to see me, with the gloss that I was not important enough for him to be punctual for the appointment. Once my analysis had got going, perhaps he should have tried to find out why I did not complain, since he was not a good time-keeper.

With my own patients, I discovered that surmises or guesses about lateness are usually wrong. They are power-ploys: an analyst has to try not to be in the grip of his or her own unconscious fantasies of omniscience or omnipotence. A know-all professional is worse than an ordinary know-all person.

During much of the time that I was in analysis with Murray Jackson, discovering a great deal about my personal psychology and especially my inner life, my outside life continued much as it had been during recent years. It could be called both good and not so good. I was teaching in a coaching establishment for girls, the Westminster Tutors. It was owned and run by Miss Freeston, who was skilful at finding both suitable part-time scholarly teachers willing to work for less than our market value, and the brightest daughters of well-off people keen for them to get to one of the ancient universities. My pupils wrote essays for "the general paper", questions on any subject at all, so that reading widely, thinking clearly, writing well and being enterprising were important. I also taught several periods of English and European history. It was convenient work for me to combine with my analysis, three times a week at first, then four times. The work with small groups was congenial and stimulating.

Once I had qualified as an analytical psychologist, and had begun to run seminars for trainee analysts, the experience of coaching girls who were likely to be academic enough to get into an Oxford or Cambridge college came in useful, on the intellectual side. Both activities were built round the task of enabling people to develop their potential as far as was possible. And that was what I was myself, most painfully, doing in analysis, not having yet discovered that the Jungian work was going to help me in the direction towards individuation. Jackson was a scrupulous and clear-minded analyst, with a powerful personality.

As the months went by, perhaps two or more years of them, I found I was developing the wish to go into some sort of training to become a therapist myself. Jackson naturally analysed that wish as hard as he could, especially as in late adolescence I had wanted to follow in my father's footsteps and failed. My new desire was perhaps also fated not to be granted: I had none of the prerequisites for becoming even a counsellor, let alone a full analyst. I had never been a social worker, and never had a patient of any kind.

By that time Cassandra had been a day pupil at North London Collegiate School and gone on to Oxford, and Christopher was at the boys' boarding school Bryanston in Dorset, with an exhibition. Camilla, having among other activities made an enterprising collection of pressed wild flowers, with English and Latin names, also got into North London. David's career was getting on well. We gave the impression of being a successful family, and we were.

Where the inner me was concerned, the end of the Fifties and the early Sixties were difficult and tense. In my outer life some encouraging opportunities came my way, each worthwhile in itself, such as being invited to speak about psychology and mental health at North London Collegiate School and writing a play about Henri Dunant, the founder of the Red Cross, which was commissioned for the history department of the B.B.C.'s schools programmes. It was full of battles and I enjoyed watching the teenage boys' faces as they listened, with rapt attention, in a classroom in Dagenham, the area in the east of London where Ford cars were made: all very masculine. Battles were going on inside me: could I perhaps become mainly a writer, giving up the wild idea analysis had engendered? How could I go forward?

I think a bold ambition was beginning to take root in me. During one of our holidays in Cornwall, some good friends were staying with us, George and Katrin Stroh. He was a psychiatrist and Freudian psychoanalyst, and at that time she was looking after their two young children. I remember walking with George all along the familiar mile of fine grey sand, below our old family house there. He pressed me very hard to examine my wish to train. He was neither for nor against, but wanted to know why. I answered that it was the most difficult thing I could think of doing. That bravado understandably took him by surprise. I could not justify it rationally, and he did not try to dissuade me openly or directly. He calmly pointed out all the difficulties I would have to face. I thought I was rather a specialist in difficulties, and that conversation somehow clinched it for me. I would continue to work towards trying to train.

There were three hurdles. The first was to find one, or two, people to treat therapeutically, to show that I could. Also a supervisor to help me to learn more. The second was that Jackson should back me as suitable and ready enough. The third was to be accepted by a good-quality professional organisation. It was quite a programme.

Fourteen

Being and Becoming

Before applying to any particular training body, I knew there was a lot to do. And all the time, at home, David was disliking what I was doing. He could not reconcile himself to it. One of the difficulties was that he had always had a clear picture of what he wanted to do in life, and even with the interruption of war service he had never wavered on being a Civil Servant. I think his picture of himself was steady, mine shifted with the years. In contrast to the straight run life gave him, I had done a variety of things and changed much more than he had, both in occupations and interests. The differences between us were more than the obvious ones of the contrasts between being a father and being a mother (especially as seen at that time in the twentieth century), and we were not good at bringing the issues out into the open.

As well as being involved in psychology, and particularly the psychology of unconsciousness in individuals, I was still as interested in collective matters, the world of politics and how the country should be run, as I ever had been. David was not only interested, he was in it. Public administration, the machinery of government, had become his specialism. Complying with the Official Secrets Act, he had to be absolutely discreet about everything he was involved in and all the people he met, which was essential when he was in the Cabinet Office and in connection with most of his work in the Treasury. He never mentioned any political gossip, but he probably knew most of the goings-on and what was being planned. I only knew what the newspapers told me. Also, he did not necessarily want to talk about work once he was at home. Sadly, I did not manage to get him to see that psychology also was interesting, or could be. Unconscious things were taboo: he thought the contents of dreams were nonsense and that people only dream when they have had cheese for supper. I disagreed. I wish I had thought he was joking and teasing me. The two worlds, Whitehall and depth psychology, were really far apart. I think they still are. His work gave him most of the companionship he wanted. That situation resulted in my concentrating on matters connected with psychology and analysis. He felt left out from my interests and the books I read. They looked more learned than they really were.

I must emphasise that we shared our love for our children, and interest in how they were getting on. We greatly enjoyed our holidays out of London and hardly minded not being able to afford to go abroad to warmer places. Often David could not resist declaring, in the face of family grumpiness on days of drenching rain, that it was 'Fundamentally Fine', whether in North Wales or Cornwall, the Scilly Isles or Western Ireland. In those places our tastes were the same, and in most of them the children were with us; they had not yet started to go their own ways. I cannot tell how much they detected about our different points of view. I felt, without discussing the problem with him, that our lack of full togetherness should be kept from them as much as possible. I may have been wrong, over-protective. It became uncomfortably part of the double life I seemed to be living. In fact, during the time I was doing the training it was hardly ever mentioned in the family and, since they were all very busy with their own lives, they hardly enquired about mine. But it is probably unusual for teen-agers to ask their mother what sort of a day she has had.

Later, once I had qualified and come to know several other analysts, especially ones who were struggling to get established in the profession, I discovered that I was not the only one whose home life had been affected if the two spouses, having once been close, were going their separate ways in their work. Most of us kept quiet about the difficulty, since it was painful and private. Apart from what I observed in the analytical world, my impression was that the wives of senior Civil Servants were most of them seen as wives, rather than being women with their own individuality or profession. Some of us could be considered feminists, though not very assertively so. I knew of none who took part actively in the Women's Liberation Movement.

Where I was concerned, working towards establishing myself as the individual I felt I could become was such a protracted struggle that I left the full Liberation effort to others, mainly of the next generation, such as Camilla, who took part with many other women in the protests against Cruise Missiles at Greenham Common. The middle-aged couples I knew where, for example, both were Civil Servants, or both medical doctors, or both analysts seemed to have an easier time than we had.

As I had decided to go ahead with the aim of becoming a therapist of some sort, the problem, by 1960, was to find some way of acquiring one or more patients, as I mentioned in the previous chapter. I had never had contact with the Samaritans, having ignorantly pictured them as simply responding to calls from people in suicidal crises and deflecting them from putting the impulse into action. But I soon found that, when suitable, they referred such people on to counsellors, therapists or psychiatrists. A visit to the founder of the organisation, the impressive vicar of St. Stephen's Church in the City of London, Chad Varah, resulted in him being willing to let me meet a man and a woman who happened to be in the church just then, and to talk their problems over with them. So my first experience of work as a would-be therapist was in the dim evening light of an uncomfortable church pew. The man was a fetishist who was turned on, in underground trains, by looking as far as he could up girls' legs, revealed by the short mini-skirts fashionable at that time. He was keen to give me the impression that he did no more than look, yearn and fantasise; so even I could see that he had more a psychological than a behavioural problem. I did not know more than the first thing about the psychology of fetishism and fetishists. So before seeing him again I searched out a few relevant analytical papers, and found Anthony Storr's early one, *The Psychopathology of Fetishism and Transvesticism*. The woman at the church was a confirmed alcoholic; she had children who were suffering from her behaviour and the life problems behind the drinking.

Being intent on acquiring patients (I do not like the term

"client", which still sounds to me like someone who goes to see a lawyer), I arranged for them to see me at home, which perhaps gave them the impression that I was a bona fide therapist. There was a suitable room that I privately hoped could become a real consulting room in the future. Since I had not taken the worldly-wise precaution of being insured, it was probably foolhardy as well as ignorant to see them at home, but no harm came of it. For them, I was at least someone who would listen, and hear about their plight. For myself, I needed to learn the art and skill of interpreting what they said and what was going on between us, in ways which would be effective. As my background was in the humanities, literature and history, I already believed that treating the person was going to be more important than concentrating on the symptom. On one occasion I visited the woman in her depressing bed-sitter in a run-down part of London, wanting to get an all-round view of her life, which might have been helpful in trying to understand her drink problem. My analyst considered that quite incorrect. He was technically right, according to his strict views of what analysts should or should not do, but I did not mind being unconventional, since I fitted into no recognised category in the caring professions. I envied him, as I imagined he had never had to step out of line during his analytical training. I could trust to him analysing my envy problems whenever necessary, which was often, but he had the sense to be lenient on several occasions.

I was clued up enough to arrange to see a superviser regularly. She was Marianne Jacoby, who was a trained Jungian. She had had a very difficult time when she first came to London as a Jewish refugee during the war, and successfully struggled through to independence, bringing up two children on her own, as well as qualifying as a therapist. She and I got on well, as she encouraged me at the same time as being both firm on methods of work and tolerant of my beginner's efforts and cautious style. My confidence improved and we worked together for about a year, at the end of which she teased me in a friendly way, saying I would always wear an L-plate. She was right: I still do. (In the U.K., before anyone is licensed to drive solo, the car has to display a large L).

During that time Murray Jackson continued to analyse strictly, which I respected, and he conveyed indirectly that he believed in me. He accompanied me through several deep crises of confidence and black moods of despair. It is interesting, and moving, to look back, at a distance of many decades, on a few incidents which show how an analyst's apparently simple remark can be of lasting value. On one occasion, for example, I remember beginning a session saying 'I am in agony, but of course that is a ridiculous exaggeration'. He calmly answered, 'It's the truth'. Many times, during my years of being an analyst, I have found that interaction coming into my mind.

I recently found some notes I had recorded of thoughts about crises, written in the spring of 1962. They were already psychologically insightful, about such matters as the fundamental sense of the Self and of myself even though it felt to have only a tenuous existence; a damaged identity; repressed or inexpressible anger; and the need to redirect inner aggression into valid ways of being and relating, as compared with acting it out unsuitably in daily life. That is the kind of thing that good-quality analytical therapy helps someone to discover, not by suggestion, advice or instruction, but through experience. And it was the basis of several papers I wrote some years later. A more sceptical view, but still a valid one, was expressed by the poet T. S. Eliot (who was adept at self-observation, without having ever subjected himself to psychoanalysis):

> There is . . . only a limited value
> In the knowledge derived from experience.
> The knowledge imposes a pattern, and falsifies,
> For the pattern is new at every moment
> And every moment is a new and shocking
> Valuation of all we have been.

He may even have been putting into poetry what he had picked up from some of his intellectual Bloomsbury friends who were all influenced by Freud: that the analyst's understanding of their own personality and experience in life would be misused if they were not attending to how individual each patient is, even when several of them seem similar or fall into a known category: each one is a new person. And each session is new. The

Jungian view on that is the contrast between the archetypal pattern and the individual manifestation of it.

My first application to train, at the British Association of Psychotherapists in 1961, was turned down, after two searching interviews: the verdict was that I was too anxious, needed more analysis and anyway had too little clinical experience. I was so ignorant still of the analytical use of the word "anxious" that I said to myself, "but of course I am anxious to succeed" and I dashed off to the beautiful tree-surrounded Ladies' Swimming Pond, on Hampstead Heath, one of my favourite places, to cool my hot disappointment. That was quite effective, and I think it earned Jackson's unspoken approval, since the Association's rejection seemed to surprise him, which soothed my wounded pride. The rebuff was mortifying, but not irrevocable. More work was to be faced. I decided to apply to the only fully Jungian training body, the Society of Analytical Psychology.

To get more experience, I approached what was then called the Student Health Unit at University College, which I chose for the simple reason that it was geographically the nearest part of London University, and discussed my hopes and plans with the Director there, Dr. Christopher Lucas. The Unit consisted of two doctors and a psychologically minded nurse. He was willing to include me as a therapist, on an honorary basis, in the small team which he was building up, provided that my plan, to apply to train as an analyst at the Society of Analytical Psychology, was successful. I felt I had one foot on the ladder that I wanted to climb, although I kept my hopeful excitement hidden from everybody except Dr. Jackson.

A little while later I had interviews with two senior analysts at the Society. It was inevitable that they would grill me severely and as deeply as possible, since I had none of the usual prerequisites for becoming an analyst. Then the training committee would consider my application. At that time the selection method included the training analyst reporting to the committee in person; he or she was meant to be as objective and impartial as possible. That practice was discontinued some years later, as analysts found it too hard not to champion too keenly someone whose application they had sanctioned. Also their own work was, in effect, being scrutinised. Waiting for what felt like a verdict was excruciating, but it came at last: yes, we will have you.

That acceptance to train at the Society had been on the understanding that I would find more conventional clinical work than the Samaritans could supply, so Dr. Lucas' offer was very valuable. Perhaps I gained Brownie points for persistence, the adult version of what had been called obstinacy when I was a child. But it was obvious that I would have to go on showing that I was safe to be trusted to work with people who were very ill, resistant, defended, ambivalent or distressed, without getting too stressed myself. It was arranged that I should also be loosely attached to the adolescent department at the Marlborough Day Hospital. The doctors there would refer me one or two young patients and I could attend the weekly staff meeting. Nowadays, that amount of work in a hospital would be considered quite inadequate: and I think the present higher standard is far better than all that was expected of me.

My reminiscences of the work on offer for me at the Marlborough Day are a small personal story in the history of the huge National Health Service. The atmosphere seemed lenient but there was probably more invisible structure than I detected, and there were advantages in it not being one of the famous psychiatric hospitals. I was allocated a depressed teen-age girl as a patient to see each week, with the vague supervision of one of the doctors. Under Dr. Bierer the hospital was run on lines which were directive rather than analytical. He had an authoritarian manner; he was a follower of the early psychoanalyst Alfred Adler who had been, at the same time as Jung and the others early in the century, one of Freud's collaborators. Adler had ceased to meet with the Professor's approval, as he did not agree with all the master's theories of depth psychology, and their personal relations deteriorated. Adler developed his own idea of the inferiority complex as central to neurosis. For some people that was obviously one feature of their unsatisfactory lives. The first time I had ever heard the term *inferiority complex* had been at my boarding school, where I and some friends had discovered the term and declared that that was our trouble. The perceptive Latin teacher told us crushingly but perhaps correctly that we suffered from its opposite: a superiority complex. The importance of opposite forces, often hidden in the unconscious mind and needing to be brought up and out into the open, is a particularly Jungian contribution to psychology, which that teacher may or may not have realised.

Most of what I learned, or as it were imbibed, at the Marlborough Day was in the Friday meetings where patients came before the assembled staff and were questioned, especially by the psychiatrists and the psychologists. Less attention was given to the unconscious psyche than I was used to, after several years of analysis. Dorothy Koestler, the first wife of the writer Arthur Koestler, was the psychiatric social worker, and I found her particularly congenial. The interviews were mostly run on formal lines, and my impression was that usually the patients were not surprisingly squirming, alone at the edge of a circle of people in power over them, and experiencing it all as inquisitorial. In contrast, some of them were truculent, obstinate and resentful. It was probably inevitable that at that stage of my induction into the world of psychotherapy I should slip into identifying with the patients more than with the tough and powerful staff, who were, according to their lights, well intentioned. They did aim to listen to the individual, but I sometimes thought they were not responding to the man's or woman's feeling side enough. They were definite about knowing the kinds, or types, of patients they were dealing with; and the ones who had been selected for treatment fitted well with Dr. Bierer's theories.

When I started working under Christopher Lucas in University College the arrangement was tentative, but he and I got on well from the beginning. He was considering qualifying as a psychoanalyst, and when there was time we used to compare our rather different experiences in the two trainings. He had a calm manner and gave the impression of being less involved emotionally than I was, which was presumably due to his being already in an established position, whereas I was struggling to achieve one. He was considerate in not conveying that I was going to be a "mere" lay analyst, so we each respected the other. Dr. Arnold Linken, the other doctor, was also interested in the psychological aspects of students' lives, and there was Marion Goldsmith, the nurse, attached to the practice, who was astute, humourous and good company.

The Student Health Unit belonged both to University College and to the National Health Service. Students at all stages of their studies could be registered with the College doctors, but the academic staff could communicate with us confidentially over any particularly worrying student, either in the main college or in the Slade School of Art. The Unit had been launched during the time when the pioneer Dr. Nicholas Malleson was there, and his interest in psychosomatic medicine had laid the foundations for the doctors attending to the emotional and psychological aspects of their patients' physical illnesses, and the students had the chance of being referred for regular weekly therapy sessions in term-time. There were graduate as well as undergraduate patients, and some from overseas.

The first room to be found for student-patients to come to see me was at the back of a somewhat mysterious and gloomy building separate from the main Unit, where there never seemed to be anyone else. As it was on the ground floor and at the back, there were bars on the windows, but for me the main thing was to have been found a room at all. My sister Mariella was shocked when she saw the bars, as she was used to the prestigious suites in the Mayo Clinic in America, where she was a neurologist. She was sympathetic too, and amused to see that I had had to provide the carpet and curtains myself: they were ones which had been discarded from one of my children's rooms. The two upright chairs were far from luxurious, let alone even comfortable, but one of my present psychiatrist friends told me recently that things can still be like that in the new century. A year or two later a much more suitable room was found, and during the ten years I worked in University College the Student Health Unit was good to me.

I had mistakenly imagined I would meet the academic staff, perhaps having access to their common room. The then Principal, Noel (later Lord) Annan, and I had known each other as students at Cambridge but that was irrelevant, though he knew of my existence, since he wrote me a nice letter at the end of my ten years there. One of the professors of History was the only academic I got to know at all and he knew I had originally studied history. He was interested in any effort being made by members of the Unit to get his students through their protracted work blocks, which he could see were not due to simple laziness.

Christopher Lucas' trust in me was vindicated at the end of 1964 when I was accepted into the Society of Analytical Psychology. From then on I began to have patients referred to me for private treatment. And several of the students I had seen in therapy there went on to full analysis.

During the years that I worked for about ten hours a week in University College, we used to have fortnightly lunch-time meetings with doctors and psychotherapists from several of the other colleges in the Bloomsbury area, in Nicholas Malleson's room. The discussions were almost always valuable for me as I was cutting my teeth in a new profession; but being treated as an equal, meeting people with whom I had an affinity, and the congenial atmosphere were all especially encouraging, compared with how isolated I had felt for many years. The only other professional meetings I had ever taken part in were many years earlier, during the war, also as a raw beginner, under the authoritative Head Mistress at Godolphin and Latymer School.

The individual differences and eccentricities among the people convened by Malleson were just what I wanted. His distinctive way of being powerful could sometimes lead to friction and rivalries between him and the milder and more philosophical members, such as Dr. John Read, from the London School of Economics. But 'Though some members chose to sit on the floor nobody sat at anybody's feet in the other sense of the expression', I wrote in a chapter contributed to *Students in Need*, a book about Malleson published in 1978, after his death. His angle was a Freudian one, and my way of working did not always seem right to him. Many students have moderate or even severe growing-up problems, which usually interfere with their studies. The Nineteen Sixties were the years when sexual mores were blatantly freeing up, when drugs, dangerous in the eyes of the authorities, were getting their grip world-wide, and when revolt in several American universities was crossing the Atlantic. Our discussions ranged widely: one time it was unwanted pregnancies, another it was anorexia, or the problems of students from West Africa. Was homesickness best treatable clinically as separation anxiety? Was a study block an occupational hazard or a psychological problem, not ordinary laziness? How "deep" could a therapist go with the kind of people we were seeing, at the last stage of adolescence?

Jung had specialised with middle-aged people and held the opinion that the Freudian approach to young people's anxieties was convincing and effective, when such anxieties were clearly caused by the need to distance themselves from their parents. I thought there was a strong case to be put for a flexible method of working with students who were also depressed. They could be enabled to emerge from their work block by discovering in therapy that depression was not just something nasty to be got rid of, but a pointer to problems which needed facing.

When we were discussing what approach would be the best for treating any particular student-patient, Malleson was apt to pounce on what he considered was the therapist's tendency to fall into unconsciously accepting what the student was projecting—*transferring*—into the clinical relationship, and we agreed that needed investigating. Since I was experiencing my training with the Jungian Society as being very firm on the subject of transference-countertransference, I sometimes bridled defensively at what felt like a false accusation. I learned to stand up for myself. I was finding that the apprenticeship of an intensive analysis had helped me to develop insights which could be adapted and contribute more effectively in the short-term work in a university setting than a milder counselling training would have done.

When analytical, even if brief, therapy succeeds, the young person will probably be saved from having much more serious psychological illness later. In the turbulent Sixties keeping long-term risks in mind was essential. It seemed to me important to be fully knowledgeable about outside political upheavals as well as to empathise with the inner struggles of any particular individual, which might be their version of world-wide events.

In the Swinging Sixties and the beginnings of the psychedelic drug culture there was also world-wide and tremendous anxiety about what was then known as The Bomb. I think there was a close connection, semi-causative, between drugs and fear. The nuclear danger was one of the legacies of the recent war, and it added an extra depth and dimension to what was known about the devastation that pre-nuclear bombing had caused in other cities in so many countries. Even though I and others of my generation had struggled with working through the ethical problem and the despair brought on by the destruction of Hiroshima and Nagasaki in 1945, we had not solved it. We had had to try to reason that those bombs had shortened the Second World War. For young people from 1964 to 1975 the Vietnam war was the major source of anger and political concern. All through those many years David and I noticed that the other almost indescribable twentieth-century evils, the Nazi concentration camps and the murders in gas chambers of so many millions of people, especially Jews, were much less spoken and written about than seemed natural. Somehow they were not then in the public arena, although they had been known for many years. The same held for the Soviets' forced Labour camps in Siberia. One of our thoughts was that they had been so appalling that there was not so much a collective attempt to deny them, fend them off or postpone thinking about them, as that it was taking the human race a long time for them to be fully digested.

That decade of the Sixties was the beginning of a new stage in my personal life, a new orientation, and I continued to do clinical work for the next thirty-five years. The achievement of that major change was during the time when our three children were growing up and growing away, but also still in touch with David and me. His work often took him far abroad, such as to Japan or India, so there were times when we were not able to discuss together something needing an urgent decision with respect to one or other of them. It was long before the days of mobile phones, answerphones, e-mail or transcontinental calls.

While I was working rather minimally at the Marlborough Day Hospital and seeing up to ten student patients at University College, those activities were supportive of the core element of the training at the Society of Analytical Psychology, which was the personal analysis. There were two weekly evening seminars, run by the senior members, and given on a voluntary basis. I found it interesting to detect the very varied ways of working on offer in the course of those evenings, although the theory and major themes of analytical psychology were ostensibly similar whoever was describing and illustrating them with clinical examples. It was immediately evident that the differences stemmed from personal factors in the backgrounds of those seniors, some among the older ones having known Jung and still being close to how we gathered he had been, and others already diverging a little or specialising differently.

I think it would have been helpful if more attention than just one seminar had been given to Jung's work on the four basic personality types (thinking, feeling, intuition, and sensation) and their subsidiary ways of interacting, which he had observed and described as a result of his painful rift with Freud. Tests of the personality types had been developed first by the work of the American analysts, Horace Grey and Joseph Wheelwright in San Francisco, and later by other psychologists, June Singer and Mary Loomis. We could do a British version of those tests voluntarily with one of our analysts, Mary Williams. I found the experience a broadening one, revealing personality aspects I had not detected before. With one of the seminar leaders we did a version of Jung's association test, and it revealed several previously unidentified complexes and aspects of ourselves still lurking in the Shadow—a good practical way of discovering the workings of that archetype. I remember seeing how close that was to Christ's saying about motes in other people's eyes and beams in one's own.

There were only three of us in my training year. One had been a psychiatric social worker, but she dropped out fairly soon. The other was a psychiatrist of many years' experience, to whom I deferred as being very knowledgeable. I was surprised to discover, after a while, that she envied me having studied people, via history and literature, rather than diseases, and that she found her envy almost too difficult to conceal and tolerate.

During the first of the two years, a patient was allocated, to be seen at least three and preferably four times a week, under supervision, paying a reduced fee which went to the Society. As trainees we analysed a second patient of the different sex under the guidance of the same superviser. Later I often wished that those two people had come for analysis when I was more experienced. At the time I was even less competent with one of them than with the other—he had been forced to leave his country and both parents when he was still quite young and had even had to accept his original name being taken from him: he had never heard from them since those losses. But it was helpful to me that neither of the patients had been told I was a beginner, as training patients are nowadays. They never detected it, and one of them even commented "innocently" on the threadbare state of the carpet, which she *said* indicated how long I had been in practice. At the time I did not sense that that was her indirect way of trying to criticise my inadequacy. Since then I have developed an internal superviser, who would probably spot that kind of interaction, and help me to interpret suitably.

There was an obvious advantage in having only one superviser, who got to know how his or her future colleague worked with two quite different individuals. The disadvantage to the trainee was in not getting to know—to follow or to diverge from—the methods and styles of two more experienced members, as happens now, over and above the opinion of the personal analyst.

After two years of seminars and of more or less satisfactorily analysing the training patients, it was possible to apply for membership. There was no formal examination, which might have shown how much or how little of Jung's *Collected Works* we had read and digested, as well as other recommended books and papers. As I was not doing a full-time job during those years, I did in fact read many of Jung's large green volumes, assiduously taking notes to help me through the many passages where the meaning had to be teased out from his complicated style. His wide reading was fascinating even when the connection with present difficulties was not always clear. More weight was given, I think, to personality factors in the trainee and to the assessment of quality in clinical work than to learnedness in analytical psychology. In that feature of the training, as it was then, the Society was already showing itself as differing to some extent from how Jungian groups in other countries were developing. No written work—such as a paper illustrating a theme—was required, but this soon became one of the important parts of qualification. I did in fact write a non-clinical one simply out of interest, which developed from curiosity about Jung's hallucinatory experience of "The Seven Sermons to the Dead", which he described in *Memories, Dreams, Reflections.* I will describe it in the next chapter.

There was, as there still is, a large Analytical Group meeting each month, open to all members and trainees, which at first I found rather awe-inspiring. At that event a paper was read and discussed. It was a good way of gradually learning as much as we could imbibe. The front row with the more comfortable armchairs was implicitly reserved for the most senior and prestigious members, though one or other of them occasionally chose not to occupy them. There were none of the many committees and sections which have grown up since then. I could tell that there were various points of view but I was too unsophisticated to detect major differences and attitudes which might, and indeed did, cause a lot of trouble later. I do not remember there being any Young Turks, but I expect there were, without my having detected them. I was not in any case interested in factions or other political goings-on: I think was fully occupied psychologically with discovering step by step how I could personally adapt to my new profession. I doubt if I more than vaguely sensed there might be serious power struggles going on, under the surface.

That insensibility to crises among my seniors broke suddenly, about six months before I would be in a position to apply for membership: I received a letter from, I think, the Chairman of the Training Committee informing me in careful terms that my analyst had resigned from the Society, having undertaken a Kleinian training (that would result in him eventually becoming a member of the Freudian Institute of Psychoanalysis, completely separate from the Jungian Society of Analytical Psychology). The letter added that, since there was not very long before I could apply, the Committee was not going to require me to finish the training with another, acceptable, analyst. After that it would be up to me what I did about it. At that time in the history of the Society, it was not possible for an analyst responsible for training a future member to have an analysis with someone outside the Society. The methods and theoretical concepts differed too widely.

I could sense that there was a major crisis going on, so to speak, behind my back, but I cannot now remember whether its significance for the Society came across to me. The letter from the training committee was disturbing in a personal way, but not more than that: I had not yet developed a full community feeling with the rest of the Jungian world. It woke me up to see that the fairly recent changes in Jackson's style of analysing, for example, an increasingly sharp or more formalistic and body-based way of interpreting the contents and imagery of my dreams, had carried a meaning or a quality I had not found more than bothersome and slightly irritating. In any case he had never been one to use technical terms, such as archetypes. I did not know whether other analysts did, either in England or in other Societies. But his unpunctuality had got worse: when I knew that he was doing a Kleinian training I imagined that the bad time-keeping was an aspect of his being under strain and having to fit in the times of going to his own analysis, but I had not become any better at complaining about it than I always had been. Apart from un-punctuality he had most of the time seemed to me to be a strict person where methods of work were concerned, but also some-one with whom I could sense that he fully understood many lay-ers of suffering. He had been entirely human (to borrow a word normally used in more tragic and collective situations) whenever I was in a particularly stressful state. At the same time, I was not really as upset as, I gathered later, more experienced and politi-cally minded members of the Society assumed I would be.

It was perhaps strange that it all felt to be only a minor blip, but I think the reason may have been that the professional Jack-son had changed, meaning that his previous agreement with the main lines of the Jungian inheritance no longer held, but that he as a person in himself was still the same. And, writing about it now, so many years later and in terms he would probably not agree with, I think the archetypal Self had held validly in him as well as in me.

All that may sound extremely unsophisticated now that there are forty Societies, Associations and Groups world-wide, each with their own character, internal rivalries and variously struc-tured trainings. When I started, in the early Sixties of the twenti-eth century, the London Jungians had been running themselves as a professional organisation only since 1945, when the seven original members, each with their own personal histories and experiences, formed themselves (technically) into a Company, under the skilful guidance and powerful influence of Michael Fordham, with the specific aim of training more analytical psychologists. The general public in the mid-twentieth century knew a certain amount about Freudian psychoanalysis, especially as its influence on contemporary writers and painters was already important, but much less about analytical psychology, which was developing from Jung's work. The bitter quarrels between the two major founders were still all too alive in the profession itself, but were not part of general knowledge, including my own family, for example. If known about, they were understood in over-simple terms: Freud was scientific (which was Good) and had had no room for religion (which he had said was neurotic), Jung was unscientific (which was Bad) and *was* interested in religion.

As it turned out for me, the greater flexibility of Jungian ways of working suited me better than the Freudian orientation would have. I have appreciated the breadth of approach to all matters psychological among most of those trained to be Jungians. While trying not to miss a chance of building bridges towards "the Other Lot", I do know that simply looking for similarities can gloss over genuine and important differences. The contrasts and points of disagreement between Freudians and Jungians have something in common with those between, for example, Catholics and Protestants (Cats and Prots when I was an irreverent schoolgirl).

Fifteen

Analytical Psychologist in London

For thirty-five years, from 1964 to 1999, I was an active member of the International Association of Analytical Psychology (I.A.A.P.) through having become a member of one of its now forty constituent bodies, the London Society of Analytical Psychology (S.A.P.). This chapter describes how I grew from trainee to full analyst and learned how to listen effectively to my patients, how I felt about some Jungian ideas, such as interpreting dreams, how I viewed conflicts within the Society and how many of my papers came to be published. (Acronyms are so widely used that I have fallen for allowing them in here, and will use them when necessary. They do not always turn into useful words, and may even have flippant meanings when featuring in a different setting than their original one. For example, in an apparently friendly conversation: "You are a Sap!"— meaning a bit of an idiot.)

My path to becoming an analytical psychologist was full of twists, turns and variety, since I had started out in an apparently unrelated career, as a history teacher. Yet as I look back on how my interest in psychology developed, it seems to encompass and synthesize many ideas and activities that already were a part of my life.

My first hope, in my idealistic adolescence, had been to follow some kind of international career, seeing that possibility in wide political terms—many nation-states were trying uncomfortably to get on together under the umbrella of the League of Nations. The League was meant to be a body which would work towards reconciling its diverse and rivalrous members' needs and wishes without resorting to arms. And I would contribute to that effort. The League failed in its central aim of providing "collective security" against war, but it was one of the casualties in the struggle against Hitler. So my hope, inherited from my father, of taking part in some way or other with people who also wanted to reconcile differences, had to wait.

The second stage, during my more realistic adult life, in the middle years of the century, was to combine marriage and parenthood with contributing to bringing together men's and women's often conflicting needs and wishes, though only within admittedly restricted social limits. I wanted neither to emphasise differences nor to do away with them, but to contribute to seeing that each had its maximum chance of development. It was feminism but not sex war.

The third stage was the one of trying to find a convincing way of reconciling conflicts within and between individuals. Politics and sociology gave way to psychology. The area of activity had shrunk, but the theme was the same. History and poetry were essential parts of me.

In one of the seminars with Michael Fordham, during the training, we were discussing the chapter in Jung's very much edited memoir, *Memories, Dreams, Reflections* (which had only recently been privately translated into English), in which Jung describes the dreams, the visions and "the incessant stream of fantasies" which were released in him after distancing himself from Freud and the outbreak of the war in 1914. Those visions culminated in 1916 in the experiences recorded in the strange document with its latin title *Septem Sermones ad Mortuos.* It was written in archaic language. I asked Michael what it was, and I remember the way his face lit up in interest. He asked me if I would like to see it: it was not yet published but he had an early photo-copy of it, which I could borrow.

I found it to be very obscure and impenetrable until I discovered that by reading it as though it were poetry it came alive. I began to tease out possible interpretations of who or what the various characters were standing in for, without at once starting to research them properly. Their representations in Jung's production were versions of what he had found in early post-Christian, Gnostic, writings. Michael knew that I had studied history at Cambridge, and when I told him that I would like to find out more he offered me several of his books about gnosticism and I wrote a paper on it all, published in 1966.

One of the important outcomes, for me, of some research into the whole matter produced the important clue that Gnostics and their system of thought came from the greek word for knowledge (i.e. knowledge of religious truth, goodness, evil and so on) and that could be found through inner experience rather than as the result of imposed authority. Jung had painfully deviated from classical Freudian authority and he seems to have been a most appropriate person to soak himself, on his own, in Gnostic productions. The search for truth by means of encouraging previously unconscious, unrecognised, internal elements of the psyche to rise to the surface can be seen as one of the central features of both Freud's and Jung's overall work. But Jung wanted to go about the work in his own almost heretical way. Other Jungians later investigated the origins and meanings of *The Seven Sermons*; some of them, but not all, agreed with what I had written. The Sermons had become a subject that was of interest among Jungians, and one of the important roots of that was Jung's own keenness throughout his life to go on trying to find out more on everything he took up.

For me, bringing together my main interests was important: a historical subject, its psychological meaning, and using poetry as a way of gaining insight. I think it was at about that time that I wrote a poem which put many of my thoughts and beliefs into words. Michael's encouragement enabled me to step into the previously unknown world of people who gave papers. And, hopefully, I would go on.

Isaiah

When all is said and done,
And a great deal, under the sun,
Every day, is done and said,
Between the dawn and the moon-time bed—
When all, as I thought,
Is organized, marketed, and bought,
There is still Isaiah crying:
Ho, everyone that thirsteth,

Come ye to the waters:
Finished with selling and buying,
Finished with birth and death,
And sons, and daughters—
The thirst for life is all that is left
For the giving and the bereft.
Ho, he cries, and ho again,
And the stream still flows,
The simple rain,
The flowering rose,
The grapes of delight,
Both the sweet and the sour,
The grapes of wrath and the grapes for wine—
Life is vinegar, sharp, and a piercing hour
In the eternity of night.
Pain is yours, pain is mine,
But, come, he said, to the waters, Ho,
Find the stream, and drink, and go.

Through the wilderness they went,
For, go, he said,
And going is going on to the utmost extent:

It might be hell-for-leather, or slowly,
It might be high-and-mighty, or lowly;
And in the heart and in the head,
Joined in the words and in the silence,
Were compassion and patience.

After I had written about Jung's *Seven Sermons* I moved from the academic kind of exploration into considering how much analytical concepts could be adapted into being useful in limited psychotherapy. Most of my patients early in my years as an analyst, apart from the ones I had seen during my training, were undergraduate students and could only come to therapy once a week, in term-time. What, I wondered, could be found out about the differences and similarities between full analysis, as pursued in the Society at that time, requiring several sessions each week, and psychotherapy, since I knew them both from experience? In the next paper that I wrote I gave three short vignettes of sessions with people in brief therapy at University College. There emerged ideas about how images, contributed by the patients in a wide variety of ways, could develop into effectively symbolic and mutative forms when I listened and responded to them with an analytical attitude on the look-out for potential symbolism, even if it was what some full-blown analysts would call "only" psychotherapy. I was trying all the time to extract from simple or even apparently banal communications the potential they held for some symbolization, which, if it became conscious, would contain a healing quality.

Much was always nearly hidden, defensively, but my experience of analysis had given me the taste for that way of listening and interacting. In the training I had come across the danger of trying to get the patient to accept too soon how defensive they were being, and had learned that an enthusiasm for freeing them before they had enough trust was worse than useless. A lot seemed to hinge round a therapeutic attitude in the therapist: it was even more worth while to notice and make use of details in once-a-week short therapy than it is in analysis because there might not be another chance. Timing was important. The other "discovery" was that gently, or carefully, pointing out, early on, even small examples of negative feelings, especially ones about me, would help a patient to make the most of his or her ambivalences in other parts of life and prevent the treatment becoming cosy.

A rather well-known psychoanalyst, David Malan, had a book published about research into methods of work in brief psychotherapy at about the same time as my paper, "The Symbolic Attitude in Psychotherapy", appeared in the *Journal of Analytical Psychology* (1969). In it he described much the same approach as mine, and at first I felt a little rueful. But at that time, the Nineteen Sixties, there was almost no professional contact between Freudians and Jungians, in England, (nor was there for about forty more years, and then it was the Jungians who made the first approach), so I soon realised that my sore feelings were childish. Anyway, I was much too little known to make an impact on a powerful Freudian.

Between the times when I wrote those two rather experimental papers I had become a member of the S.A.P. Looking back now, I can see that there was not, for me, much of a psychological difference between being in training and being a member, although there was the practical one of being free to work without supervision. Belonging to a discussion group might have taken the place of that, and I knew that some sets of ex-trainees, if they felt they formed a good-enough "family", went on meeting for mutual support. But that was not available, and there was a gap where stand-in "brothers" or "sisters" might have been. As my ex-analyst was not around, for example at meetings, I could not develop a colleague way of relating to him. It was all certainly worth while, although I found myself to be in a new version of the old situation of feeling on my own. Belonging to a group would have shown me that most new analysts feel like that. Alone, but not necessarily lonely.

As I had not previously been a member of a recognised profession, except for the short time of being a school teacher many years ago, it was difficult to see myself as being an individuated person, meaning in Jungian terms the individual I could possibly be. There are some Jungians who define, or describe, individuation as being the person I really am, whole, and distinct from other people. Whatever subtleties are read into Jung's term, whether its status is a becoming or an achieved state, I realised that I was at risk of falling into an idealisation of the concept of the fulfilled individual and that it would take a long time, (most likely the rest of my life). That realization pulled me up sharp. I remembered the image that one of the lecturers at the London Institute of Education had given us students (about thirty years before): "You can't turn a cabbage into a rose, just do the best you can to produce a good cabbage". I read as much as I could, rapidly, of what Jung had written about individuation—and one of the helpful things was that it meant enriching conscious psychological life with as much as possible from the area of unconsciousness.

Those thoughts early on in my time as an analyst laid the foundation for later thinking about one of the central concepts in analytical psychology, the personal feeling of self and the archetypal Self. (The word *archetype* is often a stumbling block to understanding Jungian psychology: apart from its original, greek, philosophical sense, the shortest way of defining it is to call it a psychological instinct). In the Jungian journal I know best (the London *Journal of Analytical Psychology*), there have been more papers about the self than about any other concept we use, and over the whole Jungian world there must have been many thousands. I should think it would take most of a life-time to read *all* that has been written—by Jungians, Freudians, philosophers and others—about the many aspects of what different practising analysts, intellectual theorists and ordinary people mean by self.

Where I was concerned there was still an uncomfortable overlap between many childhood experiences of being warned not to be selfish, so I had to adapt to a much more sophisticated approach to what turned out to have multitudinous and even variable meanings. Among many other kinds, identified by analysts, there is the healthy self and the damaged one, the narcissistic self, the original one and the false one, the big Self and the day-by-day small self, the archetypal hero or heroine self, the feeling of self, the dying self, and there is even the post-modern self. The careful daily work with patients of many kinds required the effort of finding out, on their behalf, as many as possible of the variations, in each of them, of something which sounds so simple. Mastering even a little of all those learned studies might even result in having too little time for relaxing, as often as possible, into ordinary life. We need time off. In the early days of Freud himself, and Jung too, analysts used sometimes to see patients professionally during vacations, on lakeside or mountain walks. Or they would meet accidentally. Those early analysts took far longer holidays than present-day ones do, who keep much more strictly to pre-notified separations.

Another helpful discovery I made when looking up about individuation was that in the Editorial Note at the beginning of Jung's *Psychological Types* (1923), the words "fallow period" were used about his state in the years of 1913 to 1917 or 1918: it was not so much "Confrontation with the Unconscious", or even "breakdown", but an image from country life. In traditional farming, fields rested every few years, not producing a crop, and the farmer trusted the goodness of the soil to replenish the growing potential which was invisible, underground—or, for us, in the unconscious layers of the psyche. There are times when a sophisticated psychological concept, such as individuation, can be given extra meaning when supported by an image borrowed from experience and wisdom. That is humbling when there is a temptation to use four-syllabic jargon words, which are worse than useless when talking to people unconnected with our specialism.

When I was thinking, still simplistically, about individuation I also began to be especially interested in another notion, the helpful dynamic connection which Jung made between the archetype of the child and futurity. The Child is the potential. He pointed out the frequency of child gods in myths, of child figures in dreams paving the way for change, development and the healing of opposite forces in us. The popularity of the mid-winter celebration of Christmas, the birth of an archetypal baby, even among many unbelievers, preceding the hoped-for spring, continues year after year, and it is expressed in every possible symbolic representation.

I found it immediately helpful when I saw a child version of me in a dream, early in my analysis, not as representing regression to my personal and often unhappy childhood, but a much more forward-looking possibility of growing through difficulties, bringing together bits of myself which had not looked hopeful at first sight. There was one dream where chunks of harsh broken building materials, ugly in their greyness, could not possibly be reconstituted by the small girl, me, who was vainly trying to reassemble them, but at the same time she was unwilling to see any value in broken grey stuff. Her confusion and ambivalence were obvious. And it can easily be seen that greyness in the dream was standing in for depression, as it often does. Moreover, when I was young "they" often said I was an obstinate child, which was depressing. But if there was, according to the dream, a rather crazy determined version of me, even invisible, there was still a hope of doing the probably impossible.

The typically Jungian idea of there being an unconscious hopeful possibility of moving forwards—hidden within what had seemed to be an all-too-obvious feeling of being stuck in broken greyness, which could not be mended and seemed irrevocably valueless—was just what I needed. The possibility of change hidden in the archetype of the Child could be of use. I even discovered the idea, surprising to me at that time, that being depressed could be valuable if it was accepted: I reproached my analyst, who seemed pleased with the grey dream, whereas I had been working hard to get rid of depression, thinking that was what my analysis was for. I had considered I was doing well, dashing about keenly, full of valuable ideas. He asked: "What have you done with your depression?" I felt he had asked: "What have you done with your *lovely* depression?" He must be crazy. Alas, I had been using a manic energy as a defence against accepting the painful task of finding out more about my troubles.

Among the general public it is well known that analysts are interested in dreams. That is of course because the stories and images in them are pointers to what is going on at the unconscious level in the mind. Among any other reasons for seeking analysis, the patient probably needs to find out what he or she did not realise, matters which were seriously affecting their conscious lives. So for analysts the more dreams the merrier.

Some patients dream many times each night and remember a great deal; others do not. Some people remember much more during the time when they are in analysis than they do later. But if the analyst asks for dreams, that may be counter-productive for a patient whose intimate privacy is centrally important to him or her, and who is not yet trustful, perhaps having had confidences required during adolescence by an intrusive or anxious mother. Also, for someone who is very anxious to please, being asked for dreams can be persecutory or make him merely compliant and thereby distort the relationship, even making the two of them into teacher and pupil. Or it can produce another reaction, an overproduction of them, which floods the analyst, rendering him or her useless. I am not myself in favour of asking a patient to write down the dream, because the spontaneity of it can easily be lost. The way a dream is told may be the most important factor. The therapy can turn into an investigation of the dream content rather than an analysis of the dreamer. It is often important to wait for a dream to be told, perhaps near the end of the session, when it will on its own illuminate what had been going on between the two people. Another patient might remember a dream, apparently out of the blue, when some new feature is beginning to emerge, carrying its own dynamism and perhaps reinforcing a connection to some new insight.

I once had a patient who was an artist, in many ways well adapted to the life style she had adopted. She dreamed, from time to time, but not excessively: I was taken by surprise when she appeared one day with a bulging portfolio of so many pictures that there was not room all over every bit of the floor to display them all, let alone comment or try to interpret the meaning of any of them, or their serial quality. It was the meaning of the action, and not the content, which had to be deciphered. I thought, from time to time, that being a detective must use some of the characteristics that I needed. Curiosity, but not too much inquisitiveness: waiting was part of the job, as well as going forward quickly, even bravely, at other times. Perhaps a sixth sense: intuition is the word.

When Jung was giving a seminar on dreams, at a meeting of the Zürich Psychological Club, in the Nineteen Twenties, he stressed that

> Dream analysis is the central problem of the analytical treatment . . . the main object of this treatment is, as you know, to get at the message of the unconscious. The patient comes to the analyst usually because he finds himself in an impasse or cul-de-sac, where there seems no way out, and he assumes that the doctor will know a way . . . It is important that the doctor admit he does not know: Then both are ready to accept the impartial facts of nature, scientific realities . . . Dreams are objective facts.

Freud's view that they are the "royal road" to the unconscious is well known, presumably meaning their action as well as their content.

Analysing dreams was of course one of the many bases of the work that I did with my patients, when we were trying cooperatively (as conveyed by Jung) to unravel the meaning of the images in them. Any analyst is probably also keen to find out what work the patient is unconsciously doing, perhaps via dreams, in the area of overlap between the dreamer's and the analyst's psyches. And it is up to the analyst to examine carefully just what that overlap or interaction consists of, and means in a personal way: in almost all cases there is much going on, not necessarily or only at the unconscious level, between both people.

What the patient has projected, mainly unconsciously, into his or her impressions of the analyst (a projection technically known, of course, as "the transference", different from rapport and from the incorrectly and popularly imagined "falling in love with the analyst") usually turns up in dreams. Other dreams either really are, or seem to be, absolutely free from any kind of current situations or people, and represent clearly the distilled essence of the archetypal background at work in the dreamer's mind. They have a mythological character, for example, or they are reminiscent of fairy tales known or half-remembered from childhood, which have come from many parts of the world. Or some kind of immediately striking quality stands out at once as immensely important.

Various writers have reported series of dreams about, for example, floods, falls, eruptions such as active volcanoes, murders, wars, and many other collective dramas. There can be an obvious connection with contemporary events, but the personal basis usually emerges as actually more significant than the obvious dramatic or world-wide character of such collective images.

I found, early in my time as an analyst, that the danger sometimes was of being fascinated by the pictures or the actions in such dreams and of being seduced by the dramatisation to such an extent that I could fail to look out for the personal meaning hidden in it. On such occasions I had to beware of interpreting in a reductive way, which might convey to a sensitive patient that I was distanced, or not involved enough in the emotions at work in him or her. But, by way of contrast, I remember one occasion when a patient was scoffing at a comment I had made, about what seemed to her to be quite simple and meaningless: I said I had to fetch the meaning from a long way off and bring it into the present. It felt important to alert her to something she might be wanting to disregard.

A series of dreams with the same theme can be typical for many people. One of my own series was of being in a house, sometimes one I could recognise. I was exploring level after level, but invariably there was a blocked-off door, or even a wing of the house, shut off by a thick plastered partition, or double-locked, with no key. I felt unable to do anything about how to get through it, and there seemed to be no-one to help me. There was another series, more sinister, in which the central image was of broken buildings, devastation, destruction, as though a merciless air-war attack had done its worst to all possible life that had once flourished there. Optimism had been wiped out. But in one of that series there was a small, low-lying and tentative plant, a weed. Hope, and new life of some sort, did still just exist. And many years later I dreamed of walking, in the company of previous versions of myself, through my old university town (where I had learned and enjoyed so much, before moving on to fully adult life): it was being reconstructed with warm-coloured and freshly cut limestone, not because it had been bombed, but from it having reached the time for renewal.

I have to temper the optimism implicit in the extract I gave above from one of Jung's statements, made in Zürich nearly ninety years ago: there is not always such calm cooperation between analyst and patient as he seemed to convey. There are times when the patient does not want to find out what might be a sinister meaning in a dream, and in that case keeping my mouth shut was the wisest course, waiting for a time when the difficult matter could be approached with less fear.

Without specifying actual patients, dreams or times, I can remember more than one occasion when I had a hunch about the most likely negative, or even sinister, meaning of a patient's dream, and said nothing. How I saw it, too quickly, might be wrong: hunches and intuitions cannot always be trusted. An example is when the dreamer feels sure that the dream is almost magically predictive, while the analyst may be more impressed by its wish-fulfillment quality, which may be defensive against negative factors, as yet undiscovered. Parallel to that, having myself on occasion woken up just after dreaming something which shows me up in a far from flattering light, I have a tendency to put it aside, with only a vague message to myself about its probable meaning, which I will investigate when I'm not so busy. And that time does not come. So the problem has to be re-presented to me in another dream, hopefully with more emphasis.

In quite a few situations it is the psychological action and way or time of reporting a dream which are more meaningful than its content. I remember one particular patient who dreamed very little, and when she did have a dream to report she always prefaced her account of it by telling me there was nothing in it, it wasn't important, only a little dream. Also she kept on saying she was tired, she didn't know why, and everything was difficult. I thought that perhaps her attitude to her dreams, what had been happening during the unconsciousness of sleep, had some kind of connection with the way in which she used to run down all her day-time relationships, and she was apparently struggling hard to stay in the victim position. It turned out that her way of coping with losing friends was represented by further dreams where she was being the superior one, on the high moral ground, when accepting her relative ordinariness was too difficult. Rather than disregarding her statement about her dreams, paying attention to it led me to gain insight into her situation. It turned out that the denigratory scenes in the patient's earlier dreams had contained their opposites, and this information was useful in her analysis.

I also remember another patient, a man, who revealed that he had heard that people having a Jungian analysis dreamed marvellous and Big Dreams. He had thought they should be archetypal and full of impressive symbols, while his dreams did not impress him much. When that idealising and persecutory idea had been cleared out of the way, he began to reveal much more, and more often, of what had happened during the sleeping hours. The dreams were actually important in connection with his need to attend to the tensions at work in his inner life. And from then on the dream images became as it were bigger, more impressive, but not fully archetypal, and he took valiant strides ahead in the task of working through life-threatening situations. He had had to be satisfied with what he had earlier thought was banal.

In the day-to-day work of being an analyst, listening to patients' dreams, encouraging them to associate to the various images (rather than barging in at once with a clever interpretation), and in one way or another enabling the small shoots of psychological growth to flourish, so that life-enhancing progress takes place—in that process the patient is offering the analyst a really remarkable tribute of trust. The privacy of the dream is being shared, the normally hidden fears or difficult and violent emotions are revealed. The poet W. B. Yeats' well-known remark in *He Wishes for the Cloth of Heaven* needs to be remembered:

I have spread my dreams under your feet;
Tread softly because you tread on my dreams.

Another patient comes to my mind. She seemed to be hardly
engaged at any depth in the distress for which she had come to
analysis. There was a kind of blandness about her and I started
wondering why I never looked forward to her sessions. I felt
neutral towards her, which was unusual, and I had to examine
what was going on.

My thoughts turned first to thinking there might be some kind
of hidden attack or destructiveness at work. Was it hers or mine?
Putting thought into the problem, even if it was not correct,
helped me to regain some potential of being of use to her. In literally the next session, without more than a little prompting
from me, she revealed that between sessions—which she said
were difficult—she had been examining what had happened in
them, but had not wanted me to discover that she was running a
parallel self-analysis, in which everything was simple and easy. I
had in effect been "carrying" her powerful negativity and she
had been unconsciously manipulating the relationship between
her and me, in order for her to prove to herself that she was the
knowing one. There was no question of blaming her, which she
revealed she had been fearing, having imagined I was going to
be a kind of school teacher, reprimanding her. When all that
came to light she loosened up, dreamed frequently and began to
find how that kind of interaction had damaged her family relationships during her childhood. She had worked hard, psychologically, to keep me from knowing how often she had been unhappy at home, and what a relief it had been to go to boarding
school in her 'teens. After that realisation her sense of humour
developed and I began looking forward to seeing her. That improvement had not come about through working specifically on
dreams, but by means of me trying to find out more about the
interaction between her and me, which in another patient might
have shown up via how she was dreaming.

Before leaving the subject of dreams and dreaming, it is worth
writing about a TV programme I once took part in. The organis-
ers of it in the B.B.C. had made up an imaginary dream which,
in the first part of the programme, was performed by a profes-

sional actor. Then another actor, well known at that time, came first to me, meant to be a typical Jungian analyst, and lay on the couch in my consulting room. None of that had been rehearsed in advance, and in fact he himself chose the couch rather than one of the chairs—which he probably did not realise might have been more typical for a Jungian treatment. We talked about the dream and I responded to what he said, as I might with a real patient, aiming at enabling and encouraging him to expand on various bits of it and to tell me his free associations, then myself commenting on them. The "session" was soon very lively, including the "patient" becoming agitated and finding it was all too near the bone. He put his hand up to the camera, to stop me and the recording. I did not discover whether the fabricated dream had come uncomfortably near his personal complexes and my "analysis" too actually painful, or simply (which was perhaps more likely) that he was a skilled actor. He then went on to have the dream analysed by a typical Freudian analyst. That "session" was in a completely different style: he remained calm throughout. He was asked a series of questions, and then he more or less answered them. The tone was much more restrained than it had been with what I had hoped was a Jungian approach.

The next part of the programme was the "patient" going to a dream laboratory, which demonstrated scientifically how the sleeper's Rapid Eye Movements indicate that a dream is taking place. One of my real patients at the time was very angry with me at the programme having been filmed in my own consulting room, her private place with me. I apologised to her. And I regretted that I had not warned her in advance, and foreseen that she would feel I had been insensitive—it had simply been the only room to use. The next week we remedied the trouble, the wound healed and after her analysis we became long-term friends.

I was very disappointed that the Freudian analyst was unwilling to discuss the programme, either before or after it was filmed. That was typical of the distance there was between professionals of the two main trainings in London at the time. It is not quite so extreme nowadays, but there is still room for much improvement, because analytical psychologists are, on the whole, looked down on by traditionally trained psychoanalysts, who seem to believe we are woolly-minded. There is also a tendency, and in the general public too, to confuse Jungian interest in religion and spirituality with mysticism, a term often used in a derogatory way.

Human beings have dreamed ever since the earliest days of recorded history, and probably earlier. Perhaps the often-noticed twitchings of family dogs during the evening indicates (even if unscientifically) that mammals earlier in the scale of evolution also have some kind of pre-verbal mental experience. I mention that to emphasise that what I have been writing is about the activity of dreaming, not dreams in themselves. When possible I try to give verbs priority, not nouns.

The somewhat enclosed world of analytical psychology, in England, in several American centres and elsewhere, was seriously rocked during the Nineteen Seventies, when variations in ways of working, theories, concepts and affiliations turned out to be diverging in major ways. Differences in Jungian analysts' backgrounds, personalities, beliefs, friendships, loyalties and ways of working emerged from the woodwork: they had been there potentially, and even partially perceived, for about thirty years, at any rate in London, which was the centre I knew best. Ever since the early days when the main founders, Freud and Jung, discovered mostly painfully that they were too different to be able to go on working in the same organisation, such major divergencies had been likely between those in later generations of professionals.

It is ironic that certainly Freud, and perhaps to a lesser extent Jung, did not understand the other's personality at all well. It has often been remarked that neither of them had an analyst apart from and outside himself, and I can add that self-perception is not so discerning as what someone else can see. Jesus' image of motes and beams puts it well. The actual rift between the main strands of the movement (focussing round the two powerful men) was to a great extent known about from shortly before the cataclysm of the First World War—and that in itself illustrates the collective aspect of the personal antagonisms between those two and their respective followers/disciples. Many other professions have had, and will probably continue to have, the same divisions, affected to various extents by outside events.

The splits between the successors of the original specialists in psychological treatment, which it is convenient to call simply Freudians and Jungians, were repeated in various ways, within each main group, several times throughout the century. (In Britain the term *psychoanalyst* is reserved for those who have done the Freudian training). To a great extent the differences in the Jungians in the Nineteen Seventies were between those who had originally been to Zürich, working in analysis with Jung himself and/or with one of his close associates, and those of the next generation who had not been directly affected in that way, and who were being influenced by contemporary psychoanalytical ideas, as Fordham was.

Among the mainly senior London Jungians the rift was distressing in a directly personal way: for them the differences had been becoming too painfully evident to be concealed, whereas among at any rate some of those of the immediately next generation, of whom I was one, more general reactions to splits, and thoughts about them, were more important. In a very broad way the analysts on the two sides of the disputes were comparable to two people in a marriage who are not getting on at all well: each has days or times when it seems possible to work out whether they can stay together, and other days when the opposite certainty feels paramount. They are torn between the incompatible differences. In the body of Jungian analysis, the same opposite views were voiced by different people.

During 1975, '76 and '77 many meetings were held, some of the whole Society membership and others in particular committees. The series opened with the information that one of the founder members, Dr. Gerhard Adler, was setting up an alternative training to the one that had been operating since the Society had originally been organised. His earlier colleague, but by now rival, Dr. Michael Fordham, kept away from the meetings. The Society training had been master-minded by him, and he had always been chary of the danger of idealising the Great Man: Jung himself said he did not want that to happen. Fordham and those who supported his way of analysing paid much more attention to infancy and childhood than to archetypal material, which

Adler favoured. Also, the records of the meetings do not include specifically that much of the trouble lay in the personality contrast between Adler and Fordham, though that was well known. Several of the meetings were stormy, as was compatible with the fact that feelings no longer needed to be kept back. The main lines of the controversy swirled round the question of whether it was going to be possible any longer for there to be one, as compared with two, training bodies. And if there were two, could they be housed under one roof, or would they have to be separated completely?

Where the content of the trainings was concerned, the members who supported Adler's plans wanted closer attention to be given to Jung's way of working, and to those of his writings which were less closely studied, than was then current in the main Society, which was already more clinically oriented. The following subjects were to be given emphasis: the theory of complexes, myths and fairy stories or folk tales, dreams, psychological types, how Jung studied and applied the findings of the historical alchemists in clinical work, and the links between analysis and religion, art, and literature. To outsiders, much of that may sound esoteric (one of my unpsychological friends even flippantly said it reminded him of the absurd medieval conundrum of how many angels could dance on the point of a pin), but the controversy was close to most analysts' hearts and minds, their own anxieties combined with what they felt and thought was best for patients who had specifically chosen a Jungian analysis rather than a Freudian one. Among most mainstream Society analysts those cultural matters are personally very important, but as far as I know they are not very openly referred to with patients.

Other opinions were expressed round such themes as the destructive quality of the word *split* ("separation" would be better), and the description of crises in some of the sixteenth-century Reformed Churches which were later found to be not so very extreme. The moderates and optimists pointed out that the two groups would be separate, but neither superior to the other, to which the realists retorted by instancing the older rift between the followers of the two great men, which had never been repaired.

The outcome of the two years' discussions was that the people in the more traditional group sided with Adler and separated themselves completely from the Society. After that original departure, some of Adler's group left the new organisation, founded another one, and that also led to a further one being set up. The formation of those smaller groups does not only illustrate the tendency among all sets of more or less similar people to develop internal sub-sets, but is specific to the psychological descendants of Jung, who himself had two contrasted sides, the scientific researcher and the spiritual seeker. At various times in his life, those two parts of himself, two personalities even, jockeyed for supremacy. He managed, through a near-psychotic struggle and in a very individual way, to contain the two aspects. He was not a chameleon, but a psychological fighter, who had to summon all his inner strengths to sustain the tension.

Since the Nineteen Seventies at least seven other Societies that I know of have suffered similar painful splits, representing perhaps one way of growth and being pale replicas of the break between the early giants, Freud and Jung.

Later in my time as a working analyst I was a much more vocal member at meetings of the larger Society and in various discussion groups, than I was at the time of the mid-Seventies crisis. I remember being mainly interested in the themes and arguments put forward by the other members, people I knew well, but somehow I was not so emotionally involved, bitter or deeply moved in the way that they had been. Maybe it was cowardice and fear of conflict. Added to that I was more interested in individuals' ways of thinking and acting than in the collective life of the whole set-up. I did not yet feel deeply enough integrated to the S.A.P. as a group to be passionate about it all. It is also possible that the part of me which might have been capable of being really politically minded in the Nineteen Seventies had been fully exercised, even used up, in university and international student activity of the Nineteen Thirties, leading up to the Second World War. Once that had broken out, and in the succeeding years, I still had opinions but could take no open part in politics, neither as an individual nor collectively.

From the longest, or deepest, perspective the rifts among analysts are contemporary examples of the general human tendency to develop by means of differentiating: evolution and the origin of species work that way. Moving a little forward, to pre-history and the very early periods of recorded history, when people seem to have speculated, by means of myths and literature, about such fundamentals as the nature of forces which they pictured as being outside themselves—creative Good Gods and destructive Bad Devils—they saw them as warring opposites. In later times it has had to be learned, and accepted (if only with great difficulty), time and again, that the contrasts and struggles of those opposites cannot be by-passed, they are intrinsic to human beings, unavoidable, acute, sometimes terrifying, often repeated. They are inside each of us, as well as in "The Other".

During the years when I was taking part actively in the life of the S.A.P. (my stint as Honorary Secretary was extremely worthwhile for getting to know the workings of the growing Society and many individuals who became friends) I was also busy writing papers on many of the themes which clinical work throws up. There were three results from those activities, which gave me tremendous pleasure. The major ones, which I will return to, were of being Editor of the *Journal of Analytical Psychology* and of being elected to the committee of the International Association of Analytical Psychology, representing the S.A.P. The minor one was of being asked to join what was then seen as a prestigious Jung/Freud discussion group. It had been started by two prominent Jungian members, William Kraemer who was very knowledgeable and internationally minded, and Rosemary Gordon who was making her name as a clinician and writer. As well as Jungians they attracted good-quality and broad-minded psychoanalysts, and the quality of the fortnightly meetings (preceded by dinner in the houses of each of us in turn) was first-rate. We felt relaxed and brave enough to describe our work openly, confident that the atmosphere was generous even towards any member with whom we might heartily disagree. James Home, the psychoanalyst, who had written a wise and philosophical paper, *The Concept of Mind*, which earned him some criticism among Freudians at the time, wrote a flowery description (perhaps with his tongue in his cheek): 'Membership of the Jung/Freud group has always been open only to the best people—the best qualified, or the most aristocratic or the most humane, or the most beautiful, the most outrageous, the most extensively elusive, the most compactly to the point, the fittest in body and mind, the most perseveringly brave, easily the most experienced, the most practically adroit, the steadiest and most down to grassy earth, the most appropriately dressed, the most serenely and intelligently elegant, the most humanly comfortable'. That shows how analysts are not always seriously concentrating on miseries, their own and those of their unhappy patients. I have not been able to resist quoting what he wrote, out of nostalgia for those good evenings among peers.

As I look back on the years of being Editor of the *Journal of Analytical Psychology*, several things stand out, over and above the sense of responsibility mixed with excitement and apprehension when I started. My apprenticeship period was in collaboration with Fred Plaut, which sets the stage for the observation that all issues of the Journal are works of cooperation. So an important part of the day-to-day work is to combine what each worker on the team can contribute, being that particular individual, with a certain amount of editorial direction. Moreover it was always necessary to remember that the Editor was (at that time, ostensibly) in an elected position and we did not have an authoritative Board. We had a small committee, members of which were not over-keen to attend meetings more than once a year. When I sought advice (apart from help) the response was usually along the lines of 'Do what you think best, it will probably be all right'. If that sounds shocking to those in the present sophisticated anglo-american set-up, and an example of old-fashioned British muddling through, it is still a description of how it was then.

At first I found my position difficult: Michael Fordham had launched the Journal in 1955, and had been its long-time Editor, and when a new one had to be found/elected another senior member had understood that the job was going to be his. Only a few hours before the crucial meeting for the choice of his successor to be made, Michael switched his mind, and championed Plaut. I was Honorary Secretary at that time; I felt caught in the maelstrom of those senior doctors' emotions, very critical of Michael, and sympathetic to the unchosen one, who probably never forgave him. I mention that they were all three medicals, since when I later joined Plaut as Editor that made history, which had its own significance. Most of the time the Society has not been encrusted with the older medical versus non-medical rivalries.

So when Plaut's seven-year term as Editor came to an end it was I who joined him, at first for a year, which was then extended to two. And all in all I was in what certainly felt to be the exalted position of Editor for nine years, from 1978 to 1986.

The next thing that comes to mind is that the Editor is, to a great extent, at the mercy of the papers submitted. Their subject matter and quality depend closely, at any one time, on the impression potential writers have of the kinds of papers which are being published. That impression is not always as objective as an Editor could hope for: the opinion of quite a few members of the I.A.A.P.—that the S.A.P. was unduly influenced by psychoanalytic Kleinian theory—was, I thought, simplistic, and I struggled against the introduction of the term 'The London School' for that reason. A five-year Index for the Journal began to appear, in 1980, consisting of the following sections: Subjects, Authors in alphabetical order, Titles in chronological order of publication and selected Critical Notices and Book Reviews, so it has been possible to examine trends and fashions. Thorough research using the index would be very revealing of the changes there have been over the years of publication.

The next factor, which is a more positive one for an editor, is that from time to time some subject is 'in the air' which he or she can notice, or sense, and use to advantage. For example, one or more other papers might be in the pipe-line, and several new ones may be submitted about then, having something in common with each other, which can either be used in one issue, if the editor asks the earlier authors to be patient about the date of their paper's publication, or the editor can encourage other possible analyst-authors to consider making a contribution which would fit well. The assessors of submissions did not always agree on the quality or value of a paper, but I have heard that in prestigious scientific journals there is often long-drawn-out agony all round, especially for the author. I had been warned by Fordham not positively to commission a paper, because it might turn out not to be good enough, and it could be very difficult to reject it.

That proviso did not apply to organising symposia of short communications, which I found very interesting to do. We had one on 'How do I Assess Progress in Supervision?,' in April 1982, which grew out of a Brief Communication from Fred Plaut under that title, the contributors being from Haifa, San Francisco, Paris, Zollikon, New York, Berlin and London. In 1985, there was a second symposium, on the Self, which I remember being inevitably difficult and likely to arouse tense argument. There is room for occasional symposia to pick up on topics which gradually or suddenly attract us. For a paper which was obviously going to be controversial, it was interesting to think of another analyst willing to write a Comment, which would be answered in the same issue. It was not easy to get people to submit Brief Communications, or reports of Work in Progress. I tried several times, as have other editors. I am not sure what the reluctance is due to: perhaps touchiness about criticism as well as the wish for the prestige of a full paper—which may then never get written.

Those are thoughts about the art of editing an analytical journal, though they do not exhaust the topic. Only very sophisticated writers are not sensitive about the fate of their submission, which is a child they have produced, nursed, sweated and agonised over. Waiting during the time between submitting and receiving acceptance is agony for most authors. The other aspect of the work is the craft of it, or, more crudely, the technique. The all-round quality of each issue depends on both factors. And I think the Journal owes its good reputation to attending closely to both. Of course I had to learn how to do it, from scratch. It so happens that, being obsessional, I actually enjoy proof-reading. Early in my term of office, I complained to the sub-editor John Lucas (whose main work was on one of the national broadsheets but who was working for the Journal professionally) about some misprints: he came back to me most severely, telling me that the Editor was responsible for everything, from cover to cover. The onus was a heavy one, since I was not a trained journalist, but pride in producing each issue as well as possible came in useful, especially as Jim Seddon, with his loud laugh in the Society's office, was learned, devoted and vigilant, but slips did creep in.

In later years when other editors had succeeded me, it was inevitable to wish that we had continued to publish the Journal only twice annually because so much work was involved. However, after initial misgivings I thought it was probably right to publish quarterly because there were enough good submissions and the flow of them showed that analysts world-wide were being stimulated to write. But the voluntary work involved is really heavy.

When the Journal acquired Editors from both sides of the Atlantic, the responsibility for each of them became different, and what might have seemed to give it a personal slant was diluted.

During the Seventies and Eighties all sorts of now run-of-the-mill helpful technology was still in the future, there were far fewer analysts world-wide wanting to publish, and what I did now looks rather simple, slow and unsophisticated. The collective aspects and nature of analytical psychology, as shown now in the pages of the present-day Journal, puts my time into an almost pre-historic stage. I was in effect fortunate that it was manageable and enjoyable. And I have to admit that for a while I was so identified with it that the Journal *was* me. A flash of insight showed me that I had fallen into the inflation of the French seventeenth-century king Louis XIV's boast, *L'Etat, c'est moi.* That was the end of it.

Other editorial work came my way. It was the series of seven books first produced between 1973 and 1985, known collectively as the *Library of Analytical Psychology.* Although it had the blessing of the Society as its parent body, and was run, as usual, by a small committee of cronies, it was mainly inspired and continuously directed by Michael Fordham. The first two of the seven volumes which appeared over those years were collections of papers which had been published in the Journal, by a wide variety of London members. They represented the contemporary views, methods of working and theoretical developments which had grown out of the earlier and purer classical Jungian concepts. The other five volumes were by single authors and, while showing that each was obviously 'out of the same stable', typical for what was thought of in the wider Jungian world as the London version of ways of working, they gave an individual angle of their authors' breadth and depth. Since those first seven volumes, three more have been added, not so simply 'London' as the earlier ones: on child psychotherapy, on psychopathology and an up-to-date volume on maleness. It is gratifying that they all still sell well.

The title of one of the early collective ones, *Technique in Jungian Analysis*, which we had only reached after long discussion, turned out distinctly controversial: members who were not on the committee of production and came from the more classical wing of the Society disliked its flavour, seeing it as rigid and perhaps even, horror of horrors, somewhat Freudian-sounding, or derivative from the work of Melanie Klein. Her writing always reads unattractively dogmatic, even self-important. At that stage, Fordham was moving in that direction much more than were the other members of the committee. The title was meant to show how each writer worked, his or her style and methods, but it did of course convey those things rather more than the purely psychological or emotional nature of what goes on in day-to-day work with patients. On the other hand, the content of communications between the two people involved, and the successful outcome of the analysis, tends to vary according to the methods used. These matters are very subtle.

I felt rueful about the title because it had been my suggestion, and I had not realised its implications. It was not meant to be a text book on technique, but to convey ways of working, and we did in fact remember that Jung himself had eschewed anything which sounded like technique. That can be taught, style is individual. The book sold well, I think because it brought together the practical and the ideological quality of much post-Jungian work. Although there was almost nothing in it about myths or alchemy, which many classical Jungian analysts have developed over the years, based on Jung's own researches, the intrinsic quality of the psychological relationship between analyst and patient emerges as the central feature of therapy. My own view is that a continued attention, in my work, to self-analysis is the best protection for the patient against the neglect of healing in depth as compared to the "mere" cure of symptoms. The central characteristic of therapeutic work is that (hopefully) it blends head and heart: no long or learned words will ever replace those two simple ones. It is a pity if those remarks sound naïve or priggish.

My interest in all sorts of international issues, which grew from my early family background and from the world events when I was growing up, was given all the scope it needed when I attended several of the triennial I.A.A.P. congresses, and when I became a member of its executive committee. I found it an eye-opener to see how differently committee members from one or two countries behaved during meetings from what I was used to. I developed a regrettably holier-than-thou attitude towards the people who seemed to have no respect for the Chair, continually interrupting and going on talking too long. They did not always get their own way, which resulted in my privately enjoying a sort of *schadenfreude*. With the benefit of a long memory, that reminds me of an incident when I was attending an international student conference in Sweden, some time in the mid-Thirties: it had been discovered that my french was good enough for me to be used as a translator, and on one occasion a fierce participant with extremist views kept on jumping to his feet to protest, waving his arms and shouting that I was getting the speaker's meaning absolutely the wrong way round—it was monstrous, perfidious, colonialist, *british*. The audience was on my side, the chairman supported me, so a riot did not break out, though passions ran high. The issues were ideologically important, and a long way beyond any possible humour.

On several occasions attending a Congress, or some other kind of international meeting, led me to write a poem. Each time the poem grew out of a fantasy triggered either by the place or by some contemporary event. One such, in Chicago in 1992, produced itself (that was how it felt) as a result of staying in the luxurious Hilton Hotel—not my usual level of comfort— combined with the news of terrible wars in Africa. The theme of the congress was The Transcendent Function: Individual and Collective Aspects. The relevance of that theme evidently went further for me, and no doubt for others who had come from many parts of the world, than simply in connection with the professional papers. And it was at a time when some particularly tragic events were happening in Somalia. The poem, written on August 8, 1992, is as follows:

Early One Morning

Lean from the Hilton window
high in its moneyed power
facing the lake that's like my sea at home.
Look out at the rising sun
and forward to the breathtaking pictures
we'll see today on the walls of the famous gallery.

Try not to look at the far-below street
for along it there goes—to the inner eye—
a merciless stream of barely-covered skeletons,
mothers with milkless breasts,
big-bellied babies with over-large eyes,
gaunt men old before their time.

I saw them first not long before midnight.
Now it's dawn, they still drag along,
some of them fall, the rest go on.
Only death will end
the otherwise endless stream.

I can only refer in cool terms
to probably several millions.

Now I will ask for room-service breakfast,
paying later with my trusty card.

It will be wise for me not to speak,
at the Committee meeting,
of what I have seen,
staying instead with the acceptable agenda,
then enjoy a good lunch with my friends.
A few hours later we'll dine
in comfort,
with a modest bottle of wine.

The line of those people still flows on, and on, and on.
I will wave no flags.
I will only remember
the bones and rags.

Since that poem grew out of the fantasy of countless brown and black people, nameless to everybody but themselves and representing all those who have been driven from their homes by forces they cannot comprehend, the fantasy came from an archetypal level. I cannot think of a particular name among the usual lists of archetypes, which fits those people. Perhaps there is an archetype of the Family stretching from the days of palaeolithic cavemen to those of modern town-dwellers? They had nearly been driven from membership of the family of civilised mankind, and as the writer of that poem I was powerless to do anything practical to bring them back in.

On a lighter note, many other experiences came my way during the years of being a practising analyst. The regular one-to-one clinical situation, and the writing of papers, were complemented and fed by taking part in various collective activities, both in England and abroad.

One was a week-end meeting at the west country University of Exeter, where I was the only analyst among learned academic sociologists, and the unwinding in the evenings provided a good contrast to ordinary prosaic London life. The convener was as fond of Cornwall as I have always been and she encouraged me to write about what I suggested, the three-part psychology of the coast there: the tidal sea, the beaches and the cliffs. The sea represents the unconscious, with all its possible moods, beauties, misty sulks and raging storms, the home of countless marine creatures, the source of danger to people as well as of pleasures and food, and many more facts and emotions. The beach represents both family life, parents and children (happy at times, in tantrums at others), picnics, sand castles, games, and long walks in company or alone, as well as being the place where boats are pulled up out of winter dangers. The beach is the tide-ruled area where unconsciousness and consciousness overlap. I saw the cliffs as the guardians of conscious life, activity and effectiveness, leading to cultivated fields, crops, sheep, cattle, farms and coastal villages.

I remember John Layard, the anthropologist and psychologist, asserting that the beach I knew best, factually and sentimentally, was the most archetypal beach anywhere in Cornwall. Anybody can probably see that exciting quality in their particular favourite, anywhere in the world. Archetypes are shared, not private property. I have a soft spot for that paper, which became a chapter in the book of the conference.

Before moving on to describing some aspects of my life in the years after I had stopped being an active analyst, I would like to bring in the chapter I contributed to a collective book about "The paradox of disobedience in the lives of women". Its title was *To Speak or Be Silent*. The idea had been conceived by the New York Jungian analyst, Lena B. Ross, who invited a selection of women from more or less the whole world working in many different professions, each to contribute a chapter about any woman, or any set of women, who had been disobedient to the culture of their time. It was an exciting invitation: we contributors could make our choice from anywhere in myth, history or literature.

After much thought, trawling through all my interests, I chose Eve, the first woman known in the Genesis archives of Judaism and Christianity. She had sinned by disobeying God the Creator, who was said to have forbidden both Eve and her partner Adam to eat any fruit from the tree of the knowledge of good and evil in the Garden of Eden. Like millions of other people I had always found the story a fascinating one. My thought was that it conveyed, in effect, that the history of culture and the notions about enterprise have been founded on a woman's No. That was my personal, if perhaps idiosyncratic view: I showed Eve as having carried one-half of the human psyche, not just the minor one. I called her the first scientist, going bravely forward into danger—perhaps even foolhardily. I made out that she represents our natural need to find out about ethics, her environment, and the wider world, without being shackled or inhibited. I had always disliked the way in which Adam had been shown to be a wimp, giving in to a dictatorial boss, and I wrote that he should be seen as the necessarily cautious one, complementing the make-up of our joint psyches. The chapter in effect supported Jung's view of some of the opposite forces in humans, the urge towards consciousness and the need for obedience to fate. It was an expression of the contemporary view of women as receivers of life-giving potential, for example in sex and love, rather than being in mere passive attendance on men's needs.

Sixteen

Late Years and a Few Reflections

The novelist R. K. Narayan wrote at the beginning of the last chapter of his book *My Days, A Memoir*, 'I am inclined to call this the last chapter, but how can an autobiography have a final chapter? At best it can only be a penultimate one; nor can it be given a rounded off conclusion, as is possible in a work of fiction. The ending of this sort must necessarily be arbitrary and abrupt'. So it features as his chapter 17. In her autobiography, *Ask Me No More*, my sister Jenifer chose "Finale" for her last chapter, but that did not turn out to be an accurate title, since she lived on. She tells me it means the end of what she wanted to include.

In this, my last chapter, I am finding space for some items, connected with my later years, which did not fit in well before, papers, books and chapters in collections of pieces by several authors. Each of them circled in various ways, round the themes of time, development, change and age. I am also writing about some of the many places and pleasures that David and I enjoyed together, until he sadly died, unexpectedly and too soon.

In the early Nineteen Seventies my paper "Envy and the Shadow" had been published in the *Journal of Analytical Psychology*. Photocopying was not so common at that time as it became later, so that the extent to which all the available fifty offprints were asked for, from everywhere that the Journal was read, showed that the distressing emotion of envy is of great significance to analysts–as it is also to ordinary people, not only theologians, though it ranked as one of the medieval Church's Seven Deadly Sins. Without my openly admitting it, the paper was written out of my need both to keep on working on the theme, which dated of course from ordinary sibling rivalry, and to get through the difficulties it posed me, if at all possible.

It has often been noticed that some kind of personal need or residual anxiety is behind much of the objective interests and published work of analysts, without those writers revealing anything about the connection. Our writings are the sub-texts of our autobiographies. My memory of the french phrase "avoir envie de . . ." is one contribution to my way of seeing envy, since it simply means wanting something. As a child I often wanted what I could not have, though that was nothing to do with material shortages. Valid and ordinary hunger turns into anxious greed if that hunger is not met. In my attempts to see if analysis can contribute to politics, I think that that knowledge about infants can illustrate how adult victims in the political arena retaliate for the actions of those who colonised them in the past or who had been their deprivers and victimisers.

My theme was different from the one that Melanie Klein, that all-important post-Freudian psychoanalyst, had put forward, of how envy makes gratitude impossible. That is indeed an important feature of it, but she had located its presence later in the infant's psychological life than I proposed: I see hungry envy as earlier and more intrinsic than she did, part of the original endowment of all humans. From birth onwards, we have hungry impulses, which contain an element of attack (the infant "goes at" its mother's breast), and there is also the inborn potential for loving oneself, which leads to the development of concern for others than oneself, and to adult altruism. Of course upbringing and reasonably positive life experiences enable what the psychoanalyst Winnicott felicitously called "good enough" people to develop out of the original raw material of babyhood. Children can learn to alter "I want . . ." to "I need . . ." and then even to "Please can I have . . . ." I confessed to myself, when I wrote the paper, that I wanted it, one of my "children", to be better than hers. Envy at work: she was an older sibling.

I find that, as I grow older than I was when I was in practice, but while still being analytically minded, I have become more and more concerned to see whether the important insights of depth psychology learned through work with individuals can be of use when considering the stresses, violence and aggression in world affairs as they have developed in the recent half-century. Can there be an effective link between the two? Some analysts believe there can be, but I very much wonder whether our work can really be of use beyond our consulting rooms, at the public political level where hyper-murderous arms are the power behind the ordinary human endowment of aggression. Is it an illusion, or a grandiose optimistic wild-goose chase: can significant analytical observations and analysts themselves have a positive effect at national or world level? In a small discussion group of analysts from diverse backgrounds the theme was recently dismissed as obviously not worth considering.

Another example on the pessimistic side was when, in the Sixties, during the time of the Cold War and it looked possible that one or other politician of the rival states, in which there were large accumulations of nuclear weapons, might "press the button", a group of psychoanalysts ran a campaign to alert the world to the danger. It remains unknown whether the politicians took any notice. And, on the question as to whether people are more aggressive nowadays than in the past, it is a sad truth that modern weapons of all sorts are incomparably more deadly than was possible in the days of, for example, bows and arrows. So basic aggression is easily put into murderous action.

The envy paper also brought in the subject of the archetype of the Shadow. That concept is one of Jung's most valuable psychological legacies. The Shadow is that collection of unacceptable features of our characters that we individuals do not see, but others do, since it is like a physical shadow behind us when we are facing the sun (or, in another way of putting it, it is underneath, in the unconscious parts of our minds). It is expressed in that image form, rather than in an intellectual one, and that is perhaps one of the reasons why it has had so much impact. I linked the Shadow quality of envy to the concept of sin, and that was criticized, I now think rightly, since sin is not a helpful idea when anyone is working in analytical treatment on improving his or her quality of life (emotional and ethical) by getting through unnecessary guilt for what cannot be improved without more consciousness. My bringing in the idea of sin seems to me now to have been a remnant of my childhood, when I imbibed too much moralism.

Before moving to more personal aspects of my later life, some of my further analytical thinking is worth recording, since much of it is still alive in my mind. Like many analysts I have found the subject of change of almost endless interest. In broad outline, and generalising, people seek analysis through the wish to change something major in their lives. But it often emerges, as the weeks or months pass, that they have ingrained and largely unconscious defences against anything which is really going to be of much use. Some of those resistances are more evident and obvious to the analyst than to the patient. They may have been detected during the assessment and when analysis was being considered, but the analyst had decided to see if they could be worked through, or so to speak dissolved, with as frequent sessions as possible. The irony is that, without intentionally meaning to defeat the analytically more senior of the two partners who is trying to enable the less experienced one to get through the blocks, and perhaps to understand them, the suffering patient continues to think and act in a self-defeating way—which also defeats the analyst. I found it best, most often, to concentrate on drawing attention, indirectly at first, to those resistances, as compared with in any way by-passing them and giving in to the patient's evasions of painful insights. The commonest defences or self-protections against insight are denial, evasion, secrecy, repression and anxious "forgetting", as well as projecting the trouble into the analyst or some other person. There can often be manic overwork or behaviour, unconsciously designed to delay the discovery of the painful roots of depression, which will most likely recur time and again until the loss which is behind it has been accepted, or somehow come to terms with. As is well known, depression is a plague of modern life. Major change is difficult to achieve.

Those themes and ideas became of such interest to me that I not only wrote a paper in which I was trying to track down from which part of our psyches the blocks stem, but planned to turn the broad subject of Change and Resistance to Change into a full-scale book. The publisher I was in touch with at the time was interested in what I had already written and discussed with me in detail the chapter headings and contents, paid an advance and waited for the work to drop onto his desk. I never completed it, so the typescript still occupies one drawer of my old wooden filing cabinet, which is now its dusty grave.

Some time earlier I had written what later became a novel: it was a series of chapters, like acts, imagined to have taken place over the years of three generations, in the setting of the house in Cornwall that my parents had built, before the First World War, which has become the usual holiday home for many of their descendants. It had been the place where I was most happy during my childhood. In so far as there was any speaking or dialogue of any kind in the book, it was presented through what the various characters might have been thinking, but not saying out loud since it would have been too risky to speak out, in that particular family. Some of the people in the earlier episodes were based on those I had observed closely, the later ones were invented. Since one or two of the just recognisable ones were still alive, and might have been offended to see what I had made of them in print, the manuscript stayed unlooked at for several years, until a close friend jokingly asked if I had ever written a novel: and when she had read it she urged me to do something with it. I had given it the title of *The Sea Has Many Voices*, a quotation from one of T. S. Eliot's poems, *The Dry Salvages*, and an enthusiastic publisher accepted it at once, under that title. Without my knowing, he put it in for the Sagittarius prize, recently founded for the best novel written by someone over the age of sixty and published that year, to be handed out by the Society of Authors. The arrival of the winning cheque was a complete surprise.

I never enrolled in a "creative writing" course. I realised that if there was something pushing to be written, inside me, that was valid enough. Moreover I had been very well taught history and literature at school in my teen years: three members of the staff at my boarding school were especially keen that the quality of the writing should be as good as the contents. I and several of my friends adored them, they were also what is now called role models (that term had not yet been invented) who encouraged our budding skills and enthusiasms, so I owe them a great deal. I was fair game for their perfectionism, and become ambitious.

Even a few little tags of the latin poet Horace are still somewhere at the back of my mind, such as the one in which he laments the passing of the years—very suitable now.

When I was asked recently how my poems "come to me" I found that offered a very good way of describing their provenance: they do not exactly come, after waiting to be created, it is rather more that the first line happens, in my mind, in response to something I see, or hear, or feel, or think, and it sounds right, at the time, so it grows if it has potential, enough vitality to carry it forward—to bring it to birth. It was rather the same with professional papers, they needed a trigger, of course, and there usually felt to be enough cooperation between their content and my ability to develop the theme. During the Second World War there was a slogan on many billboards at railway stations: "Is your journey really necessary?" (because of the need to save fuel). I felt the same applied to papers, but poems, while not crudely necessary, had a propelling force in them, they demanded to be brought to birth. If they were not good enough, they were binned—usually.

An experienced poet can be very helpful, or very discouraging, to a writer who is tentative: I once made the mistake of asking one, well known at the time, with whom I had been talking about her interest in Jung and William Blake, if she would read one or two of my poems and offer me her opinion. She answered that more than half the population write what they mistakenly think is poetry, and she never reads any of it. End of would-be conversation. On another occasion David and I chanced to meet Cecil Day-Lewis (he was the poet laureate at the time) and his wife Jill Balcon on holiday on the west coast of Ireland, found we were all congenial and walked together along the splendid beaches, talking about poetry, life and so on, and went on sharing ideas in the evenings in front of the fire. Cecil offered to read a few of my poems, and told me which ones he thought were good, tactfully not mentioning the others. One of his, written when he was spending some time at Harvard, was entitled *On Not Saying Everything*, which is sound advice to any writer. Another, *Pegasus*, about inspiration, depends for its success on listening to a dream.

During many years together David and I especially enjoyed

times spent outside London, week-ends and longer holidays. He had inherited a cottage in North Wales, in mountainous Snowdonia. His hill-walking father had acquired it, on lease, before being killed in the First World War, and it had been kept going by various aunts and cousins. It consisted of two originally separate small dwellings, attached to a sheep farm. Water had to be fetched from the mountain stream, at that time. A century before David had it, the seven rooms were the overcrowded home of several families of very poor slate quarrymen. It became David's when the rich owner of the local Penrhyn Castle and estate was selling many of its properties. Those are illustrations of some of the local economic and social history of North Wales.

David improved the lighting, and some of the plumbing; he did not want too much modernisation. The long walks up and down the mountains, swimming in the rivers and lakes, the birds and flowers particular to the valleys and the wet slopes, the ever-changing colours of the views, all compensated for the elemental character of the cottage and the unreliable weather. One year, when we had as yet no car in which we might have escaped from the valley onto the island of Anglesea twenty miles away, off-shore from the cloud-catching mountains, it rained solidly for the whole of our fortnight's summer holiday. We were certainly stoic. Later in life I could not recapture often enough the pleasure I had had there in earlier more energetic years, but David continued to love it deeply, and in his retirement from Whitehall wrote a scholarly book about the area, *Time and the Valley*, covering its past, present and future. He researched it with informed skill, and it was worthy of much better marketing than the local publisher organised for it. Now Christopher owns the cottage, he has made it more comfortable, but not in his view unsuitably luxurious. As it is a "second home", not politically well-thought-of these days by the local Welsh people, he has to be tactful.

David and I had another cottage that we could get to easily from London and where we spent most week-ends for over twenty years. I had been left a legacy by one of my aunts, and saw it temptingly advertised, in a Sunday newspaper. I told myself to be sensible, tried to forget it but, later that week—the newspaper was still in the bin because the refuse men were on strike—I found the paper and within a few days I had bought the cottage without a second thought.

Intuition had won out over caution: it was a serendipitous act (it happened to be suitably called Garden Cottage) and it gave us much happiness for over twenty years. Rather like the history of the Welsh cottage, this new one—at least two centuries old— had originally been built as one of a row for farm labourers and then been gentrified. It was small, mellow-bricked and south-facing. The original round bread oven was still there, and the near-by woods were full of birds. For us humans also it became the place for belated nest-building: we had been to a great extent deprived of that earlier in our marriage.

Much of the year we walked through the woods and further afield, where there were all sorts of spring flowers, snowdrops and bluebells galore, wood anemones, wild raspberries, sorrel for spring-time soup, autumn fungi, and so on. In the summer we drove to swim in the Thames, entering by a rather muddy bank, not worrying about the possibly impure water. On many autumn nights it seemed as though the planets and stars could not have been brighter (the street-lights in London make them almost invisible), and in the winter evenings in front of the log fire there were the calls of owls hunting in the woods. Since then I have never had the opportunity to hear the spring dawn chorus of countless small birds. We also enjoyed seeing many varieties of moths and butterflies. We explored the ancient grass roads along the Berkshire and Wiltshire Downs and their arche-ological sites, watched the flocks of plover, listened to the sky-larks and found many of the chalk-loving plants, some already becoming rare, even then, such as the purple Pasque anemone.

I find it all too easy to be nostalgic and to idealise some aspects of the past, such as the Garden Cottage, and all that its surroundings gave us, but our family and friends, who came quite often, agree that I am not exaggerating. It was also a really quiet place where I could write, and many of my papers were composed there, without any tiresome interruptions.

The summer holidays we enjoyed most were spent in various rented cottages on three of the Isles of Scilly, off the western tip of Cornwall. Apart from the largest of them, St. Mary's, where the steamer lands and the small helicopters fly onto a diminutive field, and where only the local inhabitants were allowed cars, the others (in the years when we went there) used to be blissfully quiet. Where sea-birds are concerned and many smaller ones, and wild flowers (as well as the high-hedged fields where spring bulbs flourish, picked in bud and sent to market on the mainland), the islands were almost literally perfect for us, our children and, later, several of our grandchildren. Each of the five main islands is small enough to walk round more than once in the day, each has a gentle side facing what is a kind of lagoon, and a wild side with towering rocks reaching out into the Atlantic.

We sometimes spent a few days in the luxury of a hotel (which gave me a rest from housekeeping) on one of the best known, Tresco, with its semi-tropical gardens. But we fell in love with two of the smaller ones, Bryher near Tresco (it was possible at very low spring tide to walk over the sand banks and just return in safety) and St. Agnes, very compact and the most westerly. We believed we discovered all possible rocks to swim off, the water, when calm, was exquisitely transparent and exciting during storms. There were prehistoric remains and standing stones in several places, it may have been the legendary Atlantis—what a perfect place to be buried.

Year after year we found cottages to rent, and rather fancied ourselves as being so familiar with every little cove and corner in the rocks that many of the real islanders welcomed us from year to year. After our children had taken to going their own ways in the summer, David and I continued enjoying all our visits, even at the times when wild or misty weather took possession.

All the same, as well as writing about our enthusiasm, other things have to be said. The islands can certainly present themselves as being ideal for people on holiday such as we and our family were, but life for the islanders is hard in many ways. There are serious problems of isolation and all the usual human vicissitudes—many of the men and women there know each other's difficult characters all too well. There can be fiendish wild winter weather when the children cannot get to school or perhaps get home again, and crossing to hospital on St. Mary's can be hazardous. The islands are sometimes called the Isles of the Blessed. That is one of their characteristics, but of course there is inevitably the shadow side to all that is superficially lovely.

For David and me, the close of that chapter in our joint lives came all too suddenly. It was ironic that the news of my winning the prize for *The Sea Has Many Voices* came only a day or so after David died, he would have been pleased about it. His death marked the end of the fifty-six years that he and I had been together, ever since we met at Cambridge and shared our ideas on what felt like everything under the sun, in a circle of congenial, like-minded friends. But suddenly he was struck by what felt to be a most unnecessary death. He had had the fairly common trouble of older men, non-cancerous prostate enlargement, which had not seemed to him more than a very annoying symptom, although it was likely to get worse. He was not more than a little worried. But surgery was advisable and to be carried out fairly soon. Sadly, that meant postponing the party we had been planning, to celebrate his seventy-fifth birthday. Up till then, as in many families, each major milestone had been a good reason for a party. And there seemed to be no bad omens. The idea was that it would rank as a minor operation.

His recovery was going well and he was shortly going to be allowed home—the large and crowded old-fashioned ward in a famous London hospital left much to be desired. He did not want to move to a private room; he thought it might not be any better. One of my nephews, a recently retired surgeon, reassured me that the doctors were monitoring his progress quite correctly. But a day or so before he was meant to be discharged, a blood clot took over, so to speak, and he became very ill. Alarm set in: our children, hastily summoned, and I could sense what was happening, but it was beyond words.

During the years of the Second World War he had been in danger of injury or death in the desert campaign in North Africa, in the invasion of Sicily, on the first morning of the landings in Normandy and throughout the drive of the Allied armies through France to Belgium, but those times had to be lived through in an absolutely different way from how it was when he was in the hands of intensive care doctors in peace-time London. Trying to keep their patient alive had to be their only consideration. It felt very hard that we as people could not be with him, a person, moving from life to death, the unknown—presumably the most awe-full step any of us has to take. Our children, one of his sisters and I could only wait, stiff, speechless, feeling lost. I felt that each of us was caught in a cloud of memories of him. For them, he had been there all their lives.

The anonymous doctors had had to take over. Then in the shock of being told he had died I was intensely angry that we had not been able to be with him; to us he was of course a person, not just a patient. It was an irrational anger since I knew they had been doing their best. I felt I was a lost individual in a sea of incomprehension. Everybody was in tears, including the young doctor who had been especially interested in him on the ward, who was weeping on my shoulder.

The shock took months to wear off. Perhaps having a reliable religious belief would have made that time easier. But it was not there in any available sense. As the weeks went by, it dawned on me that from then on my life would be absolutely different from what it had been for so long. Of course that is what must be the case for any widow or widower. I knew there had been times when each of us could have been more helpful to the other, more generous about quirks and individual needs, so that the absolute impossibility of any communication with him was very hard to bear. "Out of reach" and "Too late" were adamant, final. The phrase "vain regrets" is descriptive, and it seems inadequate to convey the intense emotions. It was hard to adjust to the pain, especially as there had not been the preparatory months, or even years, that some illnesses give to those who are left, perhaps devotedly looking after the dying person, even if they had resented the effort and loss of freedom. For me it was abandonment. The benefits of independence, which did come, seemed to take their time, and the mixture of emotions was uncomfortable. I knew that I needed to re-assess who and where I was, aiming to find value in the next stage of life. Fate does not disclose its plans.

In the years after David died, in 1991, I have often felt very lonely, which has been difficult in many ways. However it has been possible to develop my interest in both the connection between, on the one hand, the material and the spiritual and psychological aspects of life, and on the other the contrasts that they enshrine. Until then I had had a kind of uncomfortable feeling about the major differences between his and my views, and had been unable to shrug them off as unimportant, which would perhaps have been wise, or at least sensible. They did not overtly come between us, but they were undiscussable. I daresay that many otherwise congenial couples have something major which is important to each of them, and even intrinsic to their sense of individuality, but which is implicitly left untouched.

Since I have been on my own—apart from many good friends, among whom I include the immediate and the extended family—one of several themes and interests which have come to the fore is that of spirituality. It is in fact as old as the proverbial hills, and as difficult to climb, unless one is bigoted and absolutely certain that one's own views are the only tenable ones. As I often see things through imagery, I can liken spiritual questions to plants, from daisies and dandelions to grand oak trees; their roots are in the earth, they need what it gives them for most of their food, and they are also above ground, evident, in the light and the air, for all that they must have as well. I am writing about spiritual matters advisedly, not about religious ones, since I do not belong to any specific religion.

I was christened (the old word for baptised) in infancy, into the Church of England, as all my sisters were. That meant in fact that our parents decided for us at that stage, which was valid as part of the kind of people they were. In childhood, like probably many of the children I knew, I made little sense of the strange mixture of myths, stories, apparent history, scandals and admonitions, in the two Testaments, and the poetically expressed, but often persecutory, reflections in the Psalms—there were cruel enemies and a god who did not necessarily do what was asked of him. Later in life I discovered that the world is still rather like that.

I was worried at being called Judith; the original of that name had been patriotic (yet to be nationalistic was frowned on) but as a murderess (exciting) she had disobeyed the Sixth Commandment. Good and Bad seemed very mixed. Perhaps it was good to learn that. At my boarding school genuine religion began to make sense. I did not resent the regular morning and evening prayers in the austere chapel there, and I admired the headmistress, who was certainly a woman with deep spiritual resources, also humourous and humane. Her sermons every Sunday morning were stimulating and wide-reaching, which satisfied an important element in teen-agers' lives. She accepted my loss of belief or faith, I did not know the difference, with a genuine discussion, as I have described earlier in this book.

My lack of religion in my university years was part of the spirit of that time. Not being a pacifist, given the wickedness of Nazism and Fascism, I could not join the Peace Pledge Union which mobilised idealism, and stood in for spirituality among some of my generation. The other alternative to religion, communism, also would not do, it was too bigoted.

When David and I fell in love my lack of religion fitted well in parallel with his. His father had come from a long line of dyed-in-the-wool Christians. One was a rural dean, another a missionary, and there was also a bishop of All-India. His mother's family were liberal Jews. Their marriage had upset both families; she once told me that one of her many cousins, the deeply philosophical Viscount Samuel, did not speak to her for twenty years. Both David's parents had abandoned the observances of their upbringing, adopting instead the nearly religious efforts of the early twentieth-century Fabians, impressive and generous left-wing intellectuals. David's and my views were those of most of our circle of Cambridge friends. In important ways he never deviated from unbelief in conventional or established religion of any kind, and to the end of his life one of his favourite quotations was Voltaire's dictum, *Écrasez l'infâme*, stamp out infamy—or abominable people. But that shortened version of his epigram misses the generous flavour of the full quotation: *Écrasez l'infâme et aimez qui vous aime.*

Not long ago, two passages in letters between my parents, written in one of their many painful First World War separations, came to my notice. They were deeply devoted to each other, but those particular letters showed that they had had differences about religion, and had not solved them. My mother had written to my father about being distressed at the changes she was experiencing in her previously strong and simple feelings about religion, how children should be introduced to it, and her anxiety about how he and she could not discuss such matters. She had noticed that each time they approached the subject, he backed off. He answered her at great length, explaining his views, which were much more rationalistic than hers. The open expression of their feelings on that subject eluded them. It was of some comfort to me to discover that, since David and I had had comparable difficulties: both conflicts seem to me now to have been typical of the traditional and over-simple idea that male = rational and female = emotional.

As the years went by of David's and my time of being close together, and the sense of intellectual equality at Cambridge, then the separations of the war, my way of seeing and experiencing all sorts of non-material things gradually changed more than his. Thanks to my analysis I found I agreed with the Jungian view of religion being an intrinsic part of the psyche, and nothing to do with neuroticism, an idea I might have come across (and would have struggled against) if I had had a Freudian analysis. David sensed that I no longer held the views I had had when we were first together, and he minded deeply, especially as he could see that the changes were connected with my analysis, which he resented, and then my change of profession. The whole thing became a no-go area, blocked off by our version of the defensiveness my parents had run into. My mother was better at retreating than I was. Our daughters, as far as I could tell, never became interested in anything connected with a personal religion, but Christopher, after being deeply affected during his university years by many of the late-Sixties movements, had a phase of Sufism and had retained much from that kind of spirituality. His daughter Charlotte has strong Quaker leanings.

As the Eighties and Nineties progressed I found I was more and more inclined to deepen my interest in various religions as expressions of spiritual values, especially the non-dogmatic ones. The aspects of them which appealed to me were part of being an analytical psychologist: spirituality is about relating either transcendentally or internally to a power other than oneself, but also to one's self, or to the archetypal Self. I saw spirituality and analysis as both involving respect for one's potential and for the Other, both the Other in the abstract and otherness in the people who seek whatever analysis can offer them. Spirituality can combine relatedness and the search for as satisfactory as possible an inner life which ultimately has to be lived on one's own. It includes the difficult gap between the material and the non-material. That may sound glib, or simplistic, or naïve, as a way of referring to those potentially profound matters. Abstract matters were given substance and imagery in a poem, written I am not sure when, entitled Non Sense Rhyme:

When I was not looking
Was the moment of vision,
When all was confused
Came sudden precision.
Against a background of noise
I heard a fresh sound,
At the ordinary meal
A new taste was found.

When I was not looking
The dark twigs budded,
While I was sleeping
Daisies opened and studded
The familiar lawn
In revolt against order,
And surprising flowers bloomed
In the dry garden border.

Those lines indicate that such spirituality as I have consists of attention to various kinds of overlap: people and ideas which move beyond the confines of one specialism to bridge different worlds, observations, knowledge or even fascination. Other "overlap people" who have appealed to me over the years, and set me reflecting, are the philosopher William James, author of *Varieties of Religious Experience* (which I discovered during my analysis), Rudolf Otto's *The Idea of the Holy* (which included the old latin *numen*, leading to the numinous, the awe-inspiring), and several scientists such as Professor Paul Davies and Dr. John Polkinghorne. I recently came across a passage in *An Experiment in Leisure* by Marion Milner, the remarkable and deeply reflecting psychoanalyst:

I've often wondered what "spiritual" meant—something remote that I could never attain to? But we use the word often—"a man of spirit", "her spirits rose", "rest to the spirit", "a spirited performance". So spiritual things are not remote things—but vital things.

To my mind the essence of spirituality is that it is non-materialism: it is potentially to be found within matter, by anyone inclined to look for it, and able to discern it. From time to time I have dipped into the more classical early and late medieval mystics' writings, but often I did not agree with their beliefs or measure up to their elevated psyches.

As a result of many years of mulling over those thoughts, partly independently and partly growing out of the wide reading which went with them, I gave a paper at the S.A.P. which was almost mistakenly entitled "Is There Room for Spirituality in the Practice of Analytical Psychology?" The answer was that of course there is, at which point the paper might have been considered unnecessary. But it was well received and led to several members suggesting that we form a discussion group round the kind of thoughts I was offering.

The group went well for several years, with each meeting starting with one or the other member suggesting a theme. And soon after that I was asked to contribute a chapter to a book called *Beyond Belief*. It was about how we had come to, or abandoned, our beliefs. It was initiated and edited by a psychiatrist friend, Samuel Stein, who was doing the Freudian-based Institute training at the time. He had lost his original Jewish beliefs during his analysis. I knew his wife Jennifer through her being an analytical psychologist as well as a psychiatrist. As all other contributors were either actually Freudian or had leanings that way, I felt my being one of the writers was a contribution to my continued efforts to build bridges between the two major lines of depth psychology.

Towards the end of the time when I was seeing patients and supervising the work of trainees I wrote a paper on some aspects of old age, which I was myself approaching. Writing it was important in the process of having to reflect seriously about my own need to face the last stage of life. I was thinking of gradually stopping clinical work with patients before making any of the major misjudgements which are possible, over and above the obvious ones of forgetting an appointment, or someone's name, or falling asleep during a session, especially in the early afternoon. And I knew that even with foreseeing and planning retirement I would need to face a period of mourning for the loss of what had been very important to me. So the paper on the theme of old age had a subjective value as well as describing some aspects of the analysis of a patient well into his eighties, who had a wife, children and grandchildren.

Jung had endowed the Senex, the elderly years, with an archetypal character. It was obviously at the opposite end of the series of life archetypes to that of the Child—he did not write about that earlier stage, infancy. He developed his theory of archetypes after Freud had famously observed the workings of the Oedipus complex, which is well known to be typical of the psychological phase through which children in a great many cultures have to navigate themselves, or be helped to navigate. Freud did not use the term *archetype*, for that or for any of the other typical human phases, whereas Jung, basing himself on what Plato had called *ideas*, applied the term to the stages of life, to typical character traits and relationships. To those unfamiliar with analytical terms, I think the simplest way to describe most of the archetypes is that they are equivalent to psychological instincts, and to the inevitable stages of life, even if that does not meet the requirement of strict scientific definition. It conveys their great power. In clinical work the value of the concept is that, on many occasions, it helps the analyst to steer his or her way through the complicated problems the patient is presenting, and opens up the possibility of making a mutative interpretation or comment.

The patient in that paper was deeply preoccupied with what he called the enigma of death. He said he was not frightened of dying, but pressed me hard to tell him what would happen to him after death. His rather minimal Christian faith had not been helpful enough, and he described how the local vicar, to whom he had turned before seeing me, could not give him what he wanted. He finally accepted my ignorance when I said I simply did not know, having not yet been there, but he got no satisfaction from, as it were, cornering and defeating me about the un-solved enigma. He could only agree with my comment that he was questioning me like the trusting child that fate had not al-lowed him to be, since his parents had sent him to school on the other side of the world, with no home holidays, before he was old enough to discover all the problems that many children and adolescents want to explore, and to be free to discuss. They had, in effect, died in relation to where he was in life when he had had to leave his childhood country. He had described his happiness there, telling me about the beauties round about his home and garden, flowers and fruit galore. It was paradise lost and the golden age in the past. England had been grey, bleak and cold. He always came to his session with a string bag of or-anges, but did not take to my suggesting that they had some kind of meaning for him. Images and symbols did not appeal to him.

Since it was a paper that had a strongly personal meaning for me, I brought in a few of the many poets throughout history who have written about old age, those who were painfully af-fected by how sad it can be, and others who were hopeful about what might happen next. I was interested in warning against the image of the idealised "wise old man" (or woman) whose opinions are sought in some cultures, and whose views are occasionally appreciated by younger people. The "wisdom" of many impressive old people lies in managing fairly well to explain rather than to complain to the younger ones about how frustrated they feel when they see that their remaining potential will not be reached. They have to try to be patient, rather than sententious like the often-ridiculed Polonius. In *East Coker* (one of the *Four Quartets*) T. S. Eliot put it well:

> The only wisdom we can hope to acquire
> Is the wisdom of humility, humility is endless.

The last paper I wrote, and that was published in the *Journal of Analytical Psychology* in 1998, was about the dynamic energy of the self (see the appendix). As I re-read it now, a few years later, it turns out to have had a valedictory quality. It does not contain an exhaustive summary of all my analytical ideas, but I

think I must have written it in a somewhat hopeful mood. It
grew out of years of reading, learning, suffering, listening and
trying to express a combination of inner and outer experiences.
That sounds rather grandiose, high and mighty, but it is what a
great number of people know about the often hidden dynamism
in their own inner lives, their sense of self. At times it is all too
easy to be rather cynical about almost all aspects of ordinary life,
both public and private. Analysts are not many of them
paragons, patients (which includes both partners) are all too
often unlikely to achieve well-being, to emerge from repeated
versions of their original wounds, to tolerate more than minimally all the usual troubles. Putting on a brave front can be
done, so long as that is known privately to be no more than the
best possible way of carrying on ordinary daily life. There may
be welcome highlights, times when optimism can partner us
through the difficulties. The round of the seasons is an annual
reminder of how changes are really enjoyable, whatever else is
happening.

An introduction to my old age happened in a very refreshing
way, near the end of the century. It was the 1998 grand celebration at Cambridge of the fiftieth anniversary of the first admission
of women to real degrees there. At the earlier time women graduates were only granted what was called, in a demeaning way, a
certificate, raised a few years later to the title of a degree. The
men members of the University had been very obstinate ever
since the campaigning for equality had begun in 1871, holding
on to their power in the face of many generations of women students who were just as academic as the men. Several of the
women had even achieved higher standards than the men in the
two subjects that were ignorantly believed to be beyond the "little women's" minds or capacities, classics and mathematics.

The only advantage I can remember about the years when I
was at Newnham College was that, being underprivileged, we
did not have to wear the short black cotton academic "gowns"
whenever we went to a lecture or to see our tutors. Graduates'
gowns were longer, more impressive. But the senior women,
such as lecturers and professors, mostly minded a great deal not
being full members. As one of those making formal speeches
said at the celebration, it is difficult now to understand why

there was so much resistance and hostility to accepting reform, even "shameful scenes of rioting" on two occasions. The number of women achieving senior academic positions is still not good enough, in the eyes of those who believe there should be real equal opportunities. "The glass ceiling" in the business world, and the ticking biological clock for all of us women, are realities. I am inclined to think that those factors have most likely still got something to do with the simple fact that child-bearing takes more out of our mid-years than becoming a father does for even the most enlightened men. Though of course that does not apply to those women who, for whatever reason, do not have the interruption of having children, or to those who quickly find someone else to look after them when they are young.

I have noticed that among the people I know some of them, men as well as women, seem to tolerate losses and disabilities without an unbearable amount of distress. Either they are actually like that, being less vulnerable than others who show it more obviously, or they conceal how troublesome they find it. I believe there are people who are really serene. But I have to rack my brains to find any who are not privately much less tolerant of old age than might appear. Being vulnerable involves not minding the loss of ordinary pride we once had, which is perhaps more difficult than it sounds. It is not, I think, cynical to believe that it suits younger people to picture us less unhappy than we probably appear. They have to defend themselves against even a little guilt, if they are relatives, or against ignorance and not being able to picture the facts if they are unimaginative. When my mother was very old, I did not really appreciate how it was for her, so I must in all fairness allow for the same lack of ideal sensitivity to anyone younger, without being critical. It is not just that the old saying of "seeing is believing" is more or less true, if banal, but much more that being old is like being in a different dimension which is still personally unknown to younger people. Many of us dread being a nuisance, a burden, we have heard people in middle age admitting that their old parent, or parent-in-law, who lived with them, had been exactly that, even though at the time of looking after them they had been fond of them and had concealed their reactions to the inevitable. In some of the more tribal societies—those that are still left—it is likely that the old can be included in extended family life more easily than they can be in typical "Western" urban circles.

There are still many things I would like to do, and to enjoy, since making amends for the countless times when I fell short of the old childhood demand to behave well cannot now be done, and would be embarrassing all round. To illustrate that there are still many possibilities as well as impossibilities, this is the poem, which was published in the *San Francisco Jung Institute Library Journal* (vol. 8, no. 1, 1988, p. 65):

To My Unwritten Poems

Lie there, unwritten poems,
yours is a beautiful graveyard:
your graves are invisible, your lines unborn,
rocks tower above you
in the recurrent evenings of my unwinding life.
Waves mesmerically flow
to and fro, along the coasts
where you are not, nor ever were.
You need no graves, you unknown words,
you unconceived, you never born,
nor died, nor grieved.

Dear amoebas, uncreated,
from an unreachable sea,
if I walk over your graves
in the summer rain,
I give you no pain.
Mountain flowers bloom over you
unconcerned and causing no stir.
Winds, rains and snows
succeed each other in your undamaged seasons.
Happiest of poems,
asking no questions, offering no reasons,
undisturbed and unperturbed
in your simplicity and silence,
you are unsurpassed essence and inordinate quietness.

You do not clamour, nor struggle, nor dispute,
you are calmer than the lilies of the field,
you neither anger nor yield.
Deep respect is your due.

With my whole heart I salute you.
To your own unforced truth
you are true.

My impression of how I am experiencing the general difficulties, pains of several kinds, restrictions, disappointments, losses and fears of future illness is similar to how the several elderly people I know are also struggling. The subject of the increasing proportion of old people in many parts of the world is well-covered in the media and it is being tackled as well as possible—or not as well, in the view of many professionals. It is right, I suppose, that in the main publicists present an optimistic picture of how positively many marvellous old people view themselves: still able to smile and joke, even if their humour is rueful. Those I read about present a picture of the impact of their troubles varying very much, and it is almost impossible to generalise about our reactions to the inevitable ending of our lives. It seems to me that, among the people I know well, the occasional outburst is necessary and helpful, while the prevailing overall ethic—which I go along with—is at least to try to present a good front, not to complain inordinately, not to spread fear and despondency. At the centre of that way of seeing all those human preoccupations (which I wish added up to being a philosophy of life) I put a hope that I will be able to hold on to combining thinking and feeling with some kind of all-round reflecting.

The outbursts are well illustrated in one of Dylan Thomas' poems (p. 128):

Do not go gentle into that good night.
Old age should burn and rave at close of day;
Rage, rage against the dying of the light.

But the all-important background to those angry lines is that he was raging on behalf of the Other, not himself: his father, whose eyesight was failing.

So a better ending to all this is Shakespeare's sonnet, appreciated by countless readers for over four hundred years:

When to the sessions of sweet silent thought
I summon up remembrance of things past,
I sigh the lack of many a thing I sought,
And with old woes new wail my dear time's waste;
Then can I drown an eye, unused to flow,
For precious friends hid in death's dateless night,
And weep afresh love's long since cancell'd woe,
And moan the expense of many a vanish'd sight.
Then can I grieve at grievances foregone,
And heavily from woe to woe tell o'er
The sad account of fore-bemoaned moan,
Which I new pay as if not paid before:
  But if the while I think on thee, dear friend,
  All losses are restored and sorrows end.

Appendix. The dynamic self

The following article is reprinted, with permission, from the *Journal of Analytical Psychology*, 1998, vol. **43**, no. 2, 277–285

The dynamic self

Judith Hubback, *London*

Abstract: The paper describes various aspects of the dynamic energy of the self, as experienced personally and in clinical work. It discusses the inherent and archetypal force there is in the self, expressed in several ways, for example in some poetry, and in spirituality. The dynamic power of the self is shown at work in the process of individuation, including its vicissitudes of pain and working through doubts, envies and other shadow factors.

The self as dynamic energy

This paper is a brief exploration of the nature and activity of the self from the standpoint of seeing it as the major, elemental, dynamic energy in the psyche. To give substance to that idea, and to keep it in line with some of Jung's many descriptions of the self, and reflections on its workings, I went back to the chapter entitled 'The Self' in *Aion* (Jung 1959). There I found numerous nouns and verbs (powerful ones) containing the elements of energy and psychological action. They are as follows, with the relevant paragraph numbers in brackets: 'integration' and 'assimilation' (43), 'discrimination' (44), 'energic tension' (53), 'confronts' (59), 'affected' (61), 'relate' (65). In the later chapter, 'The structure and dynamics of the Self', there are: the self 'a dynamic process' (411), 'move' (413), and 'Sooner or later nuclear physics and the psychology of the unconscious *will draw* [my italics] closer together as both of them … *push forward* [my italics] into transcendental territory' (412). In the 'Conclusion', there is 'the self is a union' (426). Though some of those words refer to ego activity and many convey that the movement has been completed, I submit that their essence is about psychological activity in the self. The self is experienced not only as existing, or as a concept, both of which are mainly to do with thinking, but more importantly as having

> a value quality attached to it, namely its feeling tone. This indicates the degree to which the subject is *affected* by the process or how much it means to him … In psychology one possesses nothing unless one has experienced it in reality … a purely intellectual insight is not enough.
>
> (ibid., para. 61)

Of course I had not thought of my idea as a unique discovery and it was likely that others before me had already put it forward, in either definite or implicit ways. Then as well as the fact that Jung had gone into the matter deeply in the studies collected in *Aion*, Fordham has written of the self as a dynamic system under the title 'Actions of the self' (Fordham in Hall (ed.) forthcoming). According to him the rhythms in the psyche (integration and de-integration) are the dynamic movements that lead to growth. Numerous other writers since Jung have also contributed to my thinking on this theme, and I can but select a few: Redfearn (1977, 1985), Lambert (1981), Zinkin (1987) and Stein (1996).

The archetypal force in the self

Since archetypes are in their nature unknowable, (their existence is postulated from their observable effects), it is the archetypal nature and quality of them which makes most sense of clinical material when the analyst detects extra strong forces at work. The question of such strength is one of subjective estimation by the analyst, not to be measured 'scientifically' … I would like to add a quotation from the poet Dylan Thomas (1914-1953), since

236

poets often express more effectively than anyone else what we analysts see and hear in our consulting-rooms:

> The force that through the green fuse drives the flower
> Drives my green age; that blasts the roots of trees
> Is my destroyer.
> And I am dumb to tell the crooked rose
> My youth is bent by the same wintry fever.

(Thomas 1957)

That extract from the work of a young poet who was often harshly driven by the force of inspiration picks up the collective and archetypal character of the link between man and nature, with its round of the year's recurrent seasons. The same theme, in psychological form, is in Jung's chapter 'Resurrection' in the volume of *Miscellaneous Writings*, entitled *The Symbolic Life* (Jung 1976). That chapter was written in reply to enquiries from several people who had attended a seminar on *Aion* in Los Angeles, in 1954, led by Dr James Kirsch. Jung expanded on the view of the self as a collective image of an internal archetypal drive, writing that the myth of the resurrection of Jesus is valuable in expressing the continuity and circular wholeness which feeds the deep hunger that so many people experience in the face of anxiety about individual disappearance in death. I think those ideas of Jung's contain a reference to the archetypal movement of elemental forces in the self.

The self in the individual

Within each of us as individuals, experiences of the self are connected with, or can be conceptualised as emerging from, the greater self. For religious people of any kind and in any culture archetypal God-images are sources of vitality, creativity and capacity to relate. There are also the opposite images, of ruthlessness and destruction. For non-religious people there is the spirit element in inspiration. All those characteristics can be seen in both positive and negative workings and manifestations (for example, 'bad' devils as well as 'good' gods). It is unnecessary to go into detail here on that theme since there are numerous well-

237

documented anthropological and theological writings on them. In clinical work evidences of the activities and dynamism of the self occur in many ways: in dreams, in fantasies, in paintings, and in the handling of events in daily life which may not appear remarkable unless we are attuned to notice and reflect upon them analytically with care and insight.

The self in spirituality

At the same time as Jung was beginning to develop his view of the self as compared with Freud's, the world was reeling under the gross impact of the First World War and its after-effects. That war, and all the later ones in the twentieth century, can be seen as innumerable human beings suffering from a fearful loss of ego. What has been happening is not simply a succession of mere temporal coincidences: the fate of people in the mass is the fate of individuals, cumulatively, and derives from the conflict between the positive and the negative forces in the self. The poet Robert Bridges, in the preface to his anthology called *The Spirit of Man*, wrote of the 'cruelty, terrorism, devastation … insensate and interminable slaughter, the hate and filth' (Bridges 1916). Rudolf Otto's *Das Heilige* appeared first during that war, in 1917, was reprinted ten times in the next six years and was soon translated into English (Otto 1923). It directed attention, in effect, to how close the collective numen (the word he took from the latin) is to the personal sense of self: numinous happenings can only be experienced through the medium of the self. The tremendous energy of the numen manifests itself either in primitive, manic excitement, or in calm introversion, which does not necessarily lead to malign depression. The Jungian theory of the workings of opposite forces is effectively illustrated in that historical juxtaposition of the evil of the First World War and the positively-aimed search for selfhood which happens despite the suffering experienced by so many millions, and expressed in Otto's book.

In these last few years of the twentieth century, there is a resurgence world-wide of interest in spiritual matters, happening at a time when it seems that a great many people are increasingly concerned about the fate of the planet, and the humans and animals who live on it. I think that the parallelism between those two movements is deeply significant. The collective unconscious, charged with energy from the self, is emerging into consciousness and manifesting itself in both inner psychological/spiritual ways and in outer material ones. The force of that psychological movement can validly be seen as carrying an archetypal character. And, as usually happens when there are such emergings of elements from archetypal levels, there is an urgent need for an increase in consciousness in order to integrate them safely into the area of ego functioning.

I am selecting for mention here some of the mystics and spiritual writers from the past, who are being studied increasingly these days, and more particularly by analytical psychologists, since many of their beliefs and statements about the Deity, or aspects of what God meant to them, come close to Jung's ways of writing about the self. Among Christians the Dominican friar Eckhart (1260-1327) is especially well-known for the amazing ways in which he saw himself in relation to the western mediaeval God. It is not too far-fetched to substitute the word self in passages where he is writing about God. I think it was his own self-feeling that he really knew most about, that being his response to the more collective generalizations on offer in the Church at that time. For example: 'Man should not be afraid of God. Some fear is harmful. The right sort of fear is of losing God' (Eckhart in Fleming (ed.) 1988). And: 'If I had not been, there would have been no God. I am the cause of God being God' (ibid.). Denying the transcendence of God in that way is similar to seeing the self not as an archetype in itself (even if the greatest) but as having an essentially archetypal nature or quality. Eckhart also wrote: 'I do not find God outside myself nor conceive him excepting as my own and in me' (ibid.). He was a brilliant intellectual lecturer in philosophy, and deeply versed in theology as it was then, but he did not see God, or the more abstract idea of the God-head, as understandable either through thinking or through the senses. Having a strong poetic side to him, he saw 'God' metaphorically and symbolically, delighting in paradox in a way that makes him into a precursor of Jung, who made such subtle and difficult statements about the self.

Earlier than Eckhart some of the Greek Orthodox Christians

had seen their God as 'energies' or 'activities' in the world, which is close to the view of the self that I am proposing here. According to Karen Armstrong in *A History of God*, they 'saw God making himself accessible in a ceaseless activity in which he was somehow present' (Armstrong 1993, p. 254). So 'God' (cf. The self) was there to be experienced, not to be easily located by way of concepts.

Among many mystics, whether Jewish, Christian or Moslem, it was well understood that the 'journey to the depths of the mind' should 'only be under the guidance of an expert' (ibid., p.246), somewhat equivalent to an analyst who could be expected to notice signs of the onset of manic inflation, idealizations and attacks of any kind, or dangerously depressive episodes. Some of the early Moslem Sufis were prone to fall into ecstatic states, but those who are probably better known to present-day analytical psychologists include Rumi (1207–1273), and Ibn-al-Arabi (1165–-1240) who was introspective and imaginative, searching 'for the ground of being in the depths of the self' (ibid., p. 275). Sensitive listening, on the part of the analyst, to what is going on in the patient and in the transference/countertransference is to be expected, perhaps especially when the patient is in a state of mind similar (even if only in a small way) to those described by mystics. What is valuable, irrespective of historical and cultural differences, is their emphasis on a belief that God, or in our terms the self, could only be found in subjective experiences. That holds good in analysis as well as in private meditation. If the analyst does not personally have any spiritual interest or concern, there is still room for the patient's subjective experiences to be respected as intrinsic parts of him/ or her/self. Such unspoken respect would not mean they are being left out of the analytical interaction.

The self in pain

The view of the self as dynamic and elemental energy, put forward here, has to include consideration of how both physical and emotional pain can be fitted into the whole picture. While it can be assumed that everybody in the world knows all too well pain of one or more kinds, it is pain in (or stemming from) the psyche which is particularly interwoven in the lives of those who come into analysis, and they are the people who are especially referred to here, whose communications form the basis of my comments.

Early in my own analysis I found the most impressive aspect of the Jungian approach was the positive value of the painful symptom. Good quality analysis does not include overt reassurance. When an analysand discovers, by working through repeated phases of depression and recovery, that simply getting rid of the presenting trouble is not the aim of the analysis, but that finding out what meaning it carries, and that value is to be found there—that is deeply reassuring. It is how layers of insight are laid down: the personal self is potentially in touch with the healing energy of the greater self. An image comes to mind: those 'layers' are like the underground water-table, calmly waiting there to be tapped in future times of distress. It seems to me that when the analyst has full trust (laid down in his or her own analytical experience) in the developmental value of pain, the emergence of the paradoxical and dual nature of the self is there on hand for the receptive patient to make use of, and to convert its charge of energy into, a new inner benefit. Another image, of course, is that of the self as the source of nourishment, which is then absorbed and digested, and turned into new energy for the patient. With that picture, there is a suggestion of the self archetypally activating the energy of the mother's availability for the infant, her caring, containing and feeding. The patient's receptivity needs to be activated through discovering the meaning of the earlier painful symptom, which is so often emotional hunger.

Over all the years since Freud and Jung started working, countless papers and books have been published on what are to my mind the closely connected subjects of pain, the self and the enigmatic mutative factors for the suffering patient in analysis. Many of them point either directly or implicitly to the dynamic essence of the self. In this contribution I would like to reiterate the general theme of what I wrote on the subject of change as a process in the self (Hubback 1988). Change is activity, movement, process. Psychological pain is not eliminated by analytical treatment, but it usually becomes more bearable, better understood, more effectively integrated with other aspects of life.

Those are some of the most worthwhile outcomes. In the same way as the various researchers in the 'hard' sciences try to discover the origins of physical life, so do analysts (in the human sciences) try to trace what activates the loosening of the grip of psychic pain, which so often paralyses someone's life. 'The possibility of change lies in the self and ... it moves from the possible to the actual when two selves meet. We [analysts] observe archetypal activity, not archetypes in their essence. We take part in change, it is integral to us as alive and active beings' (ibid., p. 204). If that view is accepted, I submit that it is essential for the analyst to try to monitor all intuitions of the workings of the self in him or her, even in the banal and trivial events of ordinary life. As the poet William Blake wrote in 'Auguries of Innocence' we can 'See a World in a Grain of Sand ... And Eternity in an Hour'.

The self as the dynamic force in individuation

In most analyses shadow factors have to be worked through time and again. That is one of the beneficial aspects of the repetition compulsion: repeating is in fact an archetypal manifestation and necessity, which works in harness with the developmental needs of the patient. The work of accepting, modifying and integrating shadow attitudes and behaviour goes on throughout analytical therapy, but the important factor in that working through is the presence and active participation of the analyst, the 'other' who can incarnate the forward-going movement in the psyche. Without the contrast of the two people, with different life experiences and the oppositeness of the 'other', there lacks the essential dynamism which will empower the process of individuation. I think that we should not be grandiose and believe that individuation during therapy is brought about as a result of our work only, with our trained psychological knowledge, however perceptive and sensitive we may also be: we are the assistants to the work our patients are doing, and often they are our assistants in the same task. As analysts we are picking up on the potential for individuation which we have to believe is there in anyone, and actively fostering its forward movement, however many reverses there are on the way. Individuation, as described or more often hinted at by Jung and further researched by later analytical psychologists, is not completely achieved by any of us. A healthy enough and flexible ego is necessary for a continuous movement towards individuation. Quite often it feels as though there is not much margin between the possible and the impossible. Those in whom the original self was wounded too severely, and in infancy and childhood too often re-wounded, present the analyst with an extreme problem. For them it would be persecutory to have high aspirations, and would indicate a mistaken projective optimism on our part.

Both for ourselves and for any particular patient there are times of major doubt as to whether further movement towards the much desired individuation is going to be possible. Then it is helpful to remember the positive value of symptoms, referred to above. Early in an analysis they alert the analyst to aspects of work needing attention. In my experience, for example, a frequent one is envy, of which patients may be unaware, but which shows up in the transference projections and which they defend against the analyst interpreting. It seemed so dangerous to Christian theologians in the Middle Ages that they put it among the Seven Deadly Sins. 'Sin' as seen then is better conceptualized now as a shadow problem (Hubback 1988). Even if it has been worked on at many stages, in the analytic interactions, it is likely to resume its sinister power when in other ways the process of individuation is going well and termination may be being discussed. The patient may be taken unawares by suddenly finding him or herself yet again envious of the analyst, imagining he or she to be the more 'whole' of the two. I can remember one occasion when I found myself, presumably by the process of projective identification, envious of a patient who seemed to have achieved such 'wholeness' through a long and intense analysis, although rationally I knew well enough that that was unlikely. Reflecting as well as I could, I came to think that the patient enviously pictured me as successfully 'whole' and able to be sure that the time was ripe for ending the analysis. I think that renewal of envy, which had earlier been analysed in terms of infancy and childhood, stemmed at the late stage from anxieties which were characteristic of each of the two of us when we needed to tolerate separation, and an increase in maturity, even if that could never be complete. There was of course more work for each of us, in moving towards at least relative individuation.

Envy as a shadow factor lies within the big self, when that self is conceptualized as the elemental, archetypal, all-inclusive cluster of energies, having been originally neutral but somewhat distorted within the individual by the force of narcissistically painful life events. Behind the dangerous energy operating as envy lies the idealization of individuation. If it is fully accepted as ultimately unattainable, the healing power of the self can resolve the struggle between the dynamism of those two opposing forces, and development can continue.

In conclusion, Kenneth Lambert's use of the Greek word agape is useful to denote the particular kind of love which infuses analytical work where the energy of the self is at the heart of what is going on (Lambert 1981). The interaction which is on offer to the suffering patient is energized with that sort of love. He demonstrated learnedly and sensitively the ways in which agape differs both from eros, which includes sexuality, and from the kind of love which is referred to in the prefix philo, in such a word as philosophy, meaning love of wisdom, with a strong component of intellect. Feeling needs to be brought in too, and I see agape as a crucially important component of the psyche, on offer by the analyst to the patient, so I am including it in this description of the dynamic self.

References

Armstrong, K. (1993). *A History of God*. London: Heinemann.

Bridges, R. (1916). *The Spirit of Man*. London: Longmans.

Eckhart, M. (1260–1327). *Meister Eckhart—The Man from whom God Hid Nothing*. Fleming (ed.). London: Heinemann, 1988.

Fordham, M. (forthcoming) 'Actions of the self'. In *The Changing Subject* (temporary title), J. Hall (ed.).

Gordon, R. (1985), 'Big self and little self: some reflections'. *Journal of Analytical Psychology*, 30, 3, 261–71.

Hubback, J. (1988). *People who do things to each other.* Wilmette: Chiron.

Jung, C.G. (1959/1968). *Aion.* CW 9ii.

_____ (1976). *The Symbolic Life.* CW 18.

Lambert, K. (1981). *Analysis, Repair and Individuation.* London: Academic Press. *The Library of Analytical Psychology*, 5.

Otto, R. (1917). *Das Heilige.* (*The Idea of the Holy*). Trans. J. W. Harvey. London: Humphrey Milford, 1923.

Redfearn, J. (1977). 'The self and individuation'. *Journal of Analytical Psychology*, 22, 2, 125–41.

_____ (1985). 'My Self, my many Selves'. London: Academic Press. *The Library of Analytical Psychology*, 6.

Stein, M. (1996). *Practising Wholeness.* New York: Continuum.

Thomas, D. (1957). *The Collected Poems.* New York: New Directions.

Zinkin, L. (1987). 'The hologram as a model for analytical psychology'. *Journal of Analytical Psychology*, 12, 1, 1–21.

Selected Bibliography

de Beauvoir, S. 1949. *The Second Sex*. Paris, Gallimard. 1953. London, Cape.

Day-Lewis, C. 1957. *Pegasus, and Other Poems*. London, Cape.

Day-Lewis, C. 1965. *On Not Saying Everything*, in *The Room and Other Poems*. London, Cape.

Eliot, T. S. 1954. *Four Quartets*. London, Faber & Faber.

Field, J., (Milner, M. B.) 1934. *A Life of One's Own*. London, Chatto & Windus.

Field, J., (Milner, M. B.) 1937. *An Experiment in Leisure*. London, Chatto & Windus.

Fordham, M. 'Actions of the Self', in Howell, P. R., and Hall, J.A. (eds), *Self through Art and Science*. 2001. Bloomington, IN, 1stbooks Library.

Hart, J. 1998. *Ask Me No More*. London, Halban.

Home, J. 1966. 'The Concept of Mind'. *International Journal of Psychoanalysis*, no. 47.

Hopkinson, D. 1954. *Family Inheritance, A Life of Eva Hubback*. London and New York, Staples.

Hubback, D. 1987. *Time and the Valley*. Llanrwst, Gwasg Carreg Gwalsh.

Hubback, J. 1954. *Graduate Wives*. London, Political and Economic Planning.

Hubback, J. 1957. *Wives Who Went to College*. London, Heinemann.

Hubback, J. 1964. *Islands and People*, Poems. London, Outposts.

Hubback, J. 1988. *People Who Do Things to Each Other*. Wilmette, IL, Chiron.

Hubback, J. 1988. *To My Unwritten Poems*. San Francisco Jung Institute Library Journal Vol. 8, no. 1.

Hubback, J. 1990. *The Sea Has Many Voices*. Henley-on-Thames, Aidan Ellis Publishing Ltd.

James, W. 1902. *The Varieties of Religious Experience.* (Gifford Lectures, 1901–1902). New York, London, Longmans, Green & Co.

Jung, C. G. 1921. *Psychological Types.* London, Routledge & Kegan Paul, trans. 1923.

Jung, C. G. 1925. *Septem Sermones ad Mortuos* (trans. Baynes, H.G.: The Seven Sermons to the Dead). Privately printed, John M. Watkins, 1925. 1961, London, Random House.

Jung, C. G. 1961. *Memories, Dreams, Reflections.* London, Routledge & Kegan Paul. (trans. 1923).

Malan, D. 1963. *A Study of Brief Psychotherapy.* London, Tavistock Publications.

Meares, A. 1958. *The Door of Serenity.* London, Faber.

Milner, M. See Field, J. 1934 and 1937.

Narayan, R. K. 1974. *My Days, A Memoir.* New York, Viking, 1975, London, Chatto & Windus.

Newsom, J. H. 1948. *The Education of Girls.* London, Faber & Faber.

Otto, R. 1917. *Das Heilige (The Idea of the Holy).* Trans. Harvey, J. W., 1923. London, Humphrey Milford.

Peck, W. F. 1948. *A Little Learning, or A Victorian Childhood.* London, Faber & Faber.

Pittenger, R., Hockett, C., Danehy, J. 1960. *The First Five Minutes: A Sample of Microscopic Interview Analysis.* Ithaca, NY, Paul Martineau.

Ross, L. B. (ed). 1993. *To Speak or Be Silent.* Wilmette, IL, Chiron.

Spring-Rice, M. 1939. *Working Class Wives, Their Health and Conditions.* London, Penguin (Pelican).

Stein, S. M. (ed). 1999. *Beyond Belief, Psychotherapy and Religion.* London, Karnac.

Stevenson, R. L. 1895. *A Child's Garden of Verses.* London, Longmans Green. (Many later publications).

Storr, A. 1958. 'The Psychopathology of Fetishism and Transvesticism'. *Journal of Analytical Psychology* Vol. 2, no. 2.

Thomas, D. 1957. *The Collected Poems.* New York, New Directions.

Various Authors. 1978. Nick Malleson, *Students in Need.* Society for Research into Higher Education, Guildford.

Westland, E. (ed). 1997. *Cornwall, the Cultural Construction of Place*. Penzance, Patten Press.

Wheeler-Bennett, J., in collaboration with Musgrave, B., and Herzov, Z. 1977. *Women at the Top—Achievement and Family Life*. London, Owen.

Woolf, V. 1929. *A Room of One's Own*. London, Hogarth.

Index